Writing Assessment

LONGMAN SERIES IN
COLLEGE COMPOSITION AND COMMUNICATION

Harvey S. Wiener, Series Editor

Writing Assessment

Issues and Strategies

Edited by

KAREN L. GREENBERG, *Hunter College, CUNY*

HARVEY S. WIENER, *La Guardia Community College, CUNY*

RICHARD A. DONOVAN, *Bronx Community College, CUNY*

Co-Directors, The National Testing Network in Writing

Longman
New York & London

Executive Editor: Gordon T. R. Anderson
Production Editor: Halley Gatenby
Text Design: Laura Ierardi
Cover Design: Steven August Krastin
Production Supervisor: Judith Stern
Compositor: Graphicraft Typesetters Ltd.
Printer and Binder: Maple Vail

Writing Assessment

Longman Inc.
95 Church Street
White Plains, N.Y. 10601

Associated companies:
Longman Group Ltd., London
Longman Cheshire Pty., Melbourne
Longman Paul Pty., Auckland
Copp Clark Pitman, Toronto
Pitman Publishing Inc., Boston

Library of Congress Cataloging-in-Publication Data
Main entry under title:

Writing assessment.

(Longman series in college composition and communication)
Bibliography: p.
1. English language—Rhetoric—Study and teaching—Addresses, essays, lectures. I. Greenberg, Karen L.
II. Wiener, Harvey S. III. Donovan, Richard A.
IV. Series.
PE1404.W694 1986 808'.042'076 85-23729
ISBN 0-582-28516-X

86 87 88 89 9 8 7 6 5 4 3 2 1

Contents

121, 154   v

Foreword

This book spells out the implications of the growing use of tests of writing skill in American higher education, especially in larger institutions, which affects the progress and learning of millions of students. The book is one tangible result of a project that might have been limited by its topic and merely technical in approach. Instead, the National Testing Network in Writing (NTNW) has been a rallying place for educators who share the renewed value put on written communication and who seek to resolve the controversies related to the difficult task of assessing writing ability.

The work of NTNW can be understood only in the context of recent, ongoing changes in higher education. Twenty years ago these ideas would have had little of their current complexity or urgency.

When substantial numbers of "new students" entered colleges and universities in the late 1960s and early 1970s, they changed the framework for understanding learning beyond adolescence. Their lack of preparation for traditional college work was particularly evident in writing, and by the mid-1970s educators and the press perceived a writing "crisis" in colleges and high schools.

At the same time, tightening budgets (compared to the period of expansion following World War II) and growing public doubts about all levels of education led to new demands for accountability. There was increased interest in testing at both public and private institutions.

The emergence of new students and the recent emphasis on accountability are intertwined. The great growth of community colleges; the investment in remedial programs at two-year and four-year institutions; the increased access of minorities, adults, and women, are a familiar story. The development of new means of program evaluation, budgeting tied to enrollment, the defining of standards and required competencies, new approaches to standardized testing—were all less visible but equally important.

The demand for accountability was partly a reaction to the new students. When these students performed poorly, educators took part of the blame. Students who seemed illiterate led faculty, administrators, and legislators to call for the kinds of tests discussed within NTNW, and it remains a policy question whether the tests are supposed to screen poor students out or ensure their development.

To some extent, the similar movement to reimpose curricular requirements added up to an attempt to turn back the clock.

Always at issue was how to keep the doors open, or, indeed, how to open them further, while asserting meaningful standards. Both directions have had to be clarified and related to each other. Educators of minority students, for example, consistently expect more from their students and depend on testing to improve performance. This complex history helps explain why the terrain was difficult for NTNW. The concern with testing was driven by both access and accountability.

In addition, the project touches on a deep-seated tension between testing and learning. The American practice of using teachers as testers contributes to this tension. When do teachers encourage, and when do they judge? Though the tension can be resolved in theory, in practice students rarely learn from their answers to tests. Teachers often "teach to the test," testing what is measurable and "objective," or they score by consensus from a limited perspective.

When NTNW was begun in 1981, there was some concern that the project would favor testing at the expense of learning. Much of the new research and theory saw writing as a process and a way of thinking, and new educational approaches were encouraging. Yet writing ability was difficult to define and, to some educators, impossible to measure.

In schools and colleges, writing is mainly undertaken for the purpose of assessment, and many students find the idea of a "writing test" redundant. Few teachers question that evaluation is needed in education, for various reasons. However, when writing is performed only for judgment, it may not reflect the real abilities of the writer.

Happily, through its major conferences and this volume, NTNW has been able to generate solutions to these dilemmas. The network draws on the best new work on the writing process and on the development of writing abilities. In addition to emphasizing process over product, there have been an insistence on assessing writing by sampling writing, not by responses to multiple-choice questions; a call for attention to whole paragraphs and essays rather than to sentences only; and an important focus on meaning more than on errors. Behind this project is a recognition that testing will continue to be a part of the educational scene, but that, just as writing ability can be enhanced, tests can be improved.

The project represents a humanistic addition to the debates on testing and has allowed plenty of room for disagreement. NTNW's most important achievement may in fact be in giving voice to writing teachers in a forum that usually has been dominated by researchers and policymakers. Most of the contributors to this volume, as well as the project organizers and editors, teach writing on a regular basis. Writing teachers today are a larger and more diverse group than 20 years ago. No longer just members of English departments, they have specialized in many related fields (including linguistics, rhetoric, psychology, education, and sociology). They are directly involved in trying to make education meaningful for all students.

A word should be said about the institutional sources of NTNW. Although the City University of New York (CUNY) was the source and original sponsor, the project has gone well beyond its boundaries. CUNY was the appropriate place of origin, given its signal work in educating new students—particularly since the 1960s—as well as its subsequent efforts to develop a fair assessment of student writing. Chancellors Robert J. Kibbee and Joseph S. Murphy gave valuable support to NTNW, and the late Mina Shaughnessy gave it some of its inspiration.

Finally, the Fund for the Improvement of Postsecondary Education (FIPSE) has supported NTNW. FIPSE is a federal grants agency that has imaginatively invested in the complex recent history of higher education and shares with NTNW a concern with opening up opportunity through meaningful standards.

Richard Hendrix
Empire State College, SUNY
Long Island Regional Center

Preface

A major outgrowth of the intensive drive to written literacy at American post-secondary institutions has been an equally intensive drive to measure the progress of students attempting to acquire that literacy. State legislatures and boards of education across the nation have mandated large-scale writing assessment programs, inspired in part by public outcry for a return to basics, and in part by a general lack of interest from teaching faculty in taking early initiatives to develop tests measuring basic skills. These legislatures, wary of committing tax dollars to educational programs whose successes and failures do not submit to measurement, have pressed chief academic officers to produce data on how students write before and after completion of writing courses. Those officers, in turn, have required administrators of writing programs in English departments to test students and to certify the student-writers' proficiency at various points in their postsecondary education. As a result, numerous tests for writers have mushroomed over the last five years, providing statistics still awaiting analysis. Some institutions are testing writers to place them in appropriate courses, and some institutions are testing writers for proficiency as literate members of society.

The rush to test writers has created serious problems for writing faculty throughout the nation who now, willingly or not, are right at the heart of the assessment effort. First, there is little consensus about the skills and processes that constitute "writing." Frequently, writing tests are developed by university testing offices or by private testing services without benefit of the insight and skill that classroom teachers can bring to the complex task of writing evaluation. Moreover, research on the writing process, still in its infancy, unfortunately has not had much influence on the shape and scope of many writing tests. The tests that are based on current knowledge in the field have not been widely disseminated. This lack of shared information has contributed to the wide variability in the definitions of "writing ability" or "writing skills."

In addition, many institutions are testing within severe budgetary and temporal constraints. For example, a testing coordinator with a small budget may choose a multiple-choice test to measure writing skills because such a test costs much less to administer than an essay test scored holistically by trained faculty. This decision can have serious negative consequences for students and for curricula, particularly if the test does not measure the behaviors and skills that faculty believe characterize writing ability. Moreover, this choice may prove less cost-efficient in the long run because of the need for test security and, hence, the need to pay for the development of new, secure forms of the test.

Finally, testing operates within a highly charged political environment. National, state, and local funding sources scrutinize data and act upon them, despite a distinct lack of consensus among scholars as to the validity of the various testing instruments. Furthermore, there may be so much pressure to produce data that students are tested after minimal exposure to formal writing instruction and are, therefore, judged as competent or incompetent writers based on programs of instruction too brief to be adequate.

Whatever one's position on current writing assessment programs and practices, few would disagree that there have been too few opportunities for the people who develop, implement, and grade tests to exchange ideas and to learn from each other. With support from the Fund for the Improvement of Postsecondary Education and from the Office of Academic Affairs of the City University of New York, the National Testing Network in Writing (NTNW) was created to address this need—to enable teachers, administrators, and researchers to pool resources, exchange ideas, and review data. NTNW has accomplished its objective in a variety of ways.

First, the NTNW clearinghouse has collected information and data concerning the measures and the procedures used to assess students' writing skills at more than 2000 member institutions. After cataloguing and storing this information, NTNW has disseminated it to network members in the form of four different types of publication: summaries of the survey of network members, a data analysis of the survey, four editions of the bulletin *Notes from the National Testing Network in Writing,* and this book.

In addition to disseminating information and charting the relatively new and very controversial areas of writing assessment, NTNW has created unique opportunities for educators involved in writing assessment to question each other face-to-face and to share observations and insights. The first NTNW conference on writing assessment was held in New York City in March 1983. Many of the experts who had written articles for *Notes* served as facilitators for the small-group workshops that composed most of the conference program. The workshops focused on specific issues such as the politics of testing, test development, research, holistic scoring and reader training, testing of minority students, and the impact of testing on curricula and pedagogy. The conference was an enormous success. More than 350 educators from 36 states and three foreign countries participated, and they returned to their schools with new ideas, new materials, new solutions to problems, and—for many—new problems. Discussion of the issues continued long after the conference ended. The response was so enthusiastic that several universities invited NTNW to cosponsor subsequent conferences. Thus began the tradition of the annual NTNW Conference. The second conference, held in Tallahassee, Florida, in March 1984, was cosponsored by NTNW, the City University of New York, and Florida State University. The third conference took place in March 1985 in San Francisco and was cosponsored by NTNW, the City University of New York, the University of California, and California State University. The fourth conference, which is scheduled to take place in April 1986 in Cleveland, will be cosponsored by NTNW, the City University of New York, and Cuyahoga Community College. The issues identified in this book grew largely out of experiences shared at the first two conferences and the responses to our Technical Assistance Program.

The NTNW Technical Assistance Program was another activity designed to support test development and refinement. Building on the momentum generated by *Notes* and the first conference, NTNW arranged follow-up assistance for members requiring on-site consultations about test programs. By linking institutions with educators experienced in assessment, we expanded our concept of cooperation in the testing of writers. Reports from both consultants and host institutions attest to the success of this activity. "It was important . . . to know that we are heading in the right direction," writes one program director to a large southern university, for example. "We are reassured that our testing program is comparable with others across the nation and that we are proceeding on sound legal and academic grounds." This reaching out for professional and collegial validation is a mark of many testing programs around the nation, and we are sure that our Technical Assistance Program provided an important service.

In order to bring detailed and current information about writing assessment programs and practices to the profession at large, NTNW launched a major effort to survey its members. The results of the survey document the ways in which institutions of higher education throughout the country are grappling with decisions about the assessment of students' writing abilities. In 1983, we mailed 600 questionnaires to network members and analyzed data from more than 325 respondents. A 1985 survey is enabling us to sample the responses of more recent network members. Results of the 1983 survey indicate that writing assessment is both widely accepted and on the rise. A majority of responding institutions (84 percent) use some kind of test to place students into their composition courses or to exempt them from those courses, and almost one-fourth of the schools (23 percent) use a subsequent test to certify writing proficiency. Only 5 percent of the NTNW sample indicated no assessment of students' writing skills. The data also reveal that universities do more testing than four- and two-year colleges in the sample, although two-year colleges do a disproportionately large amount of placement testing.

After careful analysis of the data and consideration of the growing literature on testing writers; review of conference presentations, articles and *Notes,* and responses to the Technical Assistance Program; and frequent conversations with faculty in testing all across the country, we want to share some of our observations about features of the testing effort in the hope that these observations might help institutions just starting a writing assessment program or reviewing an existing one.

First, we commend the burgeoning nationwide attempts to assess writers, but only when those attempts draw upon the efforts of the best writing teachers, researchers, administrators, and text experts and are subject to rigorous investigation and discussion. Testing compels us—teachers, researchers, statisticians, administrators—to develop and refine our definitions of good writing. Often only the reality of an imminent test has been able to force dialogues that ultimately produce a consensus on goals and standards on a particular campus. Long overdue, these statements of goals and standards explain what we believe in to our students, their parents, the general public, and the men and women in government and private industry who provide moral and financial support for the literacy effort. In an age perhaps hysterical over accountability, the proper role of those concerned with student writing is to influence the terms of the accounting, not leave it to others. We do this by saying that we know what good writing is, how to describe it, and how to assess it. There is no perfect test—and this we must say, too—but given an openness and a willingness to change, we can identify testing as a developing art that time, research, and practice will shape into a more perfect form. Regrettably, in many cases we have not willingly turned our attention to assessment, and legislatures, perceiving chaos in the void, have forced the development of tests that have not enjoyed full academic scrutiny and debate.

Fortunately, many teachers and researchers have awakened to the imperative of testing writers. Through a more active involvement in assessment during the past few years, English faculty and their professional organizations have ascertained by consensus that the only valid method of testing students' writing is, in fact, to examine students' writing. The NTNW codirectors and National Advisory Board affirm that position without reservation. Multiple-choice writing tests do measure some of the skills that writing samples measure, including the ability to recognize the conventions of grammar, sentence structure, and mechanics, and the ability to make an appropriate stylistic choice among several options. However, multiple-choice tests cannot measure the skills that most writing teachers identify as the domain of composition: inventing, revising, and editing ideas to fit purpose and audience within the context of suitable linguistic, syntactic, and grammatical forms. The 1983 NTNW survey indicates that network members support the position that writing should be assessed directly through writing samples scored by trained faculty readers. Locally developed, holistically scored writing samples were preferred over any other type of test, regardless of its purpose (placement, proficiency, minimal competency, or diagnosis). More than two-thirds (69 percent) of the tests given by the responding institutions include writing samples: half of these tests (53 percent) are writing samples alone, and the remainder are writing samples given in conjunction with some other type of test. Furthermore, survey respondents also indicated that almost all (97 percent) of their holistically scored writing sample tests are locally developed by departmental or collegewide committees.

In regard to the locally developed, holistically scored writing sample, there are enormous benefits in developing a writing assessment test at local campuses—

again, as long as the effort involves faculty members sharing ideas and working toward common goals. Here is a case in which reinventing the wheel may be the best way to assure that the vehicle will run. Many good tests exist, and many of them, complete with tested writing prompts, successful rubrics, and efficient grading sessions, can be transported easily to other campuses for adoption. However, colleagues working together at a single institution attempting to assess writers have an investment in the test development at that institution. Teachers who shape an exam believe in it and will see that its principles infuse curriculum and classroom practice. A transported test, no matter how successful, rarely can build upon this sense of investment to make an important impact on course content.

Our investigations suggest that the uses of testing generally are beneficial and aim to ensure that college students get the assistance they need to become more competent writers. Our survey revealed the manner in which institutions use the results of their writing tests. Most of the schools in the sample make placement testing mandatory for all entering students in order to provide appropriate instruction in writing. In addition, these schools certify the writing proficiency of some students, generally those students who will receive degrees. The survey also reveals that respondents provide "intensive" and "remedial" courses and other assistance for students who fail their writing tests.

Our findings also underlined the need for continued research on the instruments and procedures used to test writing as well as research on the potential abuses of testing. When writing faculty are directly involved in designing and evaluating writing tests, the potential for these abuses is reduced. But ongoing examination of the goals, procedures, and uses of writing tests is necessary to ensure that these tests are meeting the needs of students and are serving the functions for which they were created.

The chapters that comprise this book provide a close examination of issues and strategies in writing assessment. The authors offer answers to a number of complex questions about testing writers, and they present a range of perspectives, diverse methodologies, and varied problems and solutions. These topics are the core of any testing effort and, taken together, can help any institution formulate, reformulate, refine, and implement a comprehensive program for assessing student writing.

The first four chapters—by Andrea Lunsford; Stephen Witte, Mary Trachsel, and Keith Walters; Marie Jean Lederman; and Rexford Brown—present a history of writing assessment and identify its major issues and problems. We travel from the early years of the American colonies to nineteenth- and twentieth-century America to China, for remarkable insights on the nature of writing assessment. The next four chapters—by Edward White, Daniel Fader, Kenneth Bruffee, and Roscoe Brown, Jr.—identify specific procedures and problems of current writing assessment efforts. Our contributors deal with the nuts and bolts of the testing machine, large-scale tests, political pressures, and the impact of testing on minorities. The final four chapters—by Gertrude Conlan, Sybil Carlson and Brent

Bridgeman, Rosemary Hake, and Gordon Brossell—present research on writing assessment and specify directions for future studies. These chapters lay the groundwork for the work awaiting us in the next decade. The focus here on recent research and development excludes several classic essays on testing writers, but an annotated bibliography on writing assessment, by William Lutz, describes these essays for interested readers. Our sixteen authors come from a variety of disciplines (English, education, linguistics, sociology, and psychometrics), and because all the essays were written expressly for this volume, the book reflects the most current directions in writing assessment.

We hope that you will find this work provocative and useful and, moreover, that some of you will join the National Testing Network in Writing and become a part of our future.

Karen L. Greenberg
Harvey S. Wiener
Richard A. Donovan

About the Contributors

Brent Bridgeman is a research scientist in the division of educational policy studies at the Educational Testing Service. His research has centered on noncognitive factors affecting students' test performance and on criteria for student placement and the validation of placement tests. He also has experience in longitudinal investigations of children's development and has directed research projects on cognitive development. He is a reviewer for four prestigious journals in educational research and has written numerous articles on cognitive development and on educational measurement.

Gordon Brossell is associate professor of English education in the College of Education of Florida State University. He has served as a test developer for the Florida Teacher Certification Examination, creating the writing test specification and the topics, and he also designed the test specifications and topics for the Florida College-Level Academic Skills Test in Writing and the Florida State Student Assessment Test in Writing. He has published numerous articles on the teaching and testing of writing. He frequently speaks on writing assessment at conferences and workshops, and in 1983 he codirected the Second Annual NTNW Conference on Writing Assessment.

Rexford Brown is director of communications and senior policy analyst for the Education Commission of the States. For 11 years he served as test developer for the National Assessment of Education Progress and was general editor of all NAEP materials and publications. His publications include *Reading, Thinking, and Writing* and *Writing Achievement, 1969–1979*; his policy studies include "Searching for the Truth about Truth-in-Testing Legislation" and "Public Policy and Pupil Achievement." He is also current chair of the English Specifications Panel of the GED Testing Service and a member of three NCTE committees: Testing and Evaluation, Research, and Excellence in English.

Roscoe C. Brown, Jr., is president of Bronx Community College of the City University of New York and former director of the Institute of Afro-American Affairs at New York University. He has received numerous awards and honors for scholarly and community activities and has served as a consultant to the Educational Testing Service, the New York and New Jersey state education departments, and the Department of the Interior's Gateway National Recreation Area. He is the author of numerous books and essays on Afro-American issues and on the transmission of literacy.

Kenneth A. Bruffee is professor of English at Brooklyn College. He has published widely on collaborative learning, innovations in liberal education, writing assessment, and the twentieth-century crisis in the authority of knowledge. He directed an institute in training writing peer tutors supported by the Fund for the Improvement of Postsecondary Education. He is past chair of the Modern Language Association Teaching of Writing Division and a member of the editorial board of *Liberal Education.*

Sybil Carlson is a senior research associate in the Division of Measurement Research and Service of the Educational Testing Service. Her research has focused on the application of learning theory to evaluation and instruction; assessment of and instruction in problem solving; new measures for medical school admissions in problem solving, interpersonal skills, and letters of evaluation; development of new test item types; and assessment of writing skills. She has directed numerous research projects throughout the United States and has written extensively on educational measurement and writing evaluation.

Gertrude Conlan is a senior examiner at the Educational Testing Service. Her work has involved both multiple-choice and essay tests of writing ability at various levels. She has directed the scoring of writing samples produced by kindergarten pupils as well as by postgraduate students. Most of her publications are concerned with the measurement of writing ability.

Daniel Fader is professor of English at the University of Michigan, where he founded and, for seven years, chaired the English Composition Board, which is responsible for the teaching of writing in all departments of the College of Literature, Science, and the Arts. He has lectured widely throughout the country on the teaching and testing of writing and is the author of many books and essays on literacy. He is now completing a book on the rhetoric of revision.

Rosemary Hake is professor of English and coordinator of the writing program at California State University at Los Angeles. She has conducted research on applied linguistics, rhetorical theory, and the assessment of written expression, and she has authored numerous articles in all three areas.

Marie Jean Lederman is university dean in the Office of Academic Affairs of the City University of New York. She has directed CUNY's Freshman Skills Assessment Program and Instructional Resource Center since 1979. She has authored numerous articles on teaching writing to nontraditional students as well as on literature and film. In addition, she has served as consultant to various writing programs of the New York City Board of Education and has lectured widely throughout the country on the teaching and assessment of basic skills of college students.

Andrea A. Lunsford is associate professor of English and coordinator of composition at the University of British Columbia. Her major interests include the theory and pedagogy of basic writing, the history and theory of rhetoric and composition studies, and the concept of coauthorship. She is coauthor of three books and has published a number of articles on teaching writing. As a Mina Shaughnessy scholar for 1984–85, she studied the strategies and processes of group writing in seven major professional organizations.

William Lutz is associate professor and chair of the Department of English at Rutgers University-Camden. He served as executive director of the New Jersey College Basic Skills Assessment Program from 1977 to 1979, during which time he supervised the design, development, and administration of tests in reading, writing, and mathematics for all New Jersey public college and university freshmen. He is the author of numerous articles on testing, language, and rhetoric, and author or coauthor of five books. He is a frequent speaker at conferences and workshops on writing and evaluation.

Mary Trachsel is a doctoral candidate in rhetoric in the English Department at the University of Texas at Austin. Her research interests include developmental studies, pedagogy, and literacy. Her dissertation will treat connections among first-language acquisition, second-language learning, and the acquisition of literacy skills.

Keith Walters, a doctoral candidate in linguistics at the University of Texas at Austin, has done research in language use in the writing conference, transfer of organization patterns in English compositions by Arabic-speaking students, and Texas dialects. His dissertation will be a study of linguistic variation and social change in Tunisia.

Edward M. White is professor of English at California State University, San Bernardino, and was director of Research in Effective Teaching of Writing, a project funded by the National Institute of Education, from 1980 to 1985. He has been coordinator of the California State University Writing Skills Improvement Program, the principal administrator responsible for the development of the CSU English Placement Test, and director of the CSU English Equivalency Examination program for over a decade. He has written extensively on the measurement of writing ability and is a frequent speaker at conferences, director of many workshops on testing, and consultant on writing and evaluation to various educational institutions.

Stephen P. Witte is associate professor of English at the University of Texas at Austin. He has served as codirector of the Writing Program Assessment Project funded by the Fund for the Improvement of Postsecondary Education and has coauthored five monographs on the evaluation of college writing programs and two books on writing assessment. He is cofounder and coeditor of the journal *Written Communication* and is the author of many articles on writing and writing assessment, one of which received the Richard Braddock Award.

1

The Past—and Future— of Writing Assessment

ANDREA A. LUNSFORD

Correctly assessing current systems of testing depends in part on knowing the tradition out of which these systems grew. A look at the history of testing may help to inform our understanding of the present and to provide a lens through which we may view future directions in the testing of writing.

Our current attempts to test student writing stem most directly from Harvard University's decision, in 1873–74, to institute a *written* examination in English composition. Harvard's catalogue for that year informs students that "each candidate will be required to write a short English composition, correct in spelling, punctuation, grammar, and expression, the subject to be taken from such works of standard authors as shall be announced from time to time" (Hill, Briggs, and Hurlbut 55). Harvard's move set off a chain of events that led inevitably to increased standardization and reflected the growing desire to find more and more objective means of assessing student performance. As early as 1879, the Conference of New England Colleges met at Trinity College in order to set standard regional requirements, and by 1894 the first National Conference on Uniform Entrance Requirements in English had been held. Only a few years later, in 1901, the College Entrance Examination Board, which exerted profound influence on writing assessment and on increased standardization, held its first sitting. This general move toward uniformity, and the tests that necessarily accompanied it, paved the way for the role that writing tests increasingly played in higher education (see Cook; Hays; Stoddard).

But not everyone accepted standardized entrance requirements based on arbitrary composition tests. Leading the swelling ranks of the opposition was the University of Michigan's redoubtable Fred Newton Scott (see, e.g., Stewart, "Two Model Teachers" and "Some Facts Worth Knowing"). In a series of fiery speeches and articles, Scott charged that Harvard's entrance examination defied "all the accepted principles of education and the suggestions of common sense."

The tests, Scott insisted, brought forth from the student the "merest fluff and ravelings of the adolescent mind, revealing neither the student's independent thought nor command of English." Scott went even further, charging that the examinations were in fact simply a "convenience for the examiner, not an essential of secondary study" ("What the West Wants," 13–14).

At the heart of Scott's objection to Harvard's examination was his concept of how best to accredit public schools and hence how to admit students to colleges and universities. The "western" model of accreditation, developed at the University of Michigan, was at the polar extreme from what Scott saw as Harvard's "feudal" model, one that essentially aimed to "dictate" what should be taught in the public schools by providing a list of works on which examination questions would be based ("College Entrance Requirements"). In contrast to this "feudal" system, the Michigan model called for university representatives to visit public schools and cooperatively examine faculty, curriculum, and students. Scott defended this model as "organic," noting that it brought teachers from colleges and public schools together to work out mutually agreeable standards and requirements. In discussing secondary school accreditation, the 1910 edition of the *Encyclopaedia Britannica* notes, "Two hundred and fifty schools are accredited by the University of Michigan. In 1904 it was stated that the system was gaining favor in the east, and that it had been adopted more or less by all the eastern colleges and universities with the exception of Harvard, Yale, Princeton, and Columbia" (Hartog 44).

Those "exceptions" came to be the rule, however, and while secondary schools continued to be accredited in a variety of ways, we know that the Michigan cooperative or "organic" model of accreditation eventually lost out to the more arbitrary entrance examinations of the big Ivy League universities. But in the short run, Scott and his colleagues successfully challenged the efficacy of Harvard's rigidly set lists of works on which their entrance exams were based. Teachers and professors joined the revolt against the lists and their dictatorial powers over the high schools, a revolt that served as the catalyst for the 1911 formation of the National Council of Teachers of English (NCTE; see Mason; Fay).

The stormy career of these early written examinations (the great-grandparents of our contemporary placement, competency, and exit tests) and their relationship to the new and increasingly influential discipline of English has been chronicled in two recent works (Applebee; Hook). But such works generally begin in the mid-nineteenth century, since our discipline essentially dates from that era. The tremendous furor over examinations, particularly over examinations in composition, however, has a history much older than our discipline.

It probably comes as a surprise to many of us to realize that the system of testing student proficiency in terms of *written* examinations dates primarily from the same nineteenth-century period that witnessed the birth of English departments as we know them today.[1] That is not to suggest, however, that examinations are a nineteenth-century phenomenon. But the earlier examinations were oral, not written, and most Western college examinations derive, in fact, from the oral university exams of the Middle Ages, such as those at Bologna in the early thirteenth century, which are described in H. Rashdall's *Universities of Europe in the Middle Ages*, published in 1895. Most of these early oral tests consisted of two parts: one in which the candidate faced a small group of examiners, and a second, more ceremonial, which usually took the form of a public discourse. The long tradition of oral examinations invested the system with authority, and indeed oral tests still provide a powerful means of assessment, as everyone who has defended PhD examinations and theses can attest. In a 1906 study of German universities, Friedrich Paulsen notes that the formal medieval examinations increased students' alertness, their powers of comprehending new ideas, and their ability to assimilate such ideas. Hence, he concludes, the oral examinations "did more to enable a student to grasp a subject than the mute and solitary . . . modern examinations can possibly do" (251).

Certainly examinations based on oral discourse dominated early American colleges and universities and hence provide the model out of which our current system ultimately grew. To understand just how such a transition from oral to written forms of assessment evolved, however, we may most profitably turn to the oral-based eighteenth-century model of education. For as George Bohman points out in "Rhetorical Practice in Colonial America," not only examinations but most of higher education was conducted orally. In "Rhetoric in the American College Curriculum: The Decline of Public Discourse," Michael Halloran examines the effects that a strong tradition of orality had on higher education in the eighteenth century. Rhetorical education, Halloran notes, "provided students with an art [of discourse], and more importantly with copious experience and with a tacit set of values bearing directly on the use of language in managing public affairs" (257). In other words, when students spoke in oral class recitations and public disputations, they spoke on matters of personal, social, and political significance: their words held consequences.

Classroom activity, as noted, was built around "oral disputation." One student chose and presented a thesis, often taken from reading or class discussion, and defended it against counterarguments offered by other students and the teacher. In addition, students regularly gave public speeches on matters of importance to society, in forums open to the entire college and the surrounding community. Reinforcing these curricular activities were the many student speaking societies where, as the University of Aberdeen's Alexander Bain was fond of pointing out, the students learned more from their peers than from their teachers (see, e.g., Potter 238–58). Bain recognized that this model of oral evaluation and the form of student speaking societies provided an audience, a full rhetorical context, and motivation for discourse, features woefully lacking in later "set" essays and written examinations. Halloran's article, like Bohman's, presents a detailed description of the oral system of education.

The culmination of these oral activities was a three- or four-week "visitation" held in the late spring of each year. During these sessions, students who wished to advance or to graduate made themselves available for oral examination in all their subjects, presented disputations, and defended them in public. In addition to the oral presentation, students often wrote out their discourses and sometimes submitted them to the teacher. Students who, in the judgment of a group of teachers or overseers, did not pass the exam studied and disputed for another year before trying again.

Of the many important features that characterize this early system of assessment, three have particular importance. First, the system was essentially interdisciplinary in that it brought all the language skills—reading, writing and speaking—to bear on problems of public concern. Students typically read a great deal in preparation for their oral examinations, and most wrote in preparation for them as well. As a result, the communicative arts were seen not as ends in themselves but as means by which students achieved personal, social, and academic goals. A second significant feature concerns the way in which the eighteenth-century system of assessment unified theory and practice. Like the classical model on which it was based, the eighteenth-century system established a theoretical relationship among language, belief, and action, and this rela-tionship was adopted and acted out as students engaged in public discourse. The rhetorical and grammatical principles studied could be immediately applied in class disputations and society debates. Such a union of theory and practice helped achieve a major goal of the university. That goal was essentially the same as Quintilian's 1500 years earlier: to produce good citizens skilled in speaking, who could use the arts of discourse to influence the life of society. The third feature worth noting concerns the model of learning implied in the eighteenth-century oral system. This learning model was a dynamic, collaborative one, based on learning by doing in association with a teacher, who, along with peers, set up a powerful dialogue or dialectic. As one late eighteenth-century pupil reported, the object of his classes and his examinations seemed "not to fill the mind with facts, but to strengthen and discipline it" (Edinburgh University MS Gen. 769/D). The special relationship, even between teacher-examiner and student, is implied in the statement that oral examinations "are of great educative value, if they are conducted on sound principles."

> *The judicious examiner who is master of the subject, while ascertaining what the student has learned, necessarily, to some extent, shows him what he has failed to learn, either in consequence of an imperfect method of study or lack of attention to certain important parts of the subject. Thus he is taught how to make his future efforts more successful. (Donaldson 288)*

Such a teacher-student relationship and viva voce examinations that character-ized that relationship, of course, depended on small classes, on the long-term association possible when a professor normally taught students throughout their college careers, and on the understanding that what was being taught was not so much a subject as a way of life in a democracy. In his 1836 "Report on Examinations," William McGuffey praises the practice of classroom speaking and oral examination, saying that it "cultivates the memory, the reasoning powers, the powers of extemporaneous expression, and the ability to defend views" (241). Unless students can do all this, McGuffey warns, they are "not suitably educated for this country" (241). Perhaps Henry Adams best sums up the spirit of the eighteenth-century system described here. Adams notes that throughout his years in college he "had been obliged to figure daily before dozens of young men who knew each other to the last fibre. One had done little but read papers to Societies, or act comedy in the Hasty Pudding, not to speak of all sorts of regular exercises [and examinations], and no audience in future life would ever be so intimately and terribly intelligent as these" (69). As a result of all this oral practice, Adams notes that "nothing seemed stranger than the paroxysm of terror before the public which often overcame the graduates of European universities" (69). For his part, Adams declared himself "ready to stand up before any audience in America or Europe, with nerves rather steadier for the excitement" (69).

The positive features, then, of the eighteenth-century system of oral assessment are that (1) it was strongly interdisciplinary, bringing reading, writing, and speaking together to deal with issues of public concern; (2) it unified theory and practice; and (3) it reflected a dynamic, collaborative learning model. What, we may well ask, happened to this system of instruction and assessment?

A definitive answer to this question lies in the progress of education in the nineteenth century, and while I cannot pretend to offer such a definitive answer here, I do wish to suggest that four factors were intimately involved with the fragmentation of the model I have described.[2] First and perhaps most important is the fact of rapidly growing enrollments in colleges and universities. In the last quarter of the nineteenth century, enrollments doubled, and professors found themselves faced not with a small group of students whose progress they could closely guide and monitor through four years of study and with whom they could engage in daily dialogue but with larger and increasingly unwieldy classes. A second important factor was the rapid expansion of scientific knowledge and the increasingly influential voice of empiricism. Educators anxious to assume the cloak of scientism naturally grew more and more wary of inexact and imprecise eighteenth-century methods of oral examination.

Growing enrollments and rapid expansion of knowledge may be linked to a third major factor responsible for the fragmentation of the eighteenth-century system: the trend toward specialization, toward ever narrower academic disciplines, which paved the way for English departments as we know them today (see Parker). These three factors are in my view related to a fourth factor that finally broke down the eighteenth-century oral, collaborative model. Ironically enough, this final factor was a growing emphasis on writing in colleges and a concomitant shift from oral to written evaluation.[3] Large classes, the increasing value placed on "scientific" or "objective" data, and bureaucratic demands for departmentalization and narrow specialization led teachers to search for ways to save time and to standardize procedures. Hence the rise of written examinations, which were generally the norm by turn of the century. In addition, the growing popularity of the belles lettres movement shifted the focus in the new English departments from spoken to written discourse, from the productive art of public discourse to the appreciation of literary works, and from broad interdisciplinary concerns to increasingly narrow departmental concerns.

The debate between the champions of oral and written examinations was a long and acrimonious one. The results are obvious in the description of the Harvard test with which this chapter begins. Although most scholars continued to see some value in oral discourse and viva voce examinations, such tests were increasingly attacked as (1) not thorough enough, (2) difficult to prepare questions for, and (3) unfair to students, who had little time for reflection. Written exams, on the other hand, evinced more "objectivity" and hence were argued to be more fair.[4]

The resulting emphasis on written examinations and on written discourse in general, with the inevitable loss of the powerful concept of oral public discourse, weakened the ties between the emerging English discipline and the eighteenth-century model of rhetorical instruction. Where reading, writing, and speaking had once been combined in the pursuit of a student's own academic and social goals, writing was now separated from the other communicative arts. The direct result of this separation was a dramatic loss of purpose: writing became not primarily a means of influencing important public affairs but merely a way to demonstrate proficiency. Divorced from its original purpose in rhetorical instruction, writing shifted its focus from discovering and sharing knowledge to being able to produce a "correct" essay on demand; lost the theoretical framework that related language, action, and belief; and became increasingly preoccupied with standards of usage, a tendency that grew, by the turn of the century, into a virtual cult of correctness. Whatever its virtues, the new methods of written assessment seem but a pale shadow of the elegant system celebrated by Henry Adams.

The history of testing in our own century is familiar to most of us: the demise of the Harvard "lists," the move from essay to more and more "objective" or "new" examinations covering narrower and narrower categories and promising efficiency and scientific certainty, the ensuing revolt against the use of objective tests alone to measure skills in writing, the strenuous attempts to create writing exams characterized by validity and reliability, and most recently, the proliferation of writing tests at all levels and the debate that currently surrounds those tests.

Writing shortly after the turn of the century, P. J. Hartog sums up a discussion of examinations:

> *It can scarcely be doubted that in spite of the powerful objections that have been advanced against [written] examinations, they are, in the view of the majority of English people, an indispensable element in the social organization of a highly*

specialized democratic state, which prefers to trust nearly all decisions to committees rather than to individuals. But in view of the extreme importance of the matter, and especially of the evidence that, for some cause or other (which may or may not be the examination system), intellectual interest and initiative seem to diminish in many cases very markedly during school and college life . . . , the whole subject [of written examinations] seems to call for a searching and impartial inquiry. (49)

Hartog's comments seem hauntingly appropriate today. Indeed, we seem once again to be at a significant watershed in the history of testing. The objectivist assumptions, which gave rise to twentieth-century scientism, are under attack from all sides, as we reassess our understanding of what it is that we want to know. *Writing Assessment: Issues and Strategies* in fact represents a major attempt to undertake the kind of "searching inquiry" called for at the turn of the century by Hartog.

Can the view of the past provided in this brief chapter offer any instructive questions to help guide such contemporary inquiries? This look at the past has suggested some tentative questions, questions that I believe hold profound implications for the future of testing.

My first question is this: How efficacious are our efforts to achieve and maintain separate or discrete assessment in writing, reading, and speaking? I have touched briefly on the historical trends that led to this separation and would note only that the eighteenth-century system merged instruction and assessment in the three areas. In spite of our modern tendency to separate them, I believe that the issue of the relationship among these three communicative arts is far from resolved. In addition to my own recent research, the work of composition scholars and cognitive psychologists has pointed up many links between reading and writing, while research on professional or work-related writing has recently found that such writing most frequently grows out of and is closely related to speaking. And of course, even in our most "objective" assessment, we have been unable to make a complete separation of these skills. Indeed, many objective tests no doubt test memory rather than writing skills. And many essay exams, especially those based on or closely related to a reading passage, may test reading more than they do writing. A large number of schools, in fact, offer six or more topics to choose from on writing proficiency tests, yet they usually fail to realize that such a test as a test of *writing* is questionable not only because the multiple topics most often elicit varying modes of discourse and thus make comparing student responses extremely problematic and unreliable, but also because the profusion of topics demands that students be able to *read* them critically in order to choose and respond to one. In short, an "essay" test that asks students to discriminate among six or so topics and to respond specifically and appropriately to one of them is first and foremost testing their ability to read.

Although I am convinced that major differences among speaking, writing, and reading do exist and that we must continue to acknowledge and stress those differences, I am also convinced that the research and trends argue that we reassess our attempts to *test* writing as a completely separate, isolable, and discrete skill. Will our theories of assessment and our methods of testing accommodate a new focus on the importance of speech to writing on the job—or on the links between reading and writing? Can we find integrative ways of assessing reading, speaking, and writing that will also satisfy current demands for validity and reliability? Answering these questions can have profound implications not only for future directions in testing but also for a curriculum that has, over the past 50 years, persistently separated the teaching and hence the assessment of speech, writing, and reading.

My second question does not relate to the relationship among communicative arts. Rather, I want to ask what model of learning and what values current writing tests reflect. These issues are at the heart of what we might call the ethos of testing. I have argued that the eighteenth-century method reflected a collaborative, interactive model of learning. In addition, the method of oral assessment reflected the values held at that time: a high standard of public discourse, freedom of speech, and a concern for abstractions such as justice and the social good, abstractions that are at the base of our unique linguistic heritage.

Most of us no doubt would support a collaborative, interactive model of learning and would say that we also value freedom of speech and the way writing promotes it by allowing us to make and share meaning about our world. But how many of our tests actually reflect that model or those values? I believe that our insistent striving for objectivity has gone hand in hand with the demise of a truly collaborative learning model because such a model depends on measurement whose criteria are based not on national norms but on the performance of the teacher as "connoisseur" and the student as "apprentice" in a context of shared cultural values and standards. In many of our tests, the criteria for achievement are external to the teacher-student relationship and hence militate against it. Further, many tests especially suggest that we value writing *not* for making meaning or for finding our stance in regard to the crucial issues of our lives but merely for labeling things "right" or "wrong," for demonstrating something called "minimum competency." This question, of course, raises other questions about future directions in testing. Can we meet the challenge of producing tests to reflect accurately the learning model and the values that we profess? Is it important to do so, and if so, why? These vexing questions demand our most careful consideration.

My final question grows out of considering the relationship of speaking, reading, and writing, as well as questions of ethos: What implications does the latest information revolution hold for us and for assessment? Most immediately, such systems as videotext, teledata, and Telidon and such methods as teleconferencing reinforce, rather than sever, the connections among reading, speaking, and writing. The advent of voice-operated computers makes those connections even stronger. If such systems and methods move toward reuniting the arts of reading, speaking, and writing, that reunion will have profound implications both for testing and for the curriculum.

In addition, the use of computers may well affect the way we perceive structure and organization in discourse. Watching and talking with youngsters doing computer programming, I am astounded at the speed with which they make synthetic leaps and at the dense sequencing they have mastered. If computer use does affect cognition, it will also affect how we perceive "good" writing, much as the medium of print journalism radically influenced our perceptions of structure and quality in writing. Such shifts, of course, will present further challenges for assessment.

Computers may affect the process as well as the product, however, by offering powerful potential for interaction and collaborative learning, especially in terms of dialogue and group writing. A *New York Times* article recently reported a story told by a professor at Carnegie-Mellon University who came home very late one night and settled down at her computer terminal to do some work. When several students at the university, who were working on one of her assignments, noticed that she had logged on, they sent an urgent "Help!" message. She answered, and together they discussed the assignment. The teacher later said that, whereas she had never in her entire teaching career known a student who would call at 2:30 A.M. for help, the computer allowed students to communicate more openly with her. But if computers hold potential for dialogue and communication, they also open intriguing possibilities for group writing. After completing preliminary research on co-writing or group writing processes, Lisa Ede and I have found this model predominant in much on-the-job writing as well as in most academic faculties other than English. Teachers are, in general, the only ones who view writing as a solitary act, and our tests, of course, reflect this view. What could be more solitary or agonized than students hunched at their desks trying to respond to a topic about which they know little and care even less? The use of computers may force us to reexamine our concept of writing and our means of assessing it.

Finally, computers used in conjunction with word processors may alter the goals of examinations. Many tests, for example, currently aim at diagnosing problems with mechanics and usage or spelling. Yet students who routinely work on word processors tell us that these are not their major problems. In fact, good software programs on spelling and mechanics are already available. Students also report that using word processors encourages a view of trial and error as constructive and necessary to success. Students who write hesitantly for fear of making mistakes are willing to make a hundred errors in programming a game, because they know they are on the way to success. And this tolerance for error, for using error as a way to achieve particular ends, can carry over to writing on the word processor. Perhaps, then, the use of word processors in composing will help *us* perceive the instructional value of error and hence reinforce the lessons Mina Shaughnessy taught so eloquently in *Errors and Expectations.*

I have mentioned my belief that the current technological revolution holds great potential for helping us understand the connections among speaking, reading, and writing; for encouraging interaction and dialogue; for bringing distant group authors together; for fostering a constructive view of error; and for speeding the transmission of information. Yet I am inclined to believe that computers will not be the answer to our prayers in terms of assessing student writers. What they may well do instead is alter our *concept* of assessment.

What would happen if students could debate publicly, via computer, in much the same manner described by Henry Adams, issues on which they might be asked to write? What if they could work in groups, via computer, to stimulate ideas and practice with real audiences? What if they could use a simple spelling program that would allow them to focus more clearly on their major point and its logical support, much in the same way students now use calculators in order to focus more clearly on the overall mathematical problem to be solved? What if they could use trial and error profusely and still produce—almost instantly—a clean copy, thus freeing them to concentrate not on avoiding messiness but on what they want to say and giving them, in addition, more time to write the long essays holistic markers seem to love and reward?

It occurs to me that such "what ifs" will surely alter our concept of assessment. And in doing so, we may find ourselves more able to provide testing that combines reading, writing, and speaking; that reflects a truly collaborative learning model; and that stresses as the uppermost value of discourse its power to help us create and share meaning about issues important to our lives and our society. By identifying the issues addressed in this volume and by provoking us to ask—and find answers for—questions like those raised here, the National Testing Network on Writing has taken a major step forward in helping us to realize such goals. And, as I hope my foray into the eighteenth century has suggested, future directions in testing may lead us, ironically, to recapture the best of our past.

NOTES

1. The earliest evidence of any *written* examinations of which I am aware occurs in W. W. Rouse Ball's *History of the Study of Mathematics at Cambridge* (1889), p. 193, where he notes that such an examination was introduced by Professor Bentley at Trinity College in 1702. But oral examinations can be traced back thousands of years to the system of testing public service officers in China (c. 1500 B.C.).

2. For a more thorough discussion of these issues, see Halloran; Connors, Ede, and Lunsford; Lunsford.

3. Writing, especially essay writing, was not universally welcomed into rhetoric or "English" classes. For a discussion of the debate over the use of essay writing in the nineteenth century, see Andrea A. Lunsford, "Essay Writing and Teachers' Responses in Nineteenth-Century Scottish Universities," *College Composition and Communication* 32 (1981): 434–44.

4. For a variety of nineteenth-century arguments on objectivity, see Whewell; Todhunter; Jebb; Latham; *Encyclopaedia Britannica*; Cyclopaedia of Education.

REFERENCES

Adams, Henry. *The Education of Henry Adams.* Boston: Houghton Mifflin, 1961.

Applebee, Arthur. *Tradition and Reform in the Teaching of English.* Urbana, Ill.: NCTE, 1974.

Ball, W. W. Rouse. *History of the Study of Mathematics at Cambridge.* London, 1889.

Bohman, George. "Rhetorical Practice in Colonial America." *The History of Speech Education in America.* Ed. Karl Wallace. Englewood Cliffs, N.J.: Prentice-Hall, 1954. 60–79.

Connors, Robert, Lisa Ede, and Andrea Lunsford. "The Revival of Rhetoric in America." *Essays in Classical Rhetoric and Modern Discourse.* Ed. Robert Connors, Lisa Ede, and Andrea Lunsford. Carbondale, Ill.: Southern Illinois UP, 1984. 1–15.

Cook, Albert. *A Summary of the Proceedings of the Conference on Uniform Entrance Requirements in English, 1894–1899.* n.p., n.d.

The Cyclopaedia of Education. Ed. Henry Kiddle and Alexander Schem. New York and London, 1877. 290–91.

Donaldson, James. "Examinations." *The Cyclopaedia of Education.* Ed. Henry Kiddle and Alexander Schem. New York and London, 1877.

Edinburgh University. MS Gen. 769/D.

Encyclopaedia Britannica. 11th ed. Cambridge, Eng.: 1910.

Fay, Robert. "The Reorganization Movement in English Teaching, 1910–1917." Diss., Harvard University, 1967.

Halloran, Michael. "Rhetoric in the American College Curriculum: The Decline of Public Discourse." *Pre/Text* 3 (1982): 245–70.

Hartog, P. J. "Examinations." *Encyclopaedia Britannica.* 1910 ed.

Hays, Edna. *College Entrance Requirements in English: Their Effects on High Schools.* New York: Columbia UP, 1936.

Hill, A. Sherman, L. B. R. Briggs, and B. S. Hurlbut, eds. *Twenty Years of School and College English.* Cambridge, Mass.: Harvard U, 1896.

Hook, J. N. *A Long Way Together.* Urbana, Ill.: NCTE, 1979.

Jebb, John. *Remarks upon the Present Mode of Education in the University of Cambridge.* London, 1774.

Latham, H. *On the Action of Examinations.* Cambridge, Eng., 1877.

Lunsford, Andrea A. "Rhetorical Lessons from History," forthcoming in *Transactions of the Canadian Society for the History of Rhetoric.*

McGuffey, William. "Report on Examinations." *Transactions of the Western Literary Institute.* Cincinnati, 1836.

Mason, J. H. "The National Council of Teachers of English, 1911–1926." Diss., George Peabody U, 1962.

Parker, William R. "Where Do English Departments Come From?" *College English* 28 (1967): 337–51.

Paulsen, Friedrich. *The German Universities and University Study.* Trans. Frank Thilly. New York: Scribner, 1906.

Potter, David. "The Literary Society." *The History of Speech Education in America.* Ed. Karl Wallace. Englewood Cliffs, N.J.: Prentice-Hall, 1954. 238–58.

Rashdall, H. *The Universities of Europe in the Middle Ages.* London, 1895.

"Report of the Committee on College Entrance Requirements." *National Education Association Addresses and Proceedings, 1899.* Chicago, 1899.

Scott, F. Newton. "College Entrance Requirements in English." *School Review* 9 (1901): 365–78.

———. "What the West Wants in Preparatory English." *School Review* 17 (1909): 13–14.

Shaughnessy, Mina P. *Errors and Expectations.* New York: Oxford UP, 1977.

Stewart, Donald. "Some Facts Worth Knowing about the Origins of Freshman Composition." *CEA Critic* 44 (1982): 2–12.

———. "Two Model Teachers and the Harvardization of English Departments." *The Rhetorical Tradition and Modern Writing.* Ed. J. J. Murphy. New York: MLA, 1982.

Stoddard, Francis. "Conference on Uniform Entrance Requirements in English." *Educational Review* (1905): 375–83.

Todhunter, I. *Competitive Examinations.* London, 1838.

Whewell, William. *English University Education.* London, 1838.

2

Literacy and the Direct Assessment of Writing: A Diachronic Perspective

STEPHEN P. WITTE, MARY TRACHSEL,
AND KEITH WALTERS

If every man's foot is to be taken as twelve inches long, it becomes an important question by whose foot we shall measure. So of the different standards of judging in the minds of different men.
  —Horace Mann, "Report of the Annual Examining Committees of the Boston Grammar and Writing Schools, with Remarks, by the Editor" (1845)

The title of this chapter includes at least two common but problematic terms—*literacy* and *assessment of writing*. These terms are problematic in part because they refer to concepts that are likely to imply different things to different people. They are also problematic because the connection between them may for some people be obvious, important, and direct, while for others the connection may be almost incidental, of no great consequence. The

The study reported here was jointly supported by grants from the Fund for the Improvement of Postsecondary Education (FIPSE Grant No. G008005896) and the University of Texas at Austin. The opinions expressed in this chapter do not necessarily represent those of the funding agencies. This discussion is a distillation of issues treated more extensively in S. P. Witte, K. Walters, M. Trachsel, R. D. Cherry, and P. M. Meyer, *Literacy and Writing Assessment: Issues, Traditions, Directions* (Norwood, N.J.: Ablex, forthcoming), and S. P. Witte, P. M. Meyer, R. D. Cherry, and M. Trachsel, *Holistic Evaluation of Writing: Issues, in Theory and Practice* (New York: Guilford, forthcoming).
  Readers not familiar with the distinction between synchronic and diachronic studies may wish to consult the work of F. de Saussure or commentaries on his work. As used here, *diachronic*, as its etymology would imply, means "across time"; it is used in an effort to avoid any of the teleological connotations that often accompany the use of a near synonym, *chronological*.

uncertainty surrounding the two terms with respect to their meaning and their relationship pervades most of the current literature on assessment. Nothing is perhaps more telling of this uncertainty than the many questions that remain unanswered about writing assessment: How should writing be assessed? What constitutes a valid assessment of writing ability? What do scores assigned to writing performances mean? To what extent are tests of writing also, or even primarily, tests of knowledge of subject matter? How can knowledge of subject matter and writing ability be separated? Who should judge writing perform- ances? What types of writing ought to be judged? Should the focus of writing assessment necessarily be limited to the products of composing? How much of an individual's writing must be judged before an assessment can be considered valid? What are the criteria by which student writing samples should be judged? Are evaluators of student writing aware of all the criteria they invoke in evaluating student writing? What is the relationship between judgments of writing and the role of education in society? What is the relationship between writing done as part of an assessment program and the writing required beyond or apart from the assessment environment? To what extent do writing assessments and the educational decisions following from them militate against cultural pluralism? What assumptions about the meaning of literacy are made by those who create and administer writing assessments and by those who judge writing performances?

However important such questions are, they are not new ones; in various forms, they arise throughout the history of writing assessment in this country. It is our contention that an examination of this history, particularly with respect to changing notions of the relationship between literacy and writing assessments, will guide us, as present-day evaluators of writing, in our own search for answers to such questions, a search demanded by our own need to understand the assumptions we make when we claim to assess writing. Our historical perspective on the relationship between the meaning of the term *literacy* and particular writing assessments is unlikely to make the current search for answers any less difficult; it should, however, help foster an awareness of current assumptions and the historical context that has shaped these assumptions.[1]

LITERACY AS A SHAPING FORCE IN AMERICAN EDUCATION

To a great extent, many of the assumptions that underlie current assessment practices are rooted in the two principal reasons for the institution of formal education in the United States. One of these reasons was religious, the other political. Writing about the religious emphasis of early American education, W. R. Stephens and W. Van Til comment that because of the New England colonists' belief in the inherent depravity of children, "the child needed to be educated to seek a religious conversion which would bring him into the fold of God's elect and make him an acceptable member of colonial society" (2). In keeping with the generally held belief that education could lead to religious knowledge and virtue, Horace Mann, in "The Support of Schools" (1839), concluded a report on the deplorable state of public education in the United States by emphasizing the inaccessibility of Christian (i.e., Protestant) doctrine to uneducated Americans:

> *To them, the Bible is a sealed book. Though living in the light of the nineteenth century, they are thrust backwards four centuries into the darkness of the age, which preceded the Reformation of Luther and the translation of the Scriptures into the native tongue. (52)*

This same goal—producing good Christians—was among the major reasons for the institution of higher education in the United States. The founders of Harvard University were concerned, for example, with producing well-trained ministers who could read all of the Bible in Latin "to advance learning and perpetuate it to posterity" (qtd. in Stephens and Van Til 10–11).

The second motivating force in early American education was the desire to produce good citizens. According to Stephens and Van Til (4–5), this commitment resulted in the Massachusetts Bay Colony's decision to enact its first law regarding education; although this law did not mandate the establishment of schools, it is the source of a principle of American education still with us today, the right of the state to require that children be educated according to the principles and values it believes necessary for its own survival.

These civic and religious motives later led to the Deluder Satan Act (1647), which actually specified the responsibility of local communities to set up schools to provide education for children in order that they might become literate Christian citizens. These motives not only influenced colonial education but also set a policy in this country that continues to the present time: the goal of education is to produce good citizens and to improve the morality of the society by inculcating the value of human improvability, whether under the guise of religious dogma or secular humanism.

In a nation that officially subscribes to the separation of church and state, the dogma of Christian morality in the domain of public education inevitably yielded to a philosophy of secular humanism. The connection that has typically been perceived between "human improvability" in the religious and the secular senses of the expression is aptly illustrated by the continuation of Mann's discussion of the need for improved public education. Having expressed alarm that the uneducated had no access to Scripture, Mann points out that such individuals likewise have no access to the moral, philosophical, and political ideas of Western history. Moreover, Mann argues, the consequences of a poor education extend to the individual's ability to function as a responsible citizen:

> *For them, the sages and the men of genius of our own and of former times have not lived. We open a book, and straightway a new train of delightful motions, of instructive thoughts takes possession of our mind, and, if the book has been well*

selected, we rise from its perusal with mental invigoration and purified feelings. But to those who cannot read, a book is only as a block, a stone, a clod of earth. What other sources of political information can they have, than the mutilated, perverted and fragmentary accounts, which have come, perhaps, through a hundred hands and been distorted by each in their passage, until the current and accredited copy no longer bears the slightest resemblance to the original? ("Support" 52)

It is important to note that in assessing public education, Mann singles out the acquisition of literacy skills as the criterion by which educational quality can be determined. His underlying assumption seems to be that the most important cultural values cannot be transmitted orally from one generation to the next—that if citizens can read (and write), subsequent generations will acquire the appropriate cultural, religious, and political values. This line of thought implies that a "text-based" society is necessarily more stable in all important respects than an oral one.

Mann was not alone in subscribing to a formula that equates literacy with education and illiteracy with ignorance; nor is it uncommon to encounter the same equations expressed, either explicitly or implicitly, in the present day. For instance, Stubbs (50) and Oxenham (42–57) give numerous examples of the ways in which the term *illiterate* is commonly used interchangeably with terms such as *stupid* and *ignorant*, while Farrell clearly subscribes to the equation himself, arguing that literacy is virtually equivalent to "intelligence"—that is, equivalent to the capability of abstract thought as presumably measured by standard IQ tests. Like Mann, Farrell claims that literacy necessarily improves the individual's ability to think. In Mann's view, access to written texts opens up to the reader a more reliable source of information and instruction than oral transmission provides. The literate individual's life is therefore improved because it can be patterned according to the "right" principles. Farrell, on the other hand, sees the corrective power of literacy as its ability to effect a change not merely in the content but, more important, in the form of the individual's thinking.

The tendency to define reading and writing as something more than academic subjects or skills to be learned at school makes the study of academic assumptions about literacy a necessary part of efforts to comprehend, evaluate, and, perhaps, improve the quality of education and the methods developed to evaluate its success.[2]

ASSESSMENT OF LITERACY SKILLS

The earliest detailed discussion of the use of direct written assessment in the United States is Mann's report on testing in the Boston public grammar schools. In 1845 written examinations were used for the first time as an expedient means of evaluating the academic performance of students too numerous to be tested in the traditional fashion—orally and individually for less than five minutes by "respected" members of the community. Until that time, academic writing had been essentially a literary skill, developed through the translation and imitation of classical authors and evaluated according to the prevailing standards of literary excellence.

The extent to which writing ability has traditionally been associated with familiarity with classic literacy models is apparent in Harvard University's 1896 report on high school and college English in the mid-nineteenth century. The opening essay in the report is A. Sherman Hill's "An Answer to the Cry for More English." In his essay, Hill refers to writing as "literary skill" and endorses the claim of Harvard's president that "an accurate and refined use of the mother tongue" is "the single mental acquisition that is an essential part of the education of a lady or gentlemen" (7). Hill goes on to describe instruction in English composition at Harvard—instruction that culminated with essay exams that required students to write on a subject selected from specified works of such literary masters as Shakespeare, Goldsmith, and Scott. The rationale behind the use of this type of exam was the need to develop in students an improved capacity for thought and expression, as Hill makes clear: "the student, by becoming familiar with a few works holding a high place in English literature, would acquire a taste for good reading, and would insensibly adopt better methods of thought and better forms of expression" (8).

In a different section of the same report, Briggs criticizes the failure of teachers at all levels of education to emphasize proper use of the mother tongue. In general, he argues, students develop proficiency in the reading and writing of classical literatures and languages at the expense of gaining an adequate command of English, one of the complaints against "traditional" education that led to the formation of the Modern Language Association in 1883 (see Parker). Because of the widespread overemphasis on the classics, Briggs notes, the writing of many college students was marred by "translation English," a perversion of the mother tongue that was especially deplorable because "no illiterate boy could produce it" (21).

The call for more instruction in the mother tongue in the second half of the nineteenth century led to the replacement of Latin and Greek literary models by the classic works of English literature. As Kinneavy notes, the development of English departments as a separate entity within the academy coincided with the tendency to view all forms of discourse as ideally literary. In his discussion of the teaching of discourse modes in nineteenth-century English instruction, Kinneavy makes the following observation:

> *The coincident occurrence of an accepted classification of the modes with the frequent narrowing of the field of English to literature caused the modes to be given from the outset . . . almost solely literary orientations. Thus narrative usually meant literary narrative, and description meant the sort of description one found in the novels of Cooper or the sketches of Washington Irving. Exposition meant the near*

literary expositions of stylists like Newman or Arnold or Ruskin; and the same writers typified argumentation. (12)

The emphasis on literary reading and writing as the subject of instruction in English departments continued, of course, well into the twentieth century, reflecting the increasing influence of the Modern Language Association (see Parker). This emphasis on the study and production of literary texts has not, however, continued unchallenged. In 1936 Stalnaker, for example, criticized the "elegant writing" encouraged by imitation of literary masters, calling it one of the primary weaknesses of then current instruction in writing. This instructional method, according to Stalnaker, resulted in the purposelessness of students' writing and encouraged a conformity to "literary standards" of language use that were at odds with the needs and interests of many students who were going to secondary schools and colleges in the industrial age. As a consequence, Stalnaker complained, "students who do not know the difference between active and passive voice, whose verbs and subjects only occasionally agree, are encouraged to imitate Lamb, Goldsmith, or Steele in writing polished essays about nothing" ("Measurement" 207).

Written examinations as first used in the Boston schools, however, seem to have demanded that academic writing assume the new expository function of demonstrating the student's knowledge in a variety of subjects such as physics, history, and philosophy. As the literature on testing indicates, this shift in the function of academic writing, from a purely literary to an expository skill, was not matched by an equally sudden shift in the literacy standards used to judge the quality of academic writing, for complaints about the use of "literary standards" to evaluate nonliterary writing continue to be heard to the present day (see Shaughnessy).

The mismatch between writing function and the criteria used to evaluate writing apparently went unnoticed by those who organized and administered early tests of writing. Addressing the virtues of the new written examinations, Mann focuses primarily on their administrative advantages, failing to concern himself with a central issue inherent in this form of direct assessment, namely, whether and to what extent the writer's knowledge of subject is separate from the written expression of that knowledge. Accordingly, Mann simplifies the issues by subsuming both skill in writing and knowledge of the thing written about under the more general category of "the state and condition of the pupils' minds" ("Boston" 334)—an assumption not unlike the one underlying Carton's recent speculations about the "inabilities" of college freshmen enrolled in writing courses.

In his 1845 discussion of the advantages of the new written exams over oral tests, Mann is primarily concerned with the clarity and objective certainty with which written tests represent the quality of a given student's mind. He offers the following seven reasons for the written exam's capability to accomplish this end:

It is impartial. (Boston 330)

This method is far more just than any other to the pupils themselves. (331)

The method under consideration is the most thorough. (331)

The new method prevents the officious interference of the teacher. (331)

It does determine, beyond appeal or gainsaying, whether the pupils have been faithfully and competently taught. (332)

It takes away all possibility of favoritism, and all ground for the suspicion of favoritism. (333)

[It results in] a transcript, a sort of Daguerreotype likeness, as it were, of the state and condition of the pupils' minds, [which] is taken and carried away, for general inspection. (334)

Mann expounds on these advantages in great detail, explaining in each case the numerous ways in which written examinations are superior to oral ones and demonstrating a sophisticated understanding of many of the critical issues in large-scale assessment. The impartiality that Mann attributes to written exams corresponds to contemporary assumptions about the advantages of standardized testing: all students, regardless of class or school, receive the same questions in a sufficient number to permit a fair sampling of each student's knowledge. In commenting on impartiality, Mann notes that "pupils required to answer dissimilar questions are like runners obliged to run on dissimilar courses" and that "each question is a partial test, and the greater the number of questions, . . . the nearer does the test approach to completeness" (331). In explaining the "just" nature of written examinations, Mann comments that "in an exercise of two minutes . . . the best scholar may fail, because he loses his only opportunity while he is summoning his energies to improve it; but give him an hour, and he will have time to rally and do himself justice" (331). The thoroughness of written exams derives from their making possible numerous questions on numerous subjects. In explaining how written tests avoid the "annoying" interruptions of examiners by teachers, Mann states:

Now where a school is examined by written or printed questions, distributed on the instant, by the examining committee—questions of which the teachers themselves are as ignorant as the pupils—they must, perforce, look on at their leisure. Though they writhe in anxiety, yet their ill-judged kindness can do no harm; their improper suggestions are excluded. (332)

Written tests, for Mann, distinguish students who have been taught well from those who have not. Students who can repeat "isolated facts and . . . abstract principles" have studied their texts, but those who can connect these "with life, with action, with duty" have been competently taught (332). As Mann notes later in the report,

if the scholars fail to answer, with promptitude and correctness, such questions as are found in the books, they must bear a portion at least of the dishonor; but if they *answer from the book accurately and readily, but fail in those cases which involve relations and the application of principles, the dishonor must settle on the heads of the teachers. (334)*

These tests likewise eliminate the possibility of favoritism, saving the examining committee from "the cry of injustice" (333). Finally, the written exam permits comparisons to be made among students, classes, and schools across years. Thus administrators can determine whether their schools are "advancing or retrograding" (334). Mann concludes by declaring that "only when the question can be inspected—that is, only when the written method of examination has been employed" can such necessary and significant comparisons be made; otherwise, "the state and condition of the pupils' minds . . . shall perish with the fleeting breath that gave it life" (334).

As Mann's list of the advantages of written exams indicates, the earliest of these examinations were explicitly intended to test knowledge in various subject areas rather than to evaluate the expression of that knowledge. Much current research on language production raises a number of questions about the extent to which subject knowledge and expression of that knowledge can be distinguished (e.g., Bracewell, Frederiksen, and Frederiksen; Nystrand). In the case of these early written examinations, the measurement of "quality of thought" or "the state and condition of the pupils' minds"—as educators typically described their task—more accurately referred to the examinee's ability to translate knowledge or thought into written form.

The tendency to view writing as a direct representation of thought was no doubt largely due to the capacity of written examinations to transform knowledge and thought into a physical artifact, Mann's "Daguerreotype likeness," which could then be subjected to statistical analysis and "scientific" measurement.[3] As the use of written examinations continued to expand, education turned to the newly developed science of statistics to facilitate more and more precise measurements of student performance on such tasks. By the late 1880s, when written examinations were regularly used to test large numbers of students, statisticians began to question the reliability of then current procedures for evaluating written tests. These procedures usually involved more or less impressionistic readings by the students' own teachers. In an 1888 article titled "The Statistics of Examinations," F. Y. Edgeworth, an Englishman,[4] claimed to have discovered a means of determining the "true judgment" of the "intellectual worth" revealed by written examinations. Edgeworth believed "intellectual worth" to be a measurable, objective reality that could best be identified by calculating the mean judgment of unquestionably "competent critics," namely, literary scholars and authors of grammar and composition textbooks. The deviations of individual evaluators' ratings from this mean judgment he regarded as "statistical errors."

Underlying Edgeworth's argument was the assumption that a direct correspondence exists between physical and mental phenomena. To illustrate the similarity he perceived between the two, he described the following situation, which he believed to be analogous to the evaluation of written examinations. Several judges are asked to estimate the weight of an object; some will produce estimates that are higher than the actual weight, and others will produce lower estimates. When all the estimates are plotted on a graph, however, the resulting pattern will reveal that the estimates deviate from the true weight in a predictable fashion, forming a bell curve. The same results, Edgeworth believed, could be expected when competent judges evaluated the "intellectual worth" of students' essay responses to questions. One had only to calculate the mean score to determine the "true" judgment of the student's writing.

Typical of testing research during this period is Edgeworth's dismissal of all questions regarding the validity of his measurement system. While he acknowledges that a student's written performance might be affected by the setting in which the exam took place as well as by a student's physical and emotional condition while writing the exam, he ultimately rejects such considerations as irrelevant:

> [N]o attempt is made to estimate the large element of chance which is introduced by the possibility of a candidate being "out of sorts" on the day of the examination; or of the [assigned] paper being specifically adapted to the accidents of his [the candidate's] taste or reading. (603)

Edgeworth concludes his argument with a lengthy investigation of actual placement exam results, followed by the suggestion that scores should be interpreted with the acknowledgment of their calculated probable deviation from the true judgment of the quality of intellect displayed in the writing.

In the case of oral examinations, the examiner's competence had been a function of his status as a God-fearing citizen within the community. The competence of the evaluators of written examinations, on the other hand, was largely decided on the basis of academic and literary credentials. When written exams were first used to measure not content knowledge but writing ability, "competent judges" were typically defined as authors, grammarians, and literary scholars (see Edgeworth; Hillegas; Steel and Talman). The faith in these people's ability to recognize quality in writing was virtually unquestioned, as is revealed, for example, by an excerpt from Hillegas's 1912 study in which English professors, authors of standard composition texts, gifted teachers and psychologists, and "men of special literary merit" were employed as raters: "No attempt has been made in this study to define merit. The term as here used means just that quality which competent persons commonly consider as merit, and the scale measures just this quality" (339).

Hillegas's study of writing assessment falls into the category of "scale measurements," products of the zeal for scientific accuracy in testing around the turn of the century. In order to bring scientific respectability to the measurement of writing ability, Hillegas proposed a 1000-point quality scale, each point signifying a "unit of quality" that was represented by a writing sample that at least 75 percent of the competent evaluators had judged to be superior to the sample representing the immediately preceding point on the scale. Users of the scale had only to find the sample that most closely resembled the student essay in question and record as the score the sample's numerical position on the scale.

The influence of belletristic literacy standards on Hillegas's scale is clearly evident in the samples selected to illustrate various levels of quality. With the exception of poetry, all modes and genres, rhetorical and literary, were represented in the scale. The extreme lower end, reserved for the very poorest writing, consisted of artificial samples written by competent judges to represent "absolutely no merit as specimens of English composition" (Hillegas 342). At the other end of the scale, the very highest quality of written expression was represented by "the youthful writings of such literary geniuses as Jane Austen and the Brontës" (352). Writing by actual freshman examinees was represented only in the middle range of the scale.

Not only does the Hillegas scale betray a preference for belletristic standards, but in a more subtle fashion the scale promotes certain social conventions—a "hidden curriculum" that, according to Bizzel, typically identifies the academy as "an agent of cultural hegemony," which, by overlooking differences in discourse communities, represents certain world views and values as universals (237).

Among the higher-quality samples appear many essays and paragraphs written on standard academic topics. The sample awarded a value of 772, for example, is a historical narrative about the end of the French and Indian War; the sample valued 838 is a description of Venus of Melos, and the one valued at 937 is a eulogy to Joan of Arc. Sharply contrasted with these samples—not only on the basis of mechanical correctness, cohesion, and coherence but also on the basis of subject matter—are the artificial samples at the low end of the scale. These samples typically treat books and school and all things academic in an irreverent or otherwise unfavorable light. Rural subjects and allusions to menial labor and low pay are pervasive, as is a generally hostile and uncooperative tone. The following passages are representative.

1   *I words four and two came go billa guni sing hay cows and horses he done it good he died it goon I want yes sir yes sir oxes and sheeps he come yes sir camed and goes billum gumun oomumm goodum.*

2   *I say never mind. I say he knows all right all right dony puki I say it aint. I got one I got to noo and loo, lov and sov. Don't you care all right all right I say.*

3   *i from thre ours up in room on books and books care for childer tore a page and rite on them.*

4   *dere teacher: I like schol not like school. that man other place like make work tools. Some day you say I rede*

5   *I want to say it aint no youse they aint got no right and they aint got no man ban tan pan pan san san sen sen sun sun tun tun.*

6 *Dear Sir: I write to say that it aint a square deal Schools is I say they is I went to a school. red and gree green and brown aint it hito bit I say he don't know his business not today nor yeterday and you know it and I want Jennie to get me out.*

7 *I write to tell I like the job to work what mr. Lambert said as he giv me a dolar harf a day to do things round his plase. I not affrade to work so I say plees giv me a job and I can look after the cow all right or anything no trouble long time I work for mr. panter he knows.*

These samples are particularly interesting for the insights they provide about the type of person whom examiners expected to find unable to perform well on the composition test. The points of reference from which the subject matter for low-rated samples is drawn are distinctly nonacademic, and accordingly they represent a group of writers who come from what Bizzell describes as "communities at a distance from academe" (238).

According to Bizzell, the discourse conventions of the academic community are so unfamiliar to nonmembers as to constitute something very much like a foreign language. When the language of academic discourse is perceived by those who use it as a universal code, however, those who are not socialized into its use are likely to be categorized as innately inferior. Such was apparently the case with the creation and intended use of the Hillegas scale; Hillegas at one point even describes his scale as measuring *individuals*, not just their performance as writers. Similarly telling is his dismissal of the need to define in any detail just what the scale really measures.

In the low-quality writing samples themselves, the immature and under-developed intellect of the imaginary writers is represented by the appearance of rhyming nonsense syllables that create the illusion of the babbling of young children who have not yet learned to talk. Very young children do in fact go through periods of repeating rhymed syllables while learning to talk, but the phenomenon is strictly oral, serving as a means for the child to practice the pronunciation of significant phonemes in the language and preparing the child to be able to distinguish between morphemes such as *my* and *by*. The presence of this phenomenon, through graphic representation, in combination with standard written forms in the artificial low-quality samples reveals as much about the judges' beliefs and attitudes toward illiteracy and illiterates as it does about the inability of an individual to write good English.

Interestingly, the appearance of nonsense syllables in the samples is coupled in one instance with a listing of barnyard animals (sample 1) and in other cases with a belligerent attitude (samples 2 and 5). In another low-rated sample, this belligerence or simple unwillingness to cooperate is directed specifically toward school (sample 6); in this sample the incoherence that is elsewhere represented by nonsense syllables appears as the intrusion of a list of colors (a feature likely to be found in the discourse of a young child who is learning to identify colors). Sample 7 differs from samples 2, 5, and 6 in tone; rather than hostility or defiance, if expresses a slavish willingness to cooperate—to work for low wages, to accept whatever menial task is assigned, to be content and cause no trouble. Like sample 1, this sample makes references to a rural environment, and like sample 4, it alludes to the nonacademic world of tools and unskilled labor. Sample 3 is similarly nonacademic in its reference; the sense that does come through the tangled syntax and garbled mechanics is a childish inability to understand the function of books or the proper way to treat them.

In contrast to the earthy and pragmatic concerns of the nonacademic communities represented by the personae of the low-rated composition samples are the esoteric appreciations of the competent writers at the other end of the scale. The final lines of the high-rated samples aptly illustrate the abstract concerns of the passages from which they were taken, all of which focus on sources of wonder that uplift or transport the spirits of the writers.

8 (*diary entry about the beauties of nature*)

It seemed as if I had felt God as I never did before, and I prayed in my heart that I might keep that happy sense of nearness all my life.

9 (*eulogy to Joan of Arc*)

She was only a woman, yet she could die as bravely as any martyr who had gone before.

10 (a carpe diem *letter admonishing a friend visiting London to enjoy the wonders of the town and not to fear appearing "country-bred"*)

Make use of your own eyes for the purpose of observation now, and for the time at least, lay aside the spectacles with which authors would furnish us.

11 (*description of Venus of Melos*)

Yet to say that every feature is of faultless perfection is but cold praise. No analysis can convey the sense of her peerless beauty.

Although Hillegas makes no explicit claims as to the significance of the subject matter or the tone of the writing samples, the consistency with which certain subjects and attitudes appear exclusively at either the high-rated or the low-rated end of the scale suggests that in the minds of the "literary authorities" who created the scale, the competent writer is expected to be a particular kind of person—a person who has not only the sensitivity but also the leisure and means to appreciate art, literature, history, and a pastoral version of nature—the subjects of a classical education.

Hillegas believed that with the precision of his 1000-point scale, he could obtain a scientific measurement of writing quality, though today we would probably use the term *assessment* instead of *measurement*. Designed to measure not intellectual ability or knowledge of subject matter but writing quality in general, Hillegas's scale, unlike a number of other scales devised during the same period, did not attempt to account for the interaction of form and content.

The form-content separation espoused by Hillegas was encouraged by the development in 1910 of the "new type" examinations,[5] forerunners of modern "objective tests," including ones that provide indirect measures of writing ability. Originally designed as an efficient way to measure the student's mastery of material in "content courses," new-type exams were soon appropriated for the evaluation of writing by educators who saw them as a means of overcoming problems of rater subjectivity while providing for time-, labor-, and cost-efficient assessments. These were the major concerns of American educators such as Ellwood Cubberly and Frank Spaulding, both of whom advocated reorganization of schools on the factory model (see Stephens and Van Til 155). Consequently, the concept of literacy reflected in this form of assessment is considerably more pragmatic than the belletristic notions that had prevailed earlier. Like Professor Gradgrind, who is satirized as a representative of utilitarian education in Dickens's *Hard Times*, Paterson, an educational psychologist, valued literacy as a fact-finding activity. Because he perceived literacy in this utilitarian fashion, he heartily endorsed the new-type examinations for their all-around efficiency:

> *The questions are brief, the answers are short, and little or nothing is demanded by way of writing. Hence, most of the pupil's time is consumed in cerebral activity or in thinking, and practically none of his time is devoted to grammatical constructions, composition, or laborious handwriting. There is also a real economy of effort on the part of the student, for he is freed from the dangers of writer's cramp and is released from the laboriousness with which he has traditionally been forced to organize his lengthy answers in correct grammatical form. (Preparation 10)*

In the name of science, Paterson, as a psychologist, was concerned with separating measurements of knowledge of a specific subject from measurements of the ability to write. A concern for the *expression* of knowledge, he believed, clouded and confused one's ability to assess a student's knowledge in its pure and uncontaminated form. Consequently, he argued that writing itself should be evaluated apart from its content:

> *Composition ability, spelling ability, legibility of handwriting, and neatness and arrangement of parts of the answer are irrelevant factors and are ruled out because writing is reduced to a bare minimum [in new-type examinations]. If such abilities are believed to be important in any given course, then they should be measured separately. (8)*

An educational philosophy similar to Paterson's became increasingly prevalent in the 1920s and 1930s, when new-type tests gained popularity as a means of measuring writing ability. Not only were such measures expedient, but they also ensured a high degree of reliability and therefore provided an apparent solution to the problem of rater subjectivity. Reflected in testmakers' increased efforts to make new-type exams into more accurate measures of writing quality was a view of literacy as a mechanical ability, composed of various discrete skills that could be measured separately, to yield scores that, added together, accurately represented that ability.

This view of writing ability can be traced back to the perspectives on literacy fostered by the earlier "scale measurements," as is perhaps most clearly demonstrated by the remarks of Steel and Talman concerning the marking of compositions. Steel and Talman's study, conducted at the University of Aberdeen and published in 1936, constituted one of the earliest attempts to employ an analytic scale in direct assessment of writing. In the study, the researchers devised a scoring system for assessing written composition whereby points could be awarded or deducted for words, sentences, and sentence sequences determined to be "incorrect," "sufficient," or "efficient." The points would be totaled in the margin to produce the overall score defining the quality of the composition. Assuming a fixed standard for "sufficient" expression for any intended meaning, Steel and Talman were concerned exclusively with the measurement of expression, not content:

> There will be general agreement that composition ability is the ability to express oneself coherently, lucidly, and economically. We might argue on that ground that in valuating a composition the examiner has done all that he need do if he takes account of coherences and incoherences of expression, the lucidities and obscurities, the economies and wastes. But custom has decreed that the marker of composition shall attempt to valuate subject-matter as well as the expression of it . . . .
>
> Nothing, we believe, has done more to make the marking of composition so notoriously unreliable. The only quality of subject-matter which can be assessed with any degree of reliability is the accuracy and the amount of information it conveys, and these must be regarded by the examiner of English composition as irrelevant to his immediate purpose. Some other qualities of subject-matter, such as its interest or its importance, cannot be measured objectively, for what is of interest and importance to one person is not necessarily of the same interest and importance to another . . . . We conclude that the marker of compositions will mark all he need mark if he valuates expression, that is, if he assesses the efficiency of the expression to communicate the ideas which shape it. (1–3)

This reductionist notion of literacy was not universally accepted by educators, of course. At the same time that the trend toward using new-type exams was gaining momentum, questions about the "validity" of such tests were being raised in a number of ways. In 1929 Zelma Huxtable, an eighth-grade teacher in Los Angeles, devised a scale for measuring the quality of thought reflected in student essays because she was convinced that then current forms of writing assessment were too limited; in particular, she questioned what has come to be called the *construct validity* of such tests because she believed they did not test what they purported to.[6] Commenting on teaching at the time, she noted:

> In many courses of study, the teaching of grammar, mechanics, punctuation, and spelling is emphasized almost to the complete neglect of the thoughts to be expressed. The goal, in other words, has been lost sight of in a near-sighted effort to smooth the way toward it. (188)

Huxtable reacted against the practice of fragmenting composition into discrete subskills. To compensate for what she viewed as an excessive concern with easily measurable mechanical aspects of writing, she recommended an evaluation procedure that focused on the quality of thought demonstrated by the student's writing.

The scale that Huxtable designed to correct the flaws she perceived in then current assessment practices was composed of five categories, defined in order from lowest to highest as (1) "inarticulate thought," (2) "unrelated thoughts (on the plane of mere sensory perception)," (3) "related thoughts on the sense perception level," (4) "reflective thoughts," and (5) "creative thoughts to the extent of a real contribution to literature" (189–91). Huxtable was careful to test for *convergent validity* (not construct validity) by correlating ratings of students' essays on her thought-content scale with their scores in grammatical correctness and punctuation as well as their ratings on IQ tests.[7] Like many researchers at that time and unfortunately even now, Huxtable seems to have assumed that if a test is valid in one respect, it is equally valid in all respects.

In her belief that the ultimate goal of composition instruction was to improve the students' quality of thought, Huxtable—like Mann, Edgeworth, and Hillegas—assumes that a written product is a direct reflection of the writer's intellect. In her own words, "It is impossible, apparently, for an individual whose IQ is low, 89 or below, to think reflectively" (191). Moreover, as is evident from Huxtable's sample essays illustrating the writing quality represented by each of the five points on her scale, belletristic standards of literacy had not wholly yielded to the utilitarianism that accompanied the introduction of statistics and scientific methods into the world of educational assessment. The assignment Huxtable used in her exam to elicit student writing was neutral enough as she reported it:

> [E]ach student was to suppose himself writing to a friend who had previously attended the same school with himself, telling first, about some interesting event which had recently taken place at school; second, about something which would especially interest the friend to whom he was writing; and third, about his own plans for the summer. (188)

Her examples of sample papers, however, reveal her preference for the literary. None of the three examples of the highest score—5—treats any of the three parts of the assigned topic. The samples singled out for their excellence receive their high marks because they illustrate "creative thinking," "original reflective analysis," "figures of speech," or "experience containing original reflective excellence to the extent of a real contribution to literature" (193), as the following example constructed by Huxtable illustrates:

> Mother, perhaps I am antisocial, but there is much in this kind of existence which caused me to question its value as training for manhood's tasks. Last night I wrote these lines after I returned from the Grand Ball.

DISAPPOINTMENT

My heart was bent on gladness,
And my inner being sang;
But the gladness turned to sorrow
And a dirge was all that rang
From the temple of my soul.
(195)

Huxtable's assignment was, as she noted, "quite within the experience of every child and, consequently, could scarcely offer any impediment to individual modes of written expression" (189). The paper that she offers as an example of excellence, however, neither responds to the assignment in terms of topic and audience nor seems to typify the experiences of the average eighth grader. Rather, the alleged student's use of poetic form and diction, his contemplation of manhood's tasks, his access to functions such as the Grand Ball, and his description of his soul as a temple call to mind the social and moral values often associated in this culture with literacy and a literary education.

This country's tradition of associating certain social and moral values with literacy did not begin with Huxtable's work, nor does it end there. The examples from Hillegas's 1912 scale, for instance, demonstrate a bias toward the same academic values that Bizzell identified 70 years later. The association of literacy with social propriety and knowledge of a particular body of texts continues to the present. A striking example of modern-day versions of this belief can be found in E. D. Hirsch's observations on what he refers to as "cultural literacy." Hirsch argues that a nationwide decline in literacy skills has resulted primarily from "cultural fragmentation," and in order to improve these skills, "we shall have to restore certain common contents to the humanistic side of the school curriculum" (161). Hirsch's notion of "common contents" is a core curriculum consisting of a canon of standard literary works such as those that were typically taught in English departments during the late nineteenth century.

Concern for upholding the moral and social values of literacy underlies many of the arguments against new-type exams put forth by proponents of direct assessment of literacy skills. The 1931 report by the College Entrance Examination Board's Commission on English (Thomas) calls for the retention of the essay exam despite its limited ability to predict student performance. The commission expressed alarm at the increasingly "scientific" value system of American education and concluded that the question of appropriate forms of writing assessment "is not so much a result reducible to statistics as it is a determination to retain in American education certain factors contributing to civilization and culture rather than to the mechanical efficiency of the American college student" (138).

Underlying the commission's concerns is the belief that the form of examination by which a student is judged determines to a large extent the shape of the student's learning. The desire to preserve certain "civilizing factors" in its educational aims and methods was in essence the commission's expression of allegiance to the tradition of a liberal arts education, which, in the eyes of many educators, appeared threatened by the social and economic changes that followed the Industrial Revolution. An increasing number of students from diverse backgrounds were pursuing secondary and advanced education, and the consequent demands on these levels of education were for more specific kinds of preparation required for entry into postindustrial employment. Such conditions, according to Kandel, called into question the assumption that "the function of the elementary school was to impart literacy and the so-called fundamentals of education," whereas "the purpose of secondary education was to transmit the accepted tradition of a liberal education, considered at once as the essential education for leaders and as preparation for higher education" (13–14).

One of the methodological changes occasioned by the need for efficient and yet specialized education for an expanded student population was the secondary schools' reliance on new-type exams rather than tests that required the students' own expression of thought in writing. Critics of the new-type exams argued that because of the inevitable practice of "teaching to the test," this new form of assessment indirectly fostered a kind of classroom instruction that encouraged and rewarded memorization, rote learning, and simplification of complex issues into dualities of right and wrong. What suffered most under the influence of such an instructional philosophy, the critics maintained, was critical thought, the ability to discover relationships among diverse pieces of factual information, and the skill of applying what was learned to practical situations or problem-solving contexts.

Since the early decades of this century, when new-type exams came to be used for the assessment of literacy skills, particularly writing ability, the critics have argued that the activity of writing has been similarly oversimplified—so much so that what was being tested by these "indirect" means of assessment was not writing ability at all but the memorization of grammar, spelling, and punctuation rules. Teaching to this kind of test, they believed, meant presenting writing as a mechanical process that could be mastered by learning rules of form and usage. Students were accordingly not encouraged to approach writing as a communicative or exploratory mode of language use.

Such objections to the educational influence of indirect assessment were initially more pronounced in England than in the United States. In 1956 S. Wiseman, a British researcher and one of the most vociferous critics of indirect assessment, reported that "there seems to be no doubt that, over the past two or three decades, educational psychologists have slowly but steadily inflated the importance of reliability, perhaps at the expense of validity . . . objective tests are highly reliable. They may not always be highly valid" (178; see also Vernon and Millican; Peel and Armstrong). Explaining his misgivings about the validity of indirect assessment measures, Wiseman focused on the educational consequences, what he calls the "backwash effects," which he sees as the educational tendency to deemphasize actual writing as an ability deserving evaluation. Note that by this time, through the efforts of Wiseman and others, educators had a much more sophisticated view of *validity* than at the time of, say, Huxtable's work.

Despite the warnings of British researchers such as Wiseman, most educational research on testing in America during the 1950s and 1960s was directed toward increasing the reliability of objective tests and determining the similarity of "mental functions" measured by direct and indirect assessments. Several American studies, however, do indicate a growing disenchantment with the high reliability and statistical accuracy of new-type exams. One of the most complete and thoughtful of these studies is that of Stalnaker ("Essay Type"), who, like Wiseman, is concerned with the tendency of objective testing to devalue literacy within the school systems. According to Stalnaker, who was especially concerned with the writing quality of medical students, objective exams in many subject areas cannot tap such "higher order" mental functions as creativity, the ability to select and organize material, and the ability to establish connections among facts. Stalnaker believed that essay examinations, on the other hand, can stimulate superior study habits and encourage students to view writing as a way of learning. The notion of literacy that Stalnaker advocated in his study is an active, or interactive, one, a notion that stands in direct contrast to the utilitarian point of view, which sees literacy as enabling students to extract factual information from a text or to produce mechanically correct prose. And it stands in direct contrast to the notion of "literacy" as knowledge and the expression of knowledge of the artifacts of "high culture."

IMPLICATIONS OF HISTORY FOR CURRENT ASSESSMENT PRACTICES

As the responses of Wiseman and Stalnaker ("Essay Type") to the claims made by advocates of indirect assessment of writing such as Paterson ("Do New and Old . . . ?") illustrate, the critical issue facing the would-be assessor of student writing is the validity of the test itself. However, as we have shown, notions of validity change from one educator or researcher to the next and from one historical period to the next. Mann's insistence, for example, that a written examination provides a "Daguerreotype likeness . . . of the state and condition of the pupils' minds" makes a number of assumptions about what such a "test" is capable of measuring and what it does, in fact, measure. Although Mann insists that writing is in some sense a measure of the quality of the student's mind, his notion of quality differs dramatically from that of Huxtable, whose scale suggests that superior thought content enables the student to produce "literary" artifacts, this latter a position not too distant from that of Hirsch in our own time. Like Hirsch, both Mann and Huxtable, while differing in certain particulars, seem to view thought as a fixed commodity that one can possess as one would possess a house or a horse and to view writing as a reflection of that static entity. In contrast to this static notion of thought, both Stalnaker and Wiseman perceive writing as a measure of thought as a dynamic and interactive process, a process by which individuals come to understand the world in which they live. Accordingly, Stalnaker and Wiseman tend to see writing in terms of something like "functional" literacy, the use of reading and writing to interact productively with the larger social and intellectual context rather than as a necessary reflection of the values that the writer may or may not have assimilated from that larger context.

As the divergent claims of Mann, Huxtable, Stalnaker, and Wiseman suggest, the critical issue facing educational evaluators both historically and at the present is not the relative efficacy of indirect or direct methods of assessment but rather the question of what is being measured in any purported assessment of writing abilities. We have no reason to suspect that the historical variability in the underlying assumptions of writing assessment is any less than the variability in underlying assumptions reflected in current assessment practices. To understand what current assessment practices tell us about writing, we need to begin examining the assumptions being made in writing tasks about what it means to be literate. We suspect that such an examination will show that different assessment programs are predicated on very different assumptions.

NOTES

1. Throughout this chapter, we quote directly from many sources. These quotations are not only evidence that supports particular points but also data that merit extended attention and analysis (see Bauman 19). The ways in which particular speakers have chosen to talk about literacy and about the assessment of writing ability—the metaphors they use, the comparisons they make, the issues they raise (and often fail to raise)—offer great insight into the past; it is only by studying what was said as well as how it was said that we can understand the often contradictory nature of current assessment practices.
2. Although the term *literacy* generally refers to reading as well as to writing abilities, the scope of this discussion is ultimately limited by a motivating desire to discover the means by which writing skills can best be encouraged and taught in the schools. For this reason, important questions concerning reading instruction and assessment of reading skills will receive only secondary consideration.
3. It is not unreasonable to argue that this development ushered in the modern age of education, an era in which decreasing emphasis has been placed on an individual student's ability to interpret and express knowledge orally while increasing importance has been assigned to the translation of that knowledge into a form that can be measured and analyzed to the satisfaction of educational administrators and statisticians. Thus Mann was correct when he noted, "We venture to predict that the mode of examination, *by printed questions and written answers*, will constitute a new era in the history of our schools" ("Boston" 330; emphasis in original), although he could not have foreseen the developments that would accompany the "new era" of which he spoke.
4. Throughout the history of the debates about writing assessment in American

educational literature, the published research from England and Scotland has often provided a point of departure for work in this country.

5. "New type" tests required students to produce short answers as opposed to long, discursive ones. G. F. Miller's 1926 guide for constructing objective tests for high school subjects gives examples of matching (synonyms, terms and their definitions, literary and grammatical terms and illustrations of them), true-false (items ranging from "English compositions written by students are inferior" [95], which, according to Miller, cannot be marked as either true or false, to "The complimentary close of a letter should always consist of more than one word" [95], which he labels true), multiple choice (choose the correctly spelled version of a word from four possible spellings, select the proper part of speech for each word in a paragraph, choose from a list of 13 the punctuation rule illustrated by a particular sentence), and labeling sentences as correct or incorrect and correcting the incorrect ones. See Odell for a lengthy consideration of the advantages and disadvantages, as perceived at the time, of new-type examinations.

6. *Construct validity* is "the extent to which a particular test can be shown to measure a hypothetical construct . . . such as intelligence, anxiety, creativity" (Borg and Gall 220). For example, if we define *spelling ability* as "the ability to spell words correctly," we can test for this construct in several ways: by giving spelling tests on lists of words to which students may or may not have access in advance, by asking students to find (and perhaps correct) misspelled words in sentences or texts produced by other writers, or by checking the spelling of words in compositions they turn in. Each of these assessment methods would probably yield different results and hence correlate with the construct, as defined, to a different extent; therefore, each of the methods could be said to demonstrate differing degrees of construct validity. Note that a crucial part of the issue here is the definition of the construct; had it been defined differently (e.g., "the ability to score 95 percent on a test of spelling words chosen at random from a specified text" or "the ability to spot and correct errors in a passage with—or without—use of a dictionary"), the construct validity of each of the measures would be different.

7. The *convergent validity* of a test is determined by relating the test scores of a group of subjects to a criterion measure administered at the same time or within a short interval time (Borg and Gall 279). In this particular case, Huxtable compared ratings on her scale with other independent measures, scores on a test of grammatical correctness and punctuation, and scores on IQ tests; however, her comparisons fail to address the very important question of whether her scale measures writing ability or something else, such as general intelligence (itself a rather poorly understood construct) or knowledge of belletristic values and biases.

REFERENCES

Bauman, R. *Let Your Words Be Few: Symbolism of Speaking and Silence among Seventeenth-Century Quakers.* Cambridge, Eng.: Cambridge UP, 1983.

Bizzell, P. "Cognition, Convention, and Certainty: What We Need to Know about Writing." *Pre-Text* 3 (1982): 213–43.

Borg, W. R., and M. D. Gall. *Educational Research: An Introduction.* 4th ed. White Plains, N. Y.: Longman, 1983.

Bracewell, R. J., C. H. Frederiksen, and J. D. Frederiksen. "Cognitive Processes in

Composing and Comprehending Discourse." *Educational Psychologist* 17 (1982): 146–64.

Briggs, L. B. R. "The Harvard Admission Examination in English." *Twenty Years of School and College English.* Ed. A. S. Hill, L. B. R. Briggs, and B. S. Hurlbut. Cambridge, Mass.: Harvard U, 1896. 17–32.

Carton, E. "On Going Home: Selfhood in Composition." *College English* 45 (1983): 340–47.

Edgeworth, F. Y. "The Statistics of Examinations." *Journal of the Royal Statistical Society* 51 (1888): 599–635.

Farrell, T. "IQ and Standard English." *College Composition and Communication* 34 (1983): 470–84.

Hill, A. S. "An Answer to the Cry for More English." *Twenty Years of School and College English.* Ed. A. S. Hill, L. B. R. Briggs, and B. S. Hurlbut. Cambridge, Mass.: Harvard U, 1896. 6–16.

Hillegas, M. B. "A Scale for the Measurement of Quality in English Composition by Young People." *Teacher's College Record* 13.3 (1912): 331–84.

Hirsch, E. D., Jr. "Cultural Literacy." *American Scholar* 52 (1983): 159–69.

Huxtable, Z. "Criteria for Judging Thought Content in Written English." *Journal of Educational Research* 19 (1929): 188–95.

Kandel, I. L. *Examinations and Their Substitutes in the United States.* Bulletin No. 28. New York: Carnegie Foundation for the Advancement of Teaching, 1936.

Kinneavy, J. L. *A Theory of Discourse.* Englewood Cliffs, N.J.: Prentice-Hall, 1971.

Mann, H. "Boston Grammar and Writing Schools." *The Common School Journal* 7.21–23 (1845): 321–68.

———. "The Support of Schools: The Highest Municipal Interest." *The Common School Journal* 1.4 (1839): 49–56.

Miller, G. F. *Objective Tests in High School Subjects.* Norman, Okla.: Author, 1926.

Nystrand, M., ed. *What Writers Know: The Language, Process, and Structure of Written Discourse.* New York: Academic Press, 1982.

Odell, C. W. *Traditional Examinations and New-Type Tests.* Englewood Cliffs, N.J.: Prentice-Hall, 1928.

Oxenham, J. *Literacy: Writing, Reading and Social Organization.* London: Routledge & Kegan Paul, 1980.

Parker, W. R. "Where Do English Departments Come From?" *College English* 28 (1967): 337–51.

Paterson, D. "Do New and Old Type Examinations Measure Different Mental Functions?" *School and Society* 24 (1926): 246–48.

———. *Preparation and Use of New-Type Examinations: A Manual for Teachers.* Orlando, Fla.: Harcourt Brace Jovanovich, 1925.

Peel, E. A., and H. G. Armstrong. "The Predictive Power of English Composition in the 11+ Examination." *British Journal of Educational Psychology* 26.3 (1956): 163–71.

Saussure, F. de. *Cours de linguistique générale.* 3rd ed. Paris: Payot, 1967.

Shaughnessy, M. P. *Errors and Expectations.* New York: Oxford UP, 1977.

Stalnaker, J. M. "The Essay Type of Examination." *Educational Measurement.* Ed. E. F. Lindquist. Washington, D.C.: American Council on Education, 1951. 495–530.

———. "The Measurement of the Ability to Write." *Tests and Measurement in Higher Education.* Ed. W. S. Gray. Chicago: U of Chicago P, 1936. 203–15.

Steel, J. H., and J. Talman, *The Marking of Compositions.* London: Nisbet, 1936.

Stephens, W. R., and W. van Til, eds. *Education in American Life.* Boston: Houghton Mifflin, 1972.

Stubbs, M. *Language and Literacy: The Sociolinguistics of Reading and Writing.* London: Routledge & Kegan Paul, 1980.

Thomas, C. S. *Examining the Examinations in English: Report to the College Entrance Examination Board.* Cambridge, Mass.: Harvard UP, 1931.

Vernon, P. E., and G. D. Millican. "A Further Study of the Reliability of English Essays." *British Journal of Statistical Psychology* 7.2 (1954): 65–72.

Wiseman, S. "Symposium: The Use of Essays on Selection of 11+." *British Journal of Educational Psychology* 26.3 (1956): 172–79.

3

Why Test?

MARIE JEAN LEDERMAN

Why do we test? Some of us test because we believe we must. More of us test because boards of regents or trustees, state legislators, or high-ranking college administrators have mandated testing programs. In the mid-1980s in America, testing has become the flag raised by the troops of the Land of Academic Standards.

Today's strong belief in assessment ranges from the "quick fix" of tests in popular magazines to formal examinations in schools. The city of Minneapolis is a striking example. In its 1984 attempt to tighten academic standards, it was the first school system in the country to require competency tests for promotion out of kindergarten. To ensure preparation for testing at this level, the business community is busily developing computer materials such as Program Design's *Baby's First Software.*

America appears, at this juncture, to be a particularly test-happy culture. But what seems to be an especially American, especially contemporary phenomenon is far from unique to this one place and this one time. Today's spur to testing may be boards of regents or trustees, legislators, or local administrators, but the reasons we test and the inevitable problems involved in testing have roots that touch the beginnings of social activities.

To understand why we test today, it is instructive to go back to reasons why people throughout history and throughout the world have relied on tests. A look at other cultures and their tests provides a useful historical perspective on our own motivations for testing, our testing procedures, and the inevitable limitations of any tests we create.

Perhaps the earliest tests were *rites de passage*, tests that inducted adolescents into adulthood. These rites not only marked a sexual coming of age but also marked admission into the culture, values, and mores of the group. According to

I am indebted to Mr. Kuang-fu Chu, Chinese specialist of the Oriental Division, New York Public Library, for generously agreeing to review this manuscript. His experience and enthusiasm were of enormous help.

Otto Rank, they were educational experiences that reconciled, for boys, both sexuality and education by deferring the boy's formal education to the time of puberty. The boy's initiation marked the passing of the role of education from a person (mother) to the community; *"in place of a human being as a pattern of education*, a collective *ideology* appears *as the educational ideal"* (246). Basically, such tests permitted movement of both girls and boys from one stage to another and were inherent in the education of all members of the group. Of course, the nature of the tests varied, depending on the values of the group. These *rites de passage*, marking a transition from one stage to another according to specific tasks performed, might be seen as harbingers of proficiency tests like the "rising junior" examinations given by some colleges today. These "rising junior" examinations seek to establish a set of tasks beyond course grades that are "external" verification of students' abilities to meet the standards of the group they wish to join.

If attaining membership in a group was one early function of testing, another was the attempt to sort people or to choose the best people to perform specific tasks valued by a group. The Chinese invented the examination, "one of the more controversial of their contributions to the world, which many centuries later adopted this method of determining qualifications" (Heren et al. 121). In China, the written examination system began in the Sui dynasty (589–618). The Chinese attempted to create a system of competitive examinations for government positions, precursors to our modern civil service examinations.

By A.D. 1370 these examinations had striking similarities to writing assessment examinations today:

> *Every three years competitors successful in the district examinations assembled in the provincial capitals for three sessions of three days and three nights each. Compositions in prose and verse revealed the extent of reading and depth of scholarship. At this level, penmanship did not count, since a bureau of examination copyists (established in 1015 A.D.) reproduced the papers in another hand before they were evaluated by two independent readers, with a third reader to receive and reconcile the sealed grades. (DuBois 4)*

In attempting to rank candidates on the basis of demonstrated merit, the examiners in China faced many of the problems that we face in designing similar assessment tasks today. One problem in essay testing now is the question of the influence of handwriting in judgments that readers make about the quality of an essay. This question seems to have been solved, at least to the satisfaction of the Chinese examiners. By rewriting candidates' papers, they ensured that handwriting would not "count" (DuBois 4). An alternative explanation, however, may be that the decision to copy the papers was made to conceal the identity of the examinees. Other historians note that in addition to using numbers instead of names on the examination papers, papers were copied to ensure that the examinees' identity would remain unknown and therefore would not influence the readers (Fairbank, Reischauer, and Craig 189). Today's examiners, similarly, seek to maintain the anonymity of examinees through substitutions such as social security numbers or other codes on student papers.

An even more striking parallel with today's concerns about instruments for writing assessment was the early recognition of the problem of tests establishing fixed forms and of the relationship between those fixed forms and the creativity of the examinees. By 1487 in China a specific form for writing examination papers was adopted, "under eight main headings, with not over 700 characters in all and with much use of balance and antithesis. This was the famous 'eight-legged essay' style, later denounced as imposing a tyranny of literary structures over thought" (Fairbank et al. 190). Some scholars now see this examination system as having "degraded education and made it a mere appendage to the examination system" (China Handbook 4). Today we continue to worry about whether or not the format of an essay examination will have a negative effect on students' creativity and thinking or, worse, that our tests may become more important than our curriculum.

Another question we debate is frequency of retesting. How often should students be asked to repeat tests that they have not passed? According to Scharfstein, the answer in nineteenth-century China was so many times that "many candidates sat for these examinations for twenty or thirty years or more. At the age of eighty or ninety, candidates who had failed repeatedly might be given a consolation degree. They were failures, but honorable ones" (17). Few of today's colleges exhibit either such patience or such compassion. Neither, for that matter, does the rest of our culture.

An additional problem is the control of cheating. As one expects when the stakes are high enough, there may be desperation on the part of some of the candidates. In nineteenth-century China, for example, "expert stand-ins were hired" or "clothing was lined with thousands of microscopically written essays to which the 'padded' candidate had an index" (Scharfstein 18). Soldiers inspected the candidates for hidden papers, sometimes going "so far as to cut open dumplings in order to examine their bean-jam fillings" (Miyazaki 44). Despite these attempts, in certain periods, cheating was rampant.

Perhaps the most fundamental question troubling testmakers throughout time has been the question of equity. After all, the assumption of the civil service tests in China was an assumption of the basic good of a merit system. Whether tests are designed to mark a transition, to assess specific knowledge, or to sort candidates, the question of equality of chance to pass the test is universally present. The attempt that the Chinese made, over 1300 years ago, to sort candidates according to merit was admirable in theory. The reality, however, differed, for despite the attempts to make each examinee equal to all others, the system still favored the sons of the rich. These examinees went to national schools at the capital. Moreover, many of these students could afford tutors and came from "scholar-official" families, which afforded them the additional advantage of a role model at home (Fairbank et al. 104, 190). Thus in the Chinese merit system, social class and wealth made some examinees more equal than others. Needless to say, the problem of equity in theory and reality persists in a variety of forms today.

We find ourselves kin to the examiners in China thousands of years ago, and as we move through the history of educational testing, we see other similarities in the examinations for university degrees awarded to the candidates of the first Western universities. Here the earliest examinations were oral; written examinations began in the thirteenth century, several centuries after the introduction of paper to the West. As Fairbank notes in *Chinabound*, "Europeans . . . had argued in their universities for hundreds of years before Gutenberg while Chinese scholars had been using paper, brush, and printed books all the time" (372).

Still later the Jesuit order, founded in 1540 by St. Ignatius of Loyola, pioneered in the systematic use of tests in education. They used written tests both for placement of students and for ascertaining proficiency after instruction. In 1599 they published their statement of procedures for examinations in the lower schools. While some of the procedures seem quaint, others have a decidedly familiar ring:

> *The writing should be done in a style befitting the grade of each class, clearly, and in the words of the assigned theme and according to the fashion prescribed. Ambiguous expressions are to be given the less favorable meaning. Words omitted or changed carelessly for the sake of avoiding a difficulty are to be counted as errors.*
>
> *After the composition is finished, each one, without leaving his place, should diligently look over what he has written, correct and improve it as much as he may wish. For, as soon as the composition is given to the prefect, if anything then has to be corrected, it should by no means be returned. (DuBois 9)*

The strictures to be specific, to avoid ambiguity, and to proofread the paper have a timeless quality and are reminiscent of directions given to students for many large-scale essay examinations today.

By the middle of the nineteenth century, both oral and written examinations were routine in England, on the Continent, and in the United States, and written examinations were recognized "as an appropriate basis for important decisions: who should be awarded degrees; who should be permitted to exercise a profession, such as law or teaching or medicine; and who should serve in a government post" (DuBois 10).

In the nineteenth century in England, various refinements of the grading procedures for essay examinations were developed. DuBois notes that in 1864 the Reverend George Fisher of Greenwich, England, collected samples of academic writing and arranged them in a "'Scale Book' with assigned values from 1, the best, to 5, the poorest. Intermediate values were indicated by fractions. Work by any student could then be graded by direct comparison with a set of specimens arranged in order of merit, thus providing a fixed standard of grading in each of the subject matter areas" (69).

Slowly, procedures were developed for measuring what students had learned by examining their writing. Fisher's "scale book" made explicit what was implicit in the minds of the examiners. Similarly, many educators who direct writing assessment programs today believe that it is important to illustrate raters' criteria through "scale books" that illustrate each point on the scale with real examples of student writing.

As we look at the growth of testing, we note that throughout history "whole" tasks were the rule: tasks performed as part of initiation rites and lengthy oral and written responses to questions. It is only in recent times that we have developed the notion of indirect measurement. When multiple-choice tests— easier to score and administer—arrived, we greeted them joyfully:

> A great stimulus for the growth of educational measurement was the invention of the multiple-choice item, first used extensively in the Army Alpha. Educational test makers soon discovered that an item consisting of a clearly written stem, followed by four or five alternative answers, of which one is correct, provides a flexible format for the measurement of both knowledge and skill. (DuBois 73)

The 1920s saw an explosion of such test construction for use in the schools and colleges. Not surprisingly, "Instructors liked the 'new examinations' because they were far more comprehensive than earlier methods of testing and because the chance of personal favoritism influencing scores was practically eliminated" (DuBois 76–77).

In 1900 the College Entrance Examination Board was founded to provide the country with a systematic testing program. Traditionally, only essay examinations had been used for college admissions, but after the development of the multiple-choice format during World War I and the uses of objective testing at Columbia College, objective tests were introduced into the board's testing program (DuBois 125). Varieties of other testing programs, such as the National Teachers Examination, soon began. In 1947 the three major education groups involved in testing, the American Council on Education, the Carnegie Foundation for the Advancement of Teaching, and the College Entrance Examination Board, founded the Educational Testing Service (Ebel 22). Multiple-choice testing was in.

The multiple-choice test has become so firmly entrenched in American life that it now seems revolutionary to call for "whole" tasks such as writing samples. But we must remind ourselves that our immediate past—a mere half century—is hardly the whole of human history. Short-answer tests, which permeate popular culture in our magazines, are but one example of a pervasive societal quest to find simple, quick answers to complex questions.

There are many other examples. Television has woven the short-question, short-answer format tightly through our lives, not merely through quiz shows and sitcoms but through news reporting itself. Nightly, much of life is also reduced to "And what did you feel when you saw the body?" "I felt scared."

Sixty-second spot commercials first became 30 and are now 15 seconds long. Worse, in classroom after classroom, educational level after educational level, short questions and short answers have become the norm. As John I. Goodlad asserts, students spend most of their time listening, some of their time reading short passages and writing short responses to questions on quizzes, and virtually none of their time reading or writing anything of some length. The destructive nature of the short-question, short-answer mode of living is apparent: not all of life's complexities can be summed up in one-sentence questions, much less one-sentence answers.

Despite the advantage of short-answer tests—the skills and knowledge that can be sampled and the ease of administration—a fundamental criticism remains. What many people consider to be the most important goal of education, coherent thought and expression of that thought, simply cannot be measured by multiple-choice or short-answer tests. Clear thinking and clear writing are inextricable. Writing makes us accountable in a way in which neither the spoken word nor short-answer tests do.

If we were to agree that coherent writing, which both produces and reflects thoughtful understanding and analysis, is the primary goal of education, the question of how to assess it would be easier to answer. But obviously we are not, as a group, in agreement on the primacy of writing in education, for both anecdotal reports and surveys tell us of the increase in both multiple-choice and short-answer testing in courses throughout colleges and universities. Even though most college faculty members know that they get a different kind of information about students' knowledge and abilities from essay tests than from short-answer tests, short-answer tests continue to proliferate.

A recent interesting experiment conducted with undergraduates at Florida International University supports the value of learning by writing. Students were divided into groups and were given a 4800-word passage to read. Each group was told to expect a different kind of test: an essay, multiple-choice, "memory," or some other unspecified kind of test. All the students took the same test, which included both multiple-choice and short-answer items. Students who were told to expect an essay test did better even on the multiple-choice items. The researchers theorize that when students prepare for an essay, they "take a broader focus" and try to organize facts by integrating them into a larger context. This kind of preparation apparently aids recall of the specific details needed to answer the multiple-choice questions (Cramer 17). Although research is not conclusive, it is hard to believe that teachers have not acknowledged the results of this study simply by intuition, if only from memories of the way in which they, as students, prepared for essay tests.

This point brings us back to the original question, Why test? The question must be answered—and with more than a short answer—before we can discuss assessment instruments. Most English teachers would immediately say that we test to place students, to diagnose specific strengths and weaknesses so that we can help writers improve, to determine growth, and, finally, to assess either competency or proficiency. Some would say that we test so that we may design courses that will help students to become better writers. A few would add that sometimes we test students to determine whether our courses have succeeded or failed.

But the more fundamental question is, What, as a society, do we value? Is the ability to write a critical skill for success in our culture? If so, assessing student writing is an appropriate ritual. What form should that ritual take? Our ultimate goal should be to improve teaching and learning. Yet testing, which should be an outgrowth of and subordinate to curriculum, in reality often drives curriculum. Therefore, our choice of assessment instruments is crucial. If we do not want to encourage students in writing classes throughout the country to sit in classes and fill in blanks in workbooks or on computer screens, we will not use short-answer or multiple-choice tests. If we want to signal to faculty in both secondary and postsecondary institutions that the business of a writing class is writing, our assessment instruments will be essay tests.

Faculty members in departments other than English bemoan the fact that students cannot write. When pressed for an explanation, teachers say that students do not know how to isolate and stick to an idea, develop that idea, and illustrate it with specific examples. They talk less about surface and mechanical errors (the elements that are measured by short-answer tests) than about issues of logic, coherency, and detail. Short-answer tests are not our answer if what we want is a primary educational focus on thinking skills rather than editing skills.

A clear relationship exists between the curriculum we teach and our assessment instruments, but we should not assume a total overlap between teaching and testing. No test, whether in a political science, biology, or writing class, can tap the entire domain of what the student has learned during an entire semester's work. No single instrument can deliver that kind of information.

A current example of the simplistic assumption of the complete overlap between curriculum and testing is the popular cry, "We teach process, but we test product." Like the 15-second spot advertisement on television, the complaint has a catchy ring but masks the complexities of assessment. Of course, the best teachers do help students learn something about their own writing processes, to overcome the points in their writing processes at which they are hopelessly stuck, to expand the repertoire of skills that students use when they write, and to learn the patience needed for creation and the joy of tinkering with their own prose. But in the end, it is a lie to tell students that "product" does not matter. As readers, for example, you are not interested in the 20-odd drafts that resulted in this chapter. The brilliant insight that may have flourished briefly before fading in the course of the writing process is of no use to anyone except, perhaps, the writer. What is altered does not matter to the reader, nor does the ease with which the writer composes. In the real world, product is all we can share with each other.

In an idealized universe, there is unending time for vision and revision. Nevertheless, curricula in our writing courses should allow time for students to explore many types of writing, from the quick and largely impromptu prose that most writing tests demand to the longer, more reflective essays for which students will have days or weeks to imagine, plan, write, discuss, tear up, revise, and write again and again. As teachers, we hope that in addition to learning skills, students somehow will learn to love a writing process that allows them to discover something of themselves and the world around them as they think through problems and learn to communicate their ideas in effective prose.

Our colleges and universities must decide what they value and what skills their students must have before they develop testing rituals. Each institution must weigh the benefits and disadvantages of different models of testing. Short-answer tests may have economic and temporal advantages, but they have gross disadvantages: they cannot assess the important rhetorical skills that students must learn, and they cannot elicit the kind of writing that our literate community professes to value.

Whatever our reasons for testing writing, the instruments that we develop will be, of necessity, imperfect. Whether we test for competence or excellence, to sort or to rank, we borrow, knowingly or unknowingly, methods used 1300 years ago to evaluate writing and thinking. And we suffer from the limitations of whatever assessment instruments we choose—as did the Chinese in centuries past. We agonize about the possibility that our tests will discriminate against students who have not had adequate preparation prior to the time we test; we worry about reader bias in essay testing; and we argue about the long-term effects of our tests on our students' writing. Is form dominating content and stifling creativity, as the Chinese feared in their "eight-legged essay"?

Ritual and testing are interrelated, as we can see in the initiation rites of early societies. The values of a group are symbolized in the tests one must pass in order to become a member of that group. We are being forced to test outside of college courses today because as educators we have refused to agree on and articulate our values within our courses. That there is a general distrust of college faculty is exemplified in the statewide and citywide involvement in testing in colleges and universities. Early societies developed *rites de passage* that reflected their values and their needs, depending on the way in which they lived, worked, and believed. Within the group, admission into adulthood depended on the ability to demonstrate mastery of specific tasks. So we in colleges and universities today must decide on the values and needs of membership in the group to which our students aspire. If they need skills in thinking and in making connections between disparate ideas, if drawing material together into a coherent written whole is vital to membership in a group of educated adults, essay tests will be part of our essential rituals.

As faculty and writing program administrators, we must assume leadership in assessment. We must clarify and profess our values. What do we want our students to know? What kind of thinkers should they be? What will they need to move into the complexities of the next century? Our tests should be *rites de passage* to help our students live well in that world.

REFERENCES

China Handbook Editorial Committee. *Education and Science.* Trans. Zhou Yicheng, Cai Guanping, and Liu Huzhang. Beijing: Foreign Languages Press, 1983.

Cramer, Richard. "Testing Multiple Study Choices." *Psychology Today* May 1984: 17.

DuBois, Philip H. *A History of Psychological Testing.* Boston: Allyn & Bacon, 1970.

Ebel, Robert L. *Essentials of Educational Measurement.* Englewood Cliffs, N.J.: Prentice-Hall, 1972.

Fairbank, John K. *Chinabound: A Fifty Year Memoir.* New York: Harper & Row, 1982.

Fairbank, John K., Edwin O. Reischauer, and Albert M. Craig. *East Asia: Tradition and Transformation.* Boston: Houghton Mifflin, 1973.

Goodlad, John I. *A Place Called School: Prospects for the Future.* New York: McGraw-Hill, 1983.

Heren, Louis. *China's Three Thousand Years: The Story of a Great Civilization.* New York: Macmillan, 1974.

Miyazaki, Ichisada. *China's Examination Hell: The Civil Service Examinations of Imperial China.* New Haven: Yale U, 1981.

Rank, Otto. *The Myth of the Birth of the Hero and Other Writings.* New York: Random House (Vintage Books), 1964.

Scharfstein, Ben-Ami. *The Mind of China.* New York: Basic Books, 1974.

4

A Personal Statement on Writing Assessment and Education Policy

REXFORD BROWN

Various tensions exist between the values of composition and the values of assessment, the values of education and the values of policy. I have felt them personally and have witnessed them professionally since my first involvement in assessment 15 years ago. They began with vague feelings of uneasiness and have moved through various phases of cognitive dissonance, emotional discontent, long argument, and a conviction, from time to time, that I am guilty of bad faith. I have not resolved the tensions—I am not even sure yet that they *need* to be or *can* be resolved—but I believe that we must understand the tensions in order either to learn to live with them more comfortably or to take steps toward imagining something like further progress in this hybrid discipline of writing assessment.

That we will be asked to make further progress you should not doubt. Education is at a crossroads today, and there is great pressure for us to make hasty decisions before the window of school reform opportunity closes. At issue for each of us is the question of whether the reforms in our states and communities will lead to further centralization, bureaucratization, and hyper-rationalization of education or whether the reforms will stimulate diverse, creative, local innovations. If the former, testing and assessment will continue their courses as handmaidens to the state and tools of the bureaucracy; there will be adjustments to make on the margin, but by and large, this will become an increasingly uninteresting field to work in. If the latter, testing and assessment could evolve into some interesting new forms and could help bring about some important changes. Each of us will have to decide how far we want to go in either direction or how long we want to ride both horses simultaneously, as we are doing now.

I first became aware of one of the tensions when, as a graduate student in English literature, I was asked to be a scorer of the first national writing assessment. Since it paid $5 an hour, I didn't hesitate. I joined a dozen other graduate students to score holistically 15,000 papers in an airplane hangar on the outskirts of Iowa City, where temperatures ranged from 100 to 106 degrees. One day early in my reading, a friend came to me with tears in his eyes and said, "You've got to read this." The papers we were scoring were about people the writers "most admired." This person wrote about her mother. She admired her mother so much, it emerged, that she had created a fantasy life with which to please her. She felt trapped now by her life of lies. She did not have any of the friends she told her mother about in great detail. She had no friends at all. She did not have a date to the prom; she would dress up for it and go to the movies. The essay went on like this until I, too, was reduced to tears. I passed the essay down the line and could register its progress the rest of the morning by the periodic sound of noses blowing.

That paper shocked us out of the sorting routine that had absorbed us hypnotically. When we talked about it at lunch, we all regretted that we didn't know the girl's name and thus couldn't reach out to help her as she had reached out to ask for our help. We were as anonymous to her as she was to us. Unlike the thousands and thousands of students who had chosen to put on their masks and write safe, boring papers, this girl used the writing opportunity to accomplish something heartfelt. She really *wrote*; and, in response, we gave her a score—a score that would be added to all the other scores and turned into a statistic.

That was my first inkling of a values conflict, but I couldn't bring it to the surface in a usable way. It had something to do with wanting to make a qualitative, thorough, personal response and having to make instead a quantitative, abstract, impersonal response. It was not that I felt there was something wrong with holistic scoring. Quite the contrary, it seemed like a perfectly sensible way to deal with a large number of essays and get a certain kind of information for certain audiences. It was more like a feeling that there was something wrong with *me*. Some principle I cared about was being betrayed by some other principle I cared about just as much.

The feeling that I was not altogether ethically consistent was reinforced when, a couple of years later and as a consequence of a strange series of events, I worked for the National Assessment of Educational Progress to write up the results of the first literature assessment. Literature and criticism had been my passions. I had intended to pursue the usual academic career to a professorship and a life of comparative ease in some sleepy English department. I felt the NAEP job would be interesting until I found the right opportunity to get back on track. And it *was* interesting. I had never thought much about testing, so there was plenty to learn. But at meetings of the Modern Language Association or the National Council of Teachers of English, I ran into cold shoulders and, sometimes, outright hostility from people I considered my colleagues. Apparently, they believed that I had "gone over to the enemy," though it was not clear what or who the enemy might be. Again, I experienced this as some kind of values conflict within myself. But it also seemed to be a conflict between the field of literature and the "science" of testing.

As I moved back and forth between both worlds, I found on the one side a community of people who believed that the methods and ideals of the hard sciences offered the only routes to truth and progress. The humanities may make life more enjoyable, but humanists cannot really march in the army of truth so long as they remain committed to "nonmeasurable outcomes"—subjectivity and hypotheses that cannot be put to empirical test. On the other side was a community of people who believed that the scientific ideal of objectivity is at best naive and at worst outright dangerous when applied to the study of real people. Scientists cannot march in the army of truth so long as they locate that truth outside human history and experience.

Neither side believed that the other could lay claim to unproblematic truths. They tended to compromise sometimes by agreeing that the scientist could have the truth of the physical world, the humanist the truth of the moral and aesthetic worlds. But it was an uneasy truce. The scientists' truths seemed so much more important and interesting to the general public. Humanists were being compelled by powerful economic and political forces to betray their values, whereas scientists were under no such compulsion.

I began to rationalize my personal tension as a struggle between two broad and proud traditions of inquiry. In my day-to-day life, the struggle was most manifest in disagreements about evaluation. People trained in the humanities tend to prefer evaluation models based on experience and intuition. They tend to prefer modes of evaluation that are qualitative rather than quantitative, context-rich rather than context-free, naturalistic rather than laboratory-oriented or artificial, aimed at understanding specific cases rather than general "truths," involving multiple points of view rather than a single point of view presumed to be objective, and aspiring to persuasiveness and credibility rather than "certainty."

Moreover, each tradition has its own forms of argument. Evidence is construed and used differently; beliefs are treated differently; warrants for beliefs in one tradition are not warrants in the other. When to these differences one adds the facts that people in each camp tend not to mix with people in the other and that arrogant claims have been made for the superiority of each, it is no wonder, I thought, that our arguments are interminable.

The next complication in my crisis of identity came with the realization that I was perceived by various academics not just as the representative of a behavioristic, objectivistic, positivistic, Enlightenment tradition but as a "Fed" as well. My colleagues and I were minions of the state, butting in where we didn't belong and encouraging various agencies and legislators to do the same.

My value conflicts multiplied. Where were my ultimate loyalties, to the sciences or the humanities? To a conception of the social sciences as continuous with the natural sciences or a conception of the social sciences as continuous with history and philosophy? Were my sympathies with teachers or with administrators? With educators or with social managers? It seemed increasingly clear that I was living my professional life in an ethical muddle. Moreover, it dawned on me slowly that we cannot understand, much less resolve, many of our theoretical and methodological disputes without taking into account this context of moral confusion.

Such an understanding might be interesting in its own right, yet not worth changing one's life over. On the other hand, it might conceivably enable us to see what we're doing in a new light, to see the school reform movement with new eyes, and to envision new ways of connecting writing assessment to the reform movement. With that faint hope in mind, I offer the following incomplete and preliminary thoughts, most of which have come to me on airplanes as I flew from one errand of education policy to another.

Policy inspires thoughts of Machiavelli. Isaiah Berlin suggests that Machiavelli's originality consists not, as so many suppose, in his separation of politics and morality; rather, it consists in his far more radical assumption that there are at least *two* systems of morality from which we may choose—a public one and a private one. In writing *The Prince*, Machiavelli chose a public morality derived from an ultimate commitment to the health and welfare of the state. His policy advice is totally consistent with this commitment. From his point of view, a citizen may well want to subscribe to a morality derived from an ultimate commitment to the individual self or soul. But if he chooses to do this, he should not be surprised if the Prince ignores him or eliminates him entirely in the service of what the Prince believes to be a superior value or virtue. Machiavelli makes it clear that the Prince who wants to be effective will never let concern for the life of an individual count for much in the calculus of power. "A man who wishes to make a profession of goodness in everything," he cautions, "must necessarily come to grief among so many who are not good" (56).

Machiavelli disturbs us because he suggests that there is a conceptual breach between a morality of policy and other moralities, Christian, humanist, or whatever. None is better than the others; all can be internally consistent; each can be lived by. His analysis explains some of the characteristics of modern debate over issues such as the Vietnam War or the nuclear freeze or state-funded abortions or the use of standardized writing tests—namely, their interminability due to the fact that each side subscribes to its own morality, derived from a different kind of commitment.

As a consequence, we go round and round in various arguments that cannot be resolved. We don't know that they are partly conflicts between incompatible moral systems or between pieces of many such moral systems lying about us like the bones of dinosaurs. We tend to think that if only we could find the most powerful chain of reasoning and the most compelling evidence, we could prove our opponents wrong and carry the day. So we worm deeper and deeper into our already overrationalized systems to find more and more powerful arguments that *still* pass each other like ships in the night.

At no time have I seen this situation acted out any more obviously than when I was writing about truth-in-testing legislation. The phrase itself revealed why the debate was acrimonious and erupted sometimes into slander and personal abuse. The opponents of standardized testing saw it as an instrument by which the state was sorting people into unequal destinies. The "truth" they wanted told was a truth anchored in a deep concern for individual feelings and rights. They wanted fairness. The defenders of standardized testing said that they, too, were concerned for the individual, but in the context of the state's need to select talent in its many institutions and sectors. They were giving tests so that the individual could rise above the crowd and get due recognition and a fair shot at success. Their desire that this recognition be "fair" led them to seek objectivity in their instruments. Their testimony involved lengthy explanations about the fairness embedded in psychometric reliability, validity, and value-free test development.

Two competing notions of fairness met head to head in the New York Assembly, the California legislature, and the U.S. Congress. And in each case they passed like ships in the night. The psychometric community paraded a Byzantine series of nineteenth-century ideas and twentieth-century statistics before the committee. Then Ralph Nader and people who looked just like him presented equally baffling figures and produced "evidence" that certain questions in certain examinations were trite or silly or had more than one right answer. Then the psychometric witnesses explained that it didn't really make any difference if some items were silly because the psychometric properties of the whole test were what really mattered. On and on they went, neither side ever grasping what the other was saying.

Many policymakers urged a plague on both their houses. And in a sense that was how the matter concluded. The testmakers now have to curtsy to a commonsense notion of fairness, and the test opponents find they have legitimated and strengthened the tests they wanted to destroy. But at no time did the competing moral notions of truth and fairness give in to each other or blend in a synthesis. They could not because they were derived from different moral systems rationalized in different ways.

The truth-in-testing debate combined all the tensions I have described: concern for the individual and concern for the group, arguments based in the humanities waged against arguments based in the sciences. It raised issues of individual freedom pitted against relentless state machinery for sorting, labeling, stigmatizing; the ideal of a pure democracy versus the idea of a managed society; the notion of a truly pluralistic kind of meritocracy versus a narrow, stacked-deck meritocracy.

It also illuminated relationships between various tensions. In particular, it revealed the importance and the sensitivity of the connections between the state and a kind of rationality of which testing and assessment are instances. Max Weber called it purposive-instrumental reason, a rationality of technique, calculation, organization, administration, and planning. Weber tried to determine how that kind of reason evolved in the West and how it came to dominate all other kinds of reasoning in the modern state—so thoroughly that other kinds of rationality, in moral and aesthetic spheres, for instance, aren't even thought of any longer as forms of reason.

Purposive-instrumental reason, focused on mastering the physical world, is the natural reason for the state, devoted as it is to the production and distribution of goods and services. The hard scientist and the policymaker share their thoroughgoing materialism and thus their belief that only purposive-instrumental rationality, with its capacity for proof and disproof, deserves the name of reason. Other forms of discourse—normative discourse about the intersubjective world, for instance, or expressive discourse about one's feelings—cannot serve the modern democratic state. It must, above all, appear to distribute its goods and services according to natural laws. Its rationality must be anchored in physical reality. Its bureaucracies must appear to be rational, purposive, and objective in their actions.

A number of studies have confirmed that this is not just *theoretically* the case; it is in *fact* the case that policymakers and other managers of the social enterprise view the physical sciences as paragons of truth. They prefer purportedly scientific and purportedly objective data to all other kinds of information whenever they need to rationalize a decision. And when they set out to reform something—education, for instance—they are most likely to do so with the interests of the state paramount and in ways that appear reasonable within a purposive-instrumental definition of rationality. It should not surprise us, therefore, that their concern about education stems from economic worries and their reform suggestions focus primarily on the managerial, administrative, organizational, and logistic aspects of the institution of education. Nor would it be surprising if the reforms did nothing to challenge the hyperrationalization and bureaucratization of education, ignoring powerful evidence that these phenomena account for much of the inefficiency policymakers complain about. From their point of view, these things are perfectly rational aspects of the system; it is very difficult for managers to see management rationality as an aspect of the problem instead of a key to its solution.

I've now come to believe that my uneasiness about policy is an uneasiness about the managerial rationality that pervades policymaking and the public institutions for which policymakers are ultimately responsible. I am not feeling a conflict between education and policy; it is a conflict between the values implicit in that managerial rationality—wherever it exists, but especially in the institutions of schooling—and a broader notion of reason that grows out of any decent education worth fighting for.

I can make the distinction clearer by using Alasdair MacIntyre's distinction between a *practice* and the institution that is the *bearer* of the practice. A practice is any complex, cooperative activity through which the goods internal to it are realized in the course of trying to achieve the standards of excellence that partially define it. Chess is a practice; so is football or farming or music or writing. Internal goods are the satisfaction, joys, or rewards inherent in the practice itself, all of which tend to become reasons for continuing in the practice and trying to excel. External goods are things like prestige, status, or money received for participating in a practice that are not intrinsic to the practice. You can get money anywhere, but you can know the joy of chess only by playing chess. Institutions are concerned only with external goods. They become the bearers of practices and thus sustain them, but they are always in tension with them. People who see education as a practice are thus always in tension with the institutional form of education, especially as it reflects the public morality of the state and gives preference to managerial rationality over other forms of reason.

Those of us in testing or assessment or policy work are rightly perceived by education practitioners (in the sense just defined) as agents of the state, its values, its preferred rationality, and its interest in goods external to educational practices. Clear-eyed practitioners do not see us as evil, as some of the truth-in-testing people did, but they see us as largely irrelevant to the practice of education. We're a nuisance.

The school reform problems and solutions of the last few years have been largely defined in terms of managerial, instrumental rationality. So thoroughly has this rationality driven normative discourse to the margins that we have no way of discussing excellence—a fine moral concept with a noble history—except in *numbers*! Excellence can only be understood as having something to do with higher test scores. We of the testing world are thus increasingly charged with the responsibility to define an essentially moral quality in essentially amoral terms. The conceptual breach between practice and institution, individual morality and state morality, the ideal of educating each child to his or her own potential and the state's need to select and sort efficiently grows wider and wider.

Many of us have been struggling for some time to develop writing tests that span the breach. We want to develop writing tests, for instance, that honor the practice of writing sufficiently to require writing samples, that honor managers enough to give them their numbers, and that honor the needs of teachers by providing instructional advice. In doing so, we're constantly being criticized: we are not collecting *real* writing; we are not collecting *enough* writing; we aren't collecting *finished* writing; we're wasting money collecting *any writing at all*; holistic scores don't tell us anything about writing; primary trait scores only tell us about one aspect of one kind of writing; interrater reliabilities aren't high enough; interrater reliabilities are so high that they suggest brainwashing; the information isn't useful to teachers, though administrators may use it; the information isn't useful to administrators, though teachers may use it—on and on and on. Efforts to make a test most reliable and most valid in the psychometric senses move it increasingly away from the concrete milieu of teaching and learning that must finally give the test meaning. Efforts to make the test most compatible with real learning situations move it increasingly away from the psychometric canons that must finally give the test its scientific and legal legitimation. Our solutions to these dilemmas have been technical muddles and compromises. They reflect the muddles and compromises of schooling and, beneath those, the muddles and compromises of a culture lacking in any coherent ethical perspective from which to examine or judge itself.

The school reform movement gives us an opportunity to understand our moral and technical muddles and speculate about how they may relate. We may want to say this: policymakers and managers of the institutional forms of education believe they need a certain kind of data, and we will continue to give it to them in its purest form, even though there is no evidence that they use it and even though it has little bearing on the practice of writing. In that case there is not much to do. Testing has stayed pretty much the same for the last 50 years, and so long as it serves managers primarily, it needn't change much over the next 50. Managers just need to know that there exists some indicator that provides a general picture of progress or decline and permits them to justify various managerial postures and steps in the public interest. The research on how policymakers use knowledge indicates that there is no point in making our information any fancier or more substantial than it already is. In fact, there is evidence that the more polished and sophisticated social science studies become, the less likely they are to be used by policymakers.

With some confidence that the needs of policymakers can rather easily be met, we might want to turn our attention to the people who need our help much more, the teachers and students. They need our help integrating evaluation back into ordinary learning experience within the concept of a practice. Although it is true that the worst tests in America are teacher-made tests, it does not follow that teachers need to learn how to make the kinds of tests that managers need. Teachers, especially writing teachers, don't even need tests in the ordinary sense, and they certainly don't need objectivity in the psychometric sense. They need qualitative, not quantitative, objectivity. Qualitative objectivity, as Michael Scriven once pointed out, has to do with making factual, defensible observations within a specific learning context. It is engaged, rather than disengaged, evaluation. When the director works with the actor, when the dance master works with the dancer, when the woodworker stands by the apprentice at the lathe, or when the editor works with the writer to move the manuscript toward its best potential form, learning and evaluation fuse. Pupil and teacher both submit to the practice and become apprentices to the work itself, which is what matters most to both of them. This kind of evaluation is nonmanipulative and unrelated to external goods such as grades or scores. Although it is clear that the evaluator's knowledge, craft, and contribution are different from those being evaluated, the two meet as equals over the work.

For years we have been trying to improve education by improving and expanding tests. The result has been somewhat improved and considerably expanded management. If you distinguish between the managerial needs of institutions and the learning needs of teachers and students, you begin to see that the same instruments and assumptions cannot serve them both. You begin to see that the reform movement represents an opportunity to change common notions about teaching and evaluation, perhaps by reversing the process to which we have become so accustomed. Education will be improved by improving and expanding evaluation within the context of specific, concrete educational practices such as writing. This will call for some quite different, and I think exciting, ways of thinking about what we are doing. Many of us will feel less tension between our values and our work if we turn in this direction.

REFERENCES

Berlin, I. *Against the Current.* New York: Random House, 1980.
Machiavelli, N. *The Prince.* Trans. Luigi Ricci. New York: Random House, 1950. 50.
MacIntyre, A. *After Virtue.* Notre Dame, Ind.: U of Notre Dame P, 1981. 175.
Scriven, M. "Objectivity and Subjectivity in Educational Research." *Philosophical Redirection of Educational Research.* Ed. L. G. Thomas. National Society for the Study of Education. Chicago: U of Chicago P, 1972.
Weber, M. *The Protestant Ethic and the Spirit of Capitalism.* New York: New American Library, 1958.

5

Pitfalls in the Testing of Writing

EDWARD M. WHITE

It is not hard to see why we test writing poorly. Most teachers of English know little or nothing of testing, and most specialists in testing know even less about the teaching and learning of writing. Furthermore, both groups of professionals suspect each other and confirm their suspicions by rarely communicating with those in distant, slightly disreputable fields. To be sure, not all of this distrust is unfounded. English teachers (rightly) believe that test specialists simplify writing and slight what is most important, while test specialists (rightly) believe that teacher ignorance of testing and teacher arrogance about that ignorance lead to unfair treatment of students. In the face of this gulf, many pitfalls are likely to confront anyone charged with the measurement of student writing ability.

This chapter discusses the pitfalls surrounding programs that test writing at three different levels: in classrooms, on campuses (placement or exit proficiency tests), and in large-scale programs multicampus, statewide, or national in scope. Of course, issues in measurement at these levels overlap. The same kinds of problems that may hamper national testing programs also tend to distort classroom teaching, or, put positively, better understanding of how to test writing at any level will improve classroom teaching at all levels. Furthermore, a teacher who knows how to use testing for more than mere grading in the classroom (to reduce writing anxiety, to encourage rewriting, to develop positive attitudes to the writing process, and so on) will be an informed and valuable member of any test committee, and a test specialist who comes to understand the intimate relationship of testing to teaching will be in demand at all levels of education.

Despite those similarities, I want nonetheless to distinguish the problems at each level, since the solutions to the problems often depend on context. Keeping these distinctions in mind, I have organized this overview chronologically, following the sequence that a testing program follows on campus: the planning stages of testing, test development and test administration, test scoring, and the pitfalls in the evaluation and use of test results.

PLANNING

The usual problem with the planning of tests or testing programs is simple: there is not enough of it, or it is done after problems develop instead of beforehand. The first large-scale test program I administered worked well until the end of the essay scoring session. As thousands of scored essay booklets emerged from the reading rooms, I realized that no one had planned a system to record or combine scores, and no one had reserved space for nearly a ton of paper that we had to store and keep accessible for at least a year.

In the classroom as well, we give scant attention to planning. Unclear and apparently purposeless assignments burden students in too many classrooms, and unreliable final exams are common in writing classes. We teachers often receive bad writing from our students because that is what we call for, despite our best intentions. For example, our most frustrating task as writing teachers is the teaching of revision; yet few students take revision seriously, because we often fail to plan time for the revision process, and we rarely plan to reward revisions as highly as first drafts.

An understanding of the kind of planning necessary for careful testing can improve classroom practice in all these areas. The issues for planning that follow are illustrative rather than inclusive; particular programs or classes will come up with different lists. But the topics illustrate the need for planning and the need to expand the team of planners (particularly where the program is large) to include both faculty and staff specialists.

Goals

A common pitfall in testing writing is the result of inattention to the purpose and function of the test. Classroom tests have a clear and well-understood goal: to find out if students have learned the materials of the class. But as we move beyond the single classroom test, goals become various and complex. Many teachers are far less clear about the purpose and sequence of their out-of-class writing assignments than they are about in-class tests. And when we move beyond the individual classroom to tests of larger groups, a clear consensus of purpose becomes harder to achieve.

Proficiency tests supposedly measure student performance on well-defined and clearly understood "proficiencies." Many state educational systems now require the passing of proficiency tests as a condition for receiving a high school diploma; numerous colleges and university systems (as in California, Georgia, and New York) require university-level writing proficiency of students who are earning degrees. It is easy for the uninformed to imagine that "writing proficiency," a concept so widely used, with such institutional and legal authority, must have some commonly accepted meaning. However, the term has such a variety of definitions, from the merest handwriting or spelling measure to a requirement for a thesis statement, that any test to measure writing proficiency must begin with a careful definition. To ignore this task or to assume that the job has been done by someone else (because someone else has produced something called a "proficiency test") is to make the most elemental and common error in testing.

Since, in one sense, a test is a means of gathering information, a sensible program will consider exactly what kind of information is to be gathered and why. Unfortunately, most testing programs proceed backward: they begin with a test and only later inquire into what the test is in fact discovering. A common error is to begin by selecting (or even constructing) an inexpensive multiple-choice test, frequently one based on an outmoded or casual understanding of linguistics, writing, or grammar. Another error is to construct an essay test of questionable validity to be scored with questionable reliability. After a few test administrations, when it is found that the test seems to be measuring social or economic or racial "proficiencies" rather than writing skills, someone gets around to asking for a serious definition of what the test is really testing.

A related pitfall of proficiency testing emerges from the common misconception that because they teach writing, English teachers know what writing competency is and how to test it. Although an important truth is buried in this assumption (and it is foolish to ignore the experience of writing teachers), we cannot proceed as if English teachers agree on the meaning of writing proficiency and know how to test it. Until the vexing issue of definition has been resolved, it is futile to launch into a testing program of any sort.

I do not intend here to resolve the issue of what constitutes writing proficiency. My point is that the institution must consider the issue and must resolve it before, not after, implementing a testing program. Since the definition should reflect the goals and standards of the institution, many campus groups should participate in defining proficiency. Without a widely accepted definition, inappropriate and flawed testing will result, and test scores will be received with some skepticism.

Unlike proficiency testing, testing for placement provides goals that are much easier to determine. A placement test has the narrow aim of fitting students into a known curriculum, and hence it calls for the active participation of the faculty members who are teaching in that curriculum. Although it is extremely difficult to reach agreement about definitions for proficiencies, it is relatively easy to define what is required for placement. For example, teachers of remedial English and freshman English at a particular college will be able to say what distinguishes a student who is ready to move on into the regular curriculum. We might hear that the significant issue is sentence construction—the ability to master the complex elements that lead to full, complete, variable, and correct sentences in

English. Perhaps the dividing line is nearer to mechanics (such as understanding the ways of connecting sentences or ideas). A placement test, in short, does not need to define or examine "proficiencies," only the skills that help identify appropriate courses for students at various places in the curriculum. Furthermore, a placement test can allow for more refined placement of students by instructors after instruction has begun, if necessary, and therefore need not be as costly or as elaborate as a proficiency test whose scores may lead to irrevocable decisions.

Equivalency testing, to take another case, is a form of proficiency testing, since it is designed to offer credit by examination to students who have learned independently what a class is designed to teach. The very specificity of such testing makes the consideration of goals inevitable. Although equivalency testing offers major advantages to all parties (the best students take more advanced work and more of it, the faculty find more homogenous classes), many faculty members are initially threatened by the concept that students can learn outside the classroom what teachers teach in class. They are also deeply concerned that an equivalency test will both trivialize their subject and debase academic standards. Thus a testing program that awards unit credit should accommodate and alleviate faculty suspicions by involving faculty members at all stages in the program.

Yet another set of goals applies when testing serves the needs of program evaluation—when a writing program, a research grant, an in-service project, or the like needs to demonstrate to a funding agency that its program has positive benefits. The most common form of program evaluation uses a simple pretest/ posttest model, employing some form of writing testing of individuals in the program. This model is generally inadequate, since most such programs have many more effects than a short multiple-choice test or even an essay test can show. Effective program evaluation calls for a multiple series of measures for the multiple effects, including the intangible ones. This more complicated and extensive evaluation process need not, however, lead to very long testing of individuals, since group scores are what count. For example, matrix testing, which divides a long test into short segments to be taken by different students, can provide reliable group scores even though no single individual takes the whole test. A three-hour test can be broken into six half-hour segments, and, if the groups are well chosen, no individual need write more than one segment. Whatever form of measurement may be used, if an evaluation is attempting to measure the comparative effectiveness of two programs or of a program in comparison with a control group, the measurement should focus on the aims of the program being evaluated and should avoid testing matters that are irrelevant to the programs. Thus a program evaluation of a freshman writing program that focuses on the development of analytic skills, say, ought not to depend on a multiple-choice usage test or an expressive writing essay.

In all cases, the most important aspect of planning is to consider with care the goals of the testing program. When that complicated job is done, much of the rest of the work flows naturally from it. When that job is not done or is done badly, we can expect most of what follows to be confused, undefined, and ineffective.

Specifications

Test specifications usually appear as a direct and unambiguous written statement of the goals of a testing program. People accustomed to putting together multiple-choice tests construct charts listing those goals in order to be sure that all are tested. Thus a reading test may have a list with specifications of skills such as "understands metaphors" or "comprehends implied meanings" down one side, while across the top will be a set of content specifications, such as "short poems" or "Shakespeare." Every item needs to fit both a skill and a content specification; the more important specifications will be represented by proportionally more items.

Such a grid is, of course, not really appropriate for essay tests, although the demand for precision of specification is always a worthy goal. Experienced writing faculty members must accept the responsibility for developing specifications for essay tests, and that responsibility should be taken seriously. These faculty members need to know that different kinds of writing assignments test different kinds of abilities and must develop clear enough specifications from the goal statement so that a test development committee will be able to evaluate its questions in the light of precise requirements. For example, a specification such as "use concrete language in descriptive prose" would lead to different questions than would "analyze the structure of a modern poem" or "summarize and then evaluate a given complex argument." The failure to articulate test specifications clearly and to record them in writing (often because at the moment they seem self-evident) is an important omission that can lead to confusion or worse, particularly after some time has passed.

Personnel

It is obviously both sensible and economical to recruit appropriate personnel for the various activities called for by a testing program. But often English teachers who wind up in charge of testing programs are not aware of how much support is at hand, sometimes just for the asking, and poor personnel planning can lead to unfortunate results. I witnessed a school district essay reading that used English teachers to handle the statistics while secretaries scored the papers. (An able statistician slipped a disc hauling boxes of essay booklets at the same reading.)

Consultation

A major deleterious result of badly planned testing programs is the separation of teaching from testing. A particular benefit of careful planning comes from the mutual support teaching and testing give each other when teachers are fully consulted. (The Advanced Placement Program is a fine example of this mutual support; the high school courses generated by the tests are more important than the tests themselves.) When teachers of writing are carefully and regularly consulted, and when their ideas are both heard and used by the developers of the test, there are many beneficial results: the test will both seem and be appropriate, the tone of classroom discussion of the test will be positive (since the teachers will gain a sense of ownership of the test), and the students will find the test a meaningful part of their education. People outside the field of education may wonder why this logical and obvious situation is exceedingly unusual; in fact, serious consultation among people working at different levels is rare in most American enterprises. If procedures for consultation are not built in to the planning process, consultation will probably not occur, and potential support will turn into covert or even overt opposition.

Budget

No one ever forgets to deal with money during the planning of a testing program. The problems are that there is never enough money to do all that one would like to do and that constant budgetary decision making threatens to dominate planning. Two national testing programs have cut budgets by eliminating second readings on test essays, for example, thereby not only reducing the scoring reliability of the test but also eliminating the way to ascertain and measure that reliability. For a grueling day of scoring papers, another national testing service pays essay readers the salary earned by a journeyman plumber for one hour's work; supervisors of the essay scoring then wonder why some of the readers resent working so hard.

After over a decade of planning testing programs, I have come to some highly personal conclusions about budgets. Since the difference in cost between a well-funded testing program and a badly funded one is relatively minor, budgeting in this area is almost always a statement of priority, not finance. If underfunding becomes a serious problem, it is a symptom, not a cause, of the weakness of the program. When the cost of a writing test, particularly the written part of a writing test, is challenged, most often it is writing itself that is under attack. If possible, the testing program should be abandoned rather than rendered ineffective or trivial by people who do not value writing. Program planners need to decide on the minimum funding allowable (including professional wages for essay readers) and to arrange for appropriate action should the money available sink below that figure.

It is important to remind the people in charge of budgets that test costs include development as well as scoring. Although multiple-choice tests cost far less to score than essay tests, it is far more costly to develop multiple-choice tests and to keep them current, secure, and valid. Thus the relatively high cost of scoring writing samples can be balanced by the relatively low developmental costs. The weakest testing programs can give very cheap tests by avoiding the development costs of a multiple-choice test through the purchase of out-of-date and inappropriate exams, which are available everywhere. But responsible professionals will have little to do with such tests.

Reporting and Using Test Results

From its inception, the plan of a testing program must attend to the reporting and use of test results. It is pointless to gather more information than can be well used; it is mischievous to report results in ways that can (and hence will) be misinterpreted and misused. No one should underestimate the concealed power of a test score, nor should anyone underestimate the readiness of various publics and the press to misread, misunderstand, oversimplify, and distort test results.

Unfortunately, it is common to postpone planning for score reporting until much too late, and it is even more common to ignore the need for program evaluation until valuable data have been lost. Evaluators for the testing program should be included in the planning process right from the start. It may, for example, be very valuable to gather information before the testing program begins so that comparison is possible later on. There may be ways of designing forms, such as essay booklets or answer sheets, so that data are available when needed by the evaluator, instead of requiring an expensive data collection effort later.

Finally, planning should attend to record keeping (distribution of rosters, machine-readable results, security, privacy laws, availability of transcripts, etc.) and storage long before the test is given. The sheer bulk of an essay test and the convoluted laws on the release of test results must be seen to be believed, and these matters ought not to come as surprises at the last moment, though they often do.

Scored essays often impress people who have labored over them as precious resources for research. Unfortunately, researchers with funding for and interest in someone else's test are rare, while great mounds of scored essays sit in faculty offices and garages from coast to coast. Unless a local study is under way, plan to ship tests more than a year old to a paper recycling center.

Time Lines

The plan for planning is an important strategy if all key issues are to be considered systematically. Participants at initial planning meetings should develop overall strategies and construct time lines for activities. This is the place to guard against a major pitfall in testing programs: the failure to allow sufficient time, money, consultation, and energy for adequate attention to planning.

Planning committees can discover many options by laying out time lines. One time line might begin with the development and printing of information about the test, the distribution of these materials, test registration, and then the printing and distribution of test results. A quite different time line, probably under the supervision of a different individual, might follow the selection and development of the test itself, beginning with the designation of a committee to draw up test specifications, move to pretesting and printing schedules (with extra proofreading!), and then to distribution of the test to test centers, the return of the materials to the central office, and the payment of the proctors. Yet another time line might consider the scoring of the test as the central temporal element. If student writing is involved, a choice site for the essay reading must be reserved many months ahead of time, and procedures for selecting current readers, for identifying a cadre of future readers, and for determining all costs for the reading must be developed. An essay reading is in many ways similar to a substantial conference and requires at least as much attention. Any posttest activities, such as publication of sample papers and scoring guides, should be part of these time lines, since nobody will think to collect these materials as a matter of course during the bustle of test administration and scoring.

The preparation of time lines is important for any testing program for several reasons: it allows the cool consideration of tasks in advance (instead of during the confusion of other activities), it calls for the establishment of clear lines of responsibility so that the people involved will know who is supposed to do what and when, and it helps to break down a complex job of administration into a series of discrete tasks with deadlines.

Planning sessions may seem cold and unimaginative, but in practice they are quite the reverse: exciting, creative, contentious meetings that blend people, theories, and practical activities into the pattern that becomes a testing program. They turn the chaos of an idea into the order of a plan, share responsibilities among the people best suited for the various tasks, and anticipate problems before they occur. Even the best-planned testing program may encounter unexpected turns and unpleasant surprises; planning can never obviate all problems, nor can it be expected to do so. Still, it can allow time and money to meet those problems should they arise.

TEST SELECTION, DEVELOPMENT, AND ADMINISTRATION

When to Select the Test

The crucial decision of what test to use often comes far too early in large testing programs. The classroom model is instructive in this area: faculty members are often frustrated to discover that last term's examination is not suitable for this term's class, despite an identical course description. The final exam must cover the material of the course, and coverage or emphasis cannot be determined too far ahead of time; if the exam is to be up to date, to be *valid*, it must deal with the actual (not the proposed) material of the course. In short, the people choosing an examination need to be sure that it meets clear test specifications and is right for the students involved, as well as for the material to be covered.

Unfortunately, the usual situation for large-scale testing programs works backward. The testing instrument is often chosen first, not after preliminary work, and decisions about its relation to instruction, its usefulness for the particular student population, or the meaning of its results all follow and depend on the particular test that has been chosen. In many cases, the test is selected for peculiar reasons—political, commercial, or merely personal, for example—and the entire testing program is distorted as a result.

It is for this reason that the odd complaint of "teaching to the test" has become a cliché in American education, a descriptor for distorted, even partially dishonest instruction. The objection is inherently paradoxical, since virtually every classroom teacher does in fact teach to his or her own tests all the time and sees that as sensible and appropriate. Indeed, testing is so naturally part of learning ("How'm I doing, teacher?") that no reasonable person questions the procedure. But when the testing seems, or in fact is, distant from or irrelevant to what is being taught and learned, teaching to the test suddenly becomes an issue. And when, as is often the case in school district testing programs, the test is not appropriate for the student population, teachers must choose between helping students learn and helping students pass tests. Sometimes, of course, school administrators believe that mandating an inappropriate test (such as one normed on a wholly different population, using a wholly different curriculum) helps raise academic standards and helps motivate greater performance. Such a procedure is, at best, a negative and damaging way to suggest curriculum reform.

The major pitfall in test selection, then, is to begin with the test, before developing test goals, specifications, and uses. In writing assessment, this problem tends to appear as two emotionally charged issues: multiple-choice testing versus essay testing and literature testing versus usage testing. But these are the wrong issues at the wrong point in the process. They occur as vexing problems and lead to acrimonious debate only when they relate to tests chosen prematurely.

The issue of multiple-choice versus essay testing of writing has become a bit dated since the development of relatively reliable and cost-effective holistic scoring procedures. Insofar as a test seeks to measure actual writing ability, the issue can be more generally defined as a conflict between direct and indirect measures. Traditionally, an indirect measure is preferred only when it shows clear advantages over the direct measure. Until recently, advocates of indirect (usually multiple-choice) measurement of writing ability pointed to high cost and low reliability in scoring writing samples, as compared to the low cost and high efficiency of multiple-choice answer sheets. Now the argument has shifted: the high development costs of multiple-choice testing, the constant security and revision expenses of multiple-choice tests under truth-in-testing laws, the lower validity of such tests, and the damage to curricula such tests cause by devaluing actual writing—all suggest the weaknesses of multiple-choice measurement in the field of writing.

The arguments just summarized boil most violently when institutions consider tests before careful planning. Passions and name-calling flower; the advocates of writing samples argue for the virtues of the past, of culture, of humanism, while the patrons of the machine-scored test fight for modern technology. But the solution to the issue is quite undramatic, once test specifications and other planning matters have been attended to. Different kinds of skills are most effectively measured by different kinds of tests. Writing as a whole is best dealt with by writing-sample testing; reading (which correlates highly with writing), sentence construction skills, ability to discern logical relationships, and the like, seem best dealt with by multiple-choice testing. Where highly refined measurement is needed (as in the award of college credit or in certification for graduation), the most responsible test combines both kinds of measures; where less refined measurement is required (as in placement testing, where testing errors can be readily rectified by teachers), one or the other kind of test might suffice, depending on local curricula, personnel, and facilities.

A similar pointless dichotomy sometimes divides educators debating the abstract advantages and disadvantages of literature (or reading) tests as opposed to usage or "grammar" tests (which usually have little to do with what linguists call grammar). Passions and postures often substitute for argument on these issues too when test selection precedes planning.

No one can avoid these pitfalls wholly, but one can ease their ill effects substantially by delaying the selection of a testing instrument until after careful program planning is under way. With a statement of goals, criteria, and uses, and with a clear connection between the instructional program and the test, it becomes possible to consider the testing instrument within a context that encourages logical and purposeful discussion.

Norm-referenced versus Criterion-referenced Tests

Norm-referenced testing, the standard method of mental measurement since the model was developed by and for aptitude testing of World War I draftees, has a superficial appeal for the testing of writing. The norm-reference model assumes a "normal" (bell curve) distribution of ability and compares an individual's performance on a test to that normal curve, reporting percentile rankings. Thus if you score at the 10th percentile on mechanical ability, 90 percent of the population has greater mechanical aptitude than you, and you should be kept away from valuable equipment. Norm-referencing suggests such virtues as objectivity, comparability, and statistical complexity. However, such testing has some serious problems, particularly for the unwary.[1]

Since norm referencing assumes a "normal" distribution of the skills it measures, it is disrupted by education; even short-term training can alter score distributions and skew the bell curve, so aptitude tests attempt to discount the effects of education in order to preserve the purity of the model. In order to produce a bell curve, the test design requires a preponderance of questions that about half the test population will answer correctly, with a few very easy questions (to produce the left-hand slope of the curve) and a few very hard questions (for the right-hand slope). If the curve becomes distorted, as it may if too many students answer too many questions incorrectly, the test is revised to reestablish the normal curve. This means that norm-referenced test questions tend inevitably toward the aptitude testing model and away from questions susceptible to learning. Such a situation is particularly unfortunate for the testing of writing, since writing "aptitude" usually reflects the economic, social, or ethnic conditions in the home when a student was learning the language; whatever discounts learning in writing testing tends to benefit the already advantaged. Furthermore, the population used to determine the points on the bell curve is crucial, since the curve (against which all other test takers will be compared) is determined by the ability and (sometimes even more significantly) the aptitude and upbringing of the norming population.

Although I am not suggesting that norm referencing is either evil or necessarily inappropriate in all cases, I am pointing out the potential problems for those who would measure writing ability by a norm-referenced test. The norming population must be a primary concern: a test normed on eastern prep school students will probably distort results when used on a less advantaged group of students, whatever their writing ability, if the test contains the usual number of questions calling for cultural advantages and an ear for the privileged dialect. Students from minority cultures score particularly poorly on such tests, despite relatively normal distributions on writing-sample tests (White and Thomas).

Even if the norming group seems an appropriate one, a careful review of the test is particularly necessary in order to check for aptitude test or social class items that often appear on norm-referenced writing tests. Here for example, is a sample question adapted from a popular test designed to measure college-level competence in English composition:

English-speaking musicians professionally use large numbers of words from which one of the following languages?

a. German
b. French
c. Spanish
d. Latin
e. Italian

The testmakers are obviously looking in this question for a scrap of information about the ways in which English uses foreign words, in this case the Italian vocabulary for some aspects of musical notation. Some students may, in fact, pick up such information in a composition course, though it seems unlikely; but the student most able to darken the proper space on an answer sheet is probably the one whose parents wanted to and could afford to give him or her classical music lessons as a child. Those not so privileged (including, no doubt, some professional musicians) are not likely to know the answer, regardless of their writing ability. And someone who knew too much—say, a specialist in medieval music—might even give the "wrong" answer, Latin.

It would be easy to select other bad items from norm-referenced tests (or any other kind), particularly items that are culture-linked, such as the one in the example, or based on dialect or usage differences of no bearing on writing ability. The particular issue here is not that such bad items exist but that norm referencing encourages such items because they "work" for certain convenient norming populations. (Essay testing has its share, and more, of bad questions, but they tend to be so difficult to score consistently—essay readers are much more vocal and opinionated than the computers that score answer sheets—that they are rarely repeated.)

It is sometimes hard for nonspecialists in testing to realize how narrowly and precisely conceived are the most professional norm-referenced tests. I once asked an ETS test specialist about a particular item on the Scholastic Aptitude Test. "It's really a stupid question," I said to him, in some exasperation. He cheerfully agreed. "Sure is. But students who succeed in the first year of college get it right, and those who don't get it wrong. And that's what the test is all about." He was right, in a narrow sense, since ETS consistently tries to make the people who use, and misuse, the SAT understand that its sole purpose is to predict first-year college success. But no amount of information seems to keep people from imagining the SAT to be a general intelligence test or, even worse, a proficiency test for the nation's high schools.

The basic problems with using norm-referenced tests to measure writing ability, then, are located both in their construction and in their norming populations. If the test in fact measures what you are seeking to find out and if the norming population is indeed appropriate, there is good reason to celebrate: someone else has borne the burden of test development for you.

If, on the other hand, you discover that existing tests do not meet your test specifications or your population, you may want to consider criterion-referenced testing—testing according to standards defined without reference to a student population. Such testing differs from norm referencing in its development and in its results: since it is based on test criteria rather than a norm population, criterion-referenced tests do not seek to obtain a normal curve. On the contrary, the specific nature of such testing leads to questions directed to the material of a course of instruction or a body of knowledge. Subjects who have not learned the material will answer few questions correctly, while those who have mastered the material will get most questions right. The particular advantage of criterion-referenced testing is obvious: the questions can be developed directly out of stated test criteria and for the specific purposes of the particular test or testing program. The disadvantage of such testing is equally obvious: since it is highly unlikely that a criterion-referenced test for your purpose will be available commercially, test development is necessary, and the statistical comfort of national normative data will not be available. Since, almost invariably, essay testing tends to be criterion-referenced, many institutions and many state programs have moved into such testing in recent years; almost without exception, they have found the effort to be well worthwhile, since the establishment of essay testing programs yields not only useful and credible scores but also major benefits in faculty development and curricular change.

Test Development

It is common enough for an institution to create an essay testing program, but it is a common pitfall to establish such a program without being fully aware that test development is absolutely necessary if the program is to meet its goals.

The most usual mistake in test development is to assume that it is easy and that most of us who teach (since we give tests regularly in our classrooms) can do it well. Unfortunately, test development is difficult to do well, and even more unfortunately, most of us do it rather badly. (One of the great benefits to an institution that moves into careful testing is to train its faculty in better evaluation techniques, indirectly.)

The most serious mistake is to ask faculty members to develop a multiple-choice test of writing skill. Professionally developed multiple-choice tests in this area tend to be at best uneven; the tests created without professional support tend to be unmitigated disasters. No individual should accept the responsibility of putting such a test together without a committee of colleagues to work regularly over a span of at least a year; the committee should have a professional test consultant, substantial computer support, clerical support for production and administration of tryout test items and norming tests, and a very large budget. None of these provisions are exaggerated; unfortunately, they guard only against the most obvious pitfalls of multiple-choice testing (ambiguity, invalidity, unreliability); they do not guarantee that a very good test will result.

The development costs of multiple-choice tests are not well known and are usually ignored when arguments for the economy of such testing are presented. As I pointed out earlier, multiple-choice tests, though cheaper to score than essay tests, are far more costly to put together; if we add in the necessary costs of multiple forms and revisions (required by many of the new truth-in-testing laws), essay tests turn out to be far more cost-effective. And when we consider the advantages to the curriculum and to the professional development of the faculty from essay testing, direct measurement of writing skill becomes a clear "best buy." Under ordinary circumstances, then, test development will mean essay test development, and that is what we will take the term to mean here.

Faculty members come to test design committees assuming that their classroom experience in testing will readily carry over into a large-scale testing program. Sometimes that is the case, but more typically the new situation demands a new approach. Questions that work well in a course setting will normally not work well in a large-scale test: when the classroom context is withdrawn, with all of its understood definitions and expectations, these questions must be entirely rewritten and will usually wind up in the heap of rejected possibilities.

The first time I was responsible for developing an essay test, I proceeded under the naive assumption that I could convene a group of excellent writing teachers, each bringing two of his or her best classroom essay topics, and could select from the riches before us. As we circulated the proposed topics (including two of my own, of which I was very proud), barely audible groans surfaced. After full discussion, every single question had been rejected, and we re-formed into test committees to salvage what we could. The second year, in the belief that the first year's experience was atypical, since it was so contrary to logical expectation, I tried the same procedure—with exactly the same result. We did not fall into the same error again.

The faculty members who form test development committees, then, must not only be excellent writing teachers but must also be flexible committee workers who can comfortably abandon favorite ideas that do not work. They need to recognize that a good question for a test will have the following components:

1. *Clarity.* Students will not waste time trying to figure out what is called for but will be able to get right down to work.
2. *Validity.* Good students will receive high scores and weak students will receive low scores. There will be a good range of scores, without too large a concentration in the middle.
3. *Reliability.* Scoring of pretest papers shows considerable agreement by readers, and a scoring guide can be readily constructed to describe score differences.
4. *Interest.* The question offers sufficient intrinsic interest so that students will write with some genuine concern and those scoring will not be bored (and hence become inaccurate).

With these principles in mind, the test development committee will consider the test specifications, the goals of the testing program, and the students to be tested. This initial step needs to occur several months before the actual test questions are chosen so that the committee will have ample time to revise its selections or abandon them and start over should none of them work.

The pretesting population need not be large—50 to 100 students will often suffice—but it must be carefully chosen. Those taking the pretest cannot be students who will take the real test but should be representative of them, with the same background, ethnic and cultural diversity, and range of abilities. Students at neighboring colleges or school districts will usually serve nicely, and pretesting questions for colleagues is becoming a routine professional courtesy.

Careful reading of the pretests usually reveals that most of the proposed questions do not work, according to the principles I have just listed: the test does not distinguish the best writers from the average ones, most students will find little to say or will produce only clichés, most scores group in the middle, clear scoring criteria do not emerge, and so on. But if the questions have been carefully designed, one or two of them will stand out from the rest; they will "work" as needed, often to the wonder of the committee, which included them reluctantly. These are the questions to be revised and clarified for further pretesting and eventually to be used in the test itself.

The fact that test questions must themselves be tested is not well understood and leads to many pitfalls in testing. Sometimes a question perfectly suitable for writing in a class situation will turn out to be wholly invalid in a large-scale test, and the committee will want to keep a sharp eye out for such questions during pretesting. Such questions are those that might require substantial prewriting exercises in class before students (particularly the best students) will move beyond the recitation of clichés: women's rights, the legal age for drinking, the draft, the value of education, and so on. Experienced test development committees avoid such questions as systematically as they do those allowing the pious to record their religious experiences; few good students will write essays on such topics that reflect their actual writing ability.

Given sufficient time and, in a large program, some statistical support, test developers will come up with test questions that will work. With such a test in hand, scoring the questions reliably becomes a manageable matter. Unfortunately, most testing programs spend insufficient time developing the questions and then expect the people scoring them to produce fair scores on an unfair test. Anyone who has been placed in such an unfortunate position will insist that those responsible for the question development need also to be responsible for the scoring. If readers rebel over a stupid or impossible question, they have the right to be able to attack the perpetrators at the reading site, without delay.

Finally, essay test development can never be considered finished as long as a testing program continues. Just as a conscientious classroom teacher is always revising his or her exams, improving, clarifying, updating, expanding, so test development committees can never rest. The challenge to these committees is not only to produce new topics on the model of successful past topics but also to keep abreast of writing research, which is now slowly moving into the area of measurement and cognition. We know much more about essay testing now than we did a decade ago, as this volume demonstrates; 5 or 10 years from now we will know much more than we do today. For example, we do not know why some students will perform much better on one kind of writing task than on another; there is a surprisingly low correlation between scores on personal experience and on analytic topics. (Personal experience topics may be more accessible to most students, but they are not "easier" for all students.) We can compensate for this by including at least two modes of discourse on any important writing test so that students will have the opportunity to do their best. But research in this area will probably lead to better answers and thus better tests than we can now produce. Even within single modes, the difficulty of topics can vary greatly: many writers find it considerably more difficult to respond to "Describe your favorite person" than to "Describe your favorite place." Essay tests need constant renewal from new topics and from new ideas for kinds of topics, and test development committees need to be alert to both obligations.

Test Administration

Many institutions have diligent test officers, sometimes with statistical or psychometric training, who can be trusted to see to the many details involved in the administration of tests. The test officer should identify and deal with such matters as the appropriate time and place for the test, the proper handling of test materials, the control of the testing environment, the hiring and paying of proctors, and the handling of dishonest test takers.

But there are other matters to deal with in this general area of test administration. How long should the test be? How many essay questions should there be, and of what kind? Should there be a multiple-choice portion of the test, and if so, how much weight should it have in the total test score? What kind of information about the test should be distributed to students ahead of time, and when? If there is a test fee, what is it to be, how is it to be managed, and under what circumstances are there to be refunds?

These questions are meant to be exemplary, not by any means inclusive. They are questions that require a professional test administrator, and no faculty member should undertake responsibility for a large testing program without such staff support.

TEST SCORING

Scoring Essay Tests

A modified system of holistic scoring is widely accepted today as producing reasonably reliable scores at an acceptable cost. In holistic reading, raters give a single score for overall quality of the writing; trained readers can produce 20 or so scores an hour for complex 45-minute essays and double or even triple that number for shorter or less complex writing. Reliability is achieved by developing a descriptive scoring guide accompanied by sample papers at the different score points, then by gaining a consensus among the readers (gathered together at a controlled essay reading) to apply those standards to all the papers they read. Our concern here, however, is with the pitfalls into which the people directing essay scoring may fall. Problems in essay scoring can be divided into three areas: procedures, personnel, and statistics.

The central concern for an essay reading must be to establish what the literary critic Stanley Fish calls an "interpretive community" (9), a community of readers responding in the same way to similar texts. The procedures involved in such a reading are all designed to set up such a community, within the constraints of a budget and a limited amount of time to accomplish a taxing and boring job. This suggests not only decent pay and comfortable working conditions but also a sense of collegiality among all people at the reading.

The most common pitfall in the management of holistic essay readings is the loss of this collegiality. It is easy to see why this delicate sense of joint participation and professional respect is so difficult to maintain. Very often, readings do not proceed by consensus and joint decision making, a requirement if readers are to feel that they are grading properly. Some test administrators see the frequent discussion of standards for grading as a waste of time better spent in generating scores. Coffee breaks, cocktail parties, and the like are seen as luxuries and frills instead of as the community-forming activities they need to be. Gracious treatment of readers and professional pay for readers are considered as expendable costs instead of essential ingredients for a professional working community. But readers are not merely employees; they must form a working team committed to group judgments and to the entire process of group scoring.

Even sensitive academics who run essay readings may fall into the same pitfall if they are not careful, since the process of determining standards puts them in a position to coerce others in a good cause. Before readers come together to score a test, the chief reader and the table leaders will meet to read through many student papers in order to get a sense of the range of papers to be scored. For a day or so, these experienced readers will read several hundred papers, will choose perhaps dozens of papers that represent this range for the readers to use as "range finders" (papers that illustrate the various score levels), and will develop the scoring guide describing the different points on the scale to be used at the reading. By the time the readers arrive, the people responsible for the reliability of the reading have already reached substantial agreement on standards. Every temptation exists, therefore, to tell the readers what to do and what standards to apply so that the reading can get under way efficiently.

But to do so is to ignore the need for a community of assent, which holistic readers must become to function responsibly. Those who understand the process will have no problem granting the representativeness of sample papers if they trust the leaders of the reading. But readers must have the opportunity to grade those papers, to argue out differences, to come to an understanding of the ranking system, and even to make changes in the scoring guide by mutual consent. The training of readers, or "calibration," as it is sometimes called, is not indoctrination into standards determined by those who know best (as it is too often imagined to be) but rather the formation of an assenting community that feels a sense of ownership of the standards and the process.

Maintaining standards of the reading and of this sense of community go hand in hand, even throughout scoring sessions that last many days. Retraining on new sample papers must occur every few hours, to prevent reader drift up or down, and readers must see this process as a group endeavor to work together, not as a check by management on the accuracy of the readings. When leaders of a long reading organize social activities such as play readings, poetry readings, special films, and the like, they are not serving as entertainment directors so much as helping to hold the group together. When chief readers can use confident humor to acknowledge legitimate differences of opinion or admit that they might change their minds or even be wrong, they are not giving in to reader demands (as I heard one hard-nosed administrator call it) but are admitting themselves to be human and part of the group, which must accept that leadership willingly.

I have been stressing the need to develop a sense of community for a holistic reading and the various pitfalls for leaders who fail to see the need for that community, but I do not mean to imply that the tone of a reading should be excessively casual. The best readings have a decidedly businesslike atmosphere, and the collegiality is part of the business to be done. No one should imagine the reading as a vacation or a social occasion: this is a hard and tedious job that must be done well in a limited amount of time. Establishing an "interpretive community" is simply the most efficient way to get the job done properly.

A further procedural problem often centers around the use and origin of the scoring guide (called by some a *rubric*). This description of the qualities to be found in papers at different score points is normally written by the people in charge of the reading after they have read a large sample of the work to be scored and after they have reached agreement on the ranking of many typical papers. That is, experienced readers with a deep understanding of the criteria for the test produce scoring guides that reflect not only the test criteria but also (by induction) the reality of the test papers to be scored. When this procedure is followed with care, holistic scoring allows the impersonality of the test criteria to be moderated by the humanity of the actual writing and also allows the populism of the score distribution to be adjusted according to the professionalism of the criteria. In this way, the test can combine the best aspects of both norm and criterion referencing. The scoring guide is particularly valuable for several reasons: it sets out the standards for judgment so that they can be explicit and debated, it establishes the theoretical grounds for the ranking, and it encourages the use of the full range of scores by giving reasonable descriptions of the strongest and the weakest papers. Since the scoring guide is derived in part from the actual range of papers written on each particular question, it reinforces the particular job to be done, that is, to rank the set of papers at hand according to specific criteria devised for the writing topic at hand.

Some essay readings proceed without a scoring guide, in the mistaken conviction that debates over abstract descriptions will distract readers from practical decisions. Since readers will rarely refer to the scoring guide after the reading is well under way (the goal is to help readers internalize the standards), these practical administrators argue that the considerable time and effort required by a scoring guide are wasted. All readers, the argument goes, can intuit common standards from sample papers just as well as the table leaders can.

This argument ignores the need for an assenting community, one that can act in agreement because its members have reached agreement. The scoring guide not only accomplishes the useful tasks I have summarized, but it also symbolizes this community and gives individual readers a stake in the outcome of the reading.

An even more common pitfall in relation to scoring guides also stems from a desire to avoid the cost and trouble of devising a new one for each reading. Some test directors will simply import a scoring guide from some other testing program on the supposition that if it worked well elsewhere, it must have some inherent virtue. Frequently, such borrowed goods will not fit the test question or the essay responses at hand. More problematic is the use of an all-purpose scoring guide, designed to meet the requirements of all questions that are designed for a particular testing program. A number of programs use such a guide not merely or even principally to avoid the creation of a new one but in the belief that the questions and student populations change so little from test to test that a new guide is simply not needed. In effect, this procedure discounts the influence of norm referencing on the scoring and makes the test wholly criterion-referenced. It also assumes that it is in fact possible to create equivalent questions by using the same question format, an assumption that I believe is unfounded; if this term's question is harder (or easier) than last term's and the scoring criteria remain the same, the meaning of the two sets of scores will be different. Raters who use the same scoring guide for a series of questions cannot simply assume that they are maintaining the same standard. They also need to be careful that the scoring guide, which cannot focus on the issues raised by particular questions, does not wind up emphasizing the more superficial aspects of writing at the expense of the more substantive ones. While it is true that such a procedure gains a standard document, it loses the discussion and revision process that makes a question-specific scoring guide contribute to the precision of scoring and the formation of an interpretive community.

The choice of personnel for the essay reading is fraught with difficulty, particularly for a new program. The ability to read essays accurately and quickly demands a peculiar skill, not necessarily associated with other academic skills. Some excellent teachers just never become good readers, while the least likely individuals can show amazing talent as readers. Teachers who are excessively rigid or insecure often have difficulty adopting group standards, and faculty members who take pride in their differences with their colleagues may resent the entire process. But even such apparently unsuited readers sometimes turn out to be delightful at readings, while some well-recommended people read erratically and inattentively.

Thus the major pitfall in choosing readers is making premature judgments about people before you watch them on the job. Careful record keeping will identify those who read inaccurately or too slowly. Over time, the natural leaders will emerge as potential chief readers and table leaders, and the best readers will form a steady cadre to help shape a new community each time a reading convenes.

The most valuable person at an essay reading should be the least visible: the administrative aide who sees to it that batches of papers move properly through the reading, that records are kept, that the coffee is ready, that travel and honorarium forms are properly filled in and promptly paid, and that unexpected problems are handled without much fuss. With such a person at hand, the reading proceeds smoothly; without such a person, nothing goes right, and small problems escalate into catastrophes. An efficient administrative aide must be identified at an early point in the planning, must have enough freedom to do the job well, and must be appropriately rewarded.

Many pitfalls are associated with the use of statistics in essay readings, but two particular problems are so common that they deserve special mention here: the temptation to score papers only once and the confusion between ranking papers and deciding on the meaning of the ranking.

Standard practice in essay scoring requires two independent readings of each paper. The first score is often concealed by a label of some sort, usually with a detachable center portion that can be torn away at the end of the scoring to reveal scores. Whatever the system, the second reader must be unaware of the first score. If the two scores differ (usually, by more than one point), a third reading is performed to resolve the discrepancy. Continuing programs use these comparisons, as they accumulate, to gather data on the reliability of the reading itself, as well as on the accuracy of individual readers. Without double readings, it is impossible to gather these figures or to verify the fairness of the test scoring. Although there is a constant temptation to reduce costs by reducing the second readings to samples or by eliminating second readings altogether, such an economy renders the reading unaccountable and unprofessional.

The second problem has to do with the setting of passing scores on the test, a complex issue with an interesting relation to the debate over the all-purpose scoring guide. Educators who prefer an entirely criterion-referenced test use such a guide for all essay scorings for a particular program, with confidence that the various scores on the guide will represent the same level of writing ability whatever the question or the student group. Under these circumstances, the passing score can be set in advance and can even be part of the scoring guide itself. On the other hand, those who prefer to introduce some norm-referenced aspects into the test or who are uneasy at the differences among questions and student groups will argue that the determination of the meaning of the holistic ranking must be made after the ranking, not before. Statements of scoring criteria that include references to passing and failing, this group argues, invite readers to go outside the scoring criteria into their own individual experience and so reduce scoring reliability; it is a difficult enough job to rank papers reliably, according to the criteria of a given reading, and that job should not be confounded with matters beyond the ranking. Certainly, if you are including a norming sample in the test scoring (to see, for example, how freshmen with certain grades score on a placement test), referring to previous pass-fail rates, comparing percentile scores, or using other norm-referenced concepts, you should delay the decision on passing scores until the ranking is completed. And if you suspect, as I do, that this year's score of 7 may represent the same level of ability as last year's score of 8 and next year's score of 6, you will want to decide on passing scores after reviewing score distributions and norming data and whatever else may be available to increase the fairness of the passing score decision.

Scoring Multiple-Choice Tests

The great convenience of multiple-choice testing is the ease of scoring. With sensible planning, well-designed answer sheets will produce a computer printout with scores arranged in several different ways (high to low, alphabetical by last name, etc.), with such student information as file number or mailing address listed next to the scores. In addition, the printout can provide a statistical package with all kinds of useful numbers about the score distribution and correlations among parts of the test.

It is tempting to believe that an impressive list of numbers provides everything we need to know about the test. Unfortunately, the printout provides only the raw material for what we need to know, and the people responsible for the test still have a great deal of work to do after the production of the numbers. The unresolved problem that remains is to determine the meaning of those numbers and their appropriate use in the context of the measurement of writing ability.

For example, one number to be examined closely is the standard error of measurement (SEM). This rarely discussed statistic is enormously important for the responsible use of a multiple-choice test score: it sets out the range of meaningful score differences. For example, the SEM of the verbal portion of the Scholastic Aptitude Test is 30 points. This means that if a student scoring, say, 500 on the test were to retake it, in two out of three instances, that student would score between 470 and 530. It also means that one out of every three retests would be likely to produce a score outside of this 60-point band. This set of numbers has important implications, normally avoided or ignored by institutions despite the statements of responsible testing agencies. Even highly reliable multiple-choice tests, such as the SAT, yield approximations of student rankings, not absolute measurements, and the scores should be read as the center of a band of scores rather than as a single point. The SEM describes the width of the band, and the possibility of greater error is always present.

It sometimes surprises people unfamiliar with multiple-choice test statistics to notice how wide the range of error is, even on the best of these tests. Everyone knows that essay test scores are approximate, but many people attribute an altogether unwarranted precision to what they like to call "objective tests." We ought to avoid that term *objective*, which is a judgment rather than a description, and remain aware that multiple-choice tests are a useful yet fallible method of testing some matters and are no better than the questions they contain, which were themselves composed and evaluated by subjective human beings, just as essay tests are.

Anyone using multiple-choice test scores, then, needs to consider them as bands of scores, not simply as absolute points, and to consider them as approximations of the skills they measure, which are likely to have an undetermined relation to writing skill. For these reasons, as well as many others (such as their effects on writing programs), the best use of multiple-choice scores in the area of writing is as a portion of a test, rather than as the test itself. The results of a careful multiple-choice test, when combined with the results of a careful essay test, will yield a more accurate measure of writing ability than either test used by itself.

If a writing score is to be combined with a multiple-choice test score to produce a single total score, a statistician will need to perform a simple operation called scale matching. This ensures that the differences in numerical scale on different kinds of tests do not distort the weight each score should have in the total score. Scale matching puts different kinds of scores on the same scales so that they can be combined properly. However, someone still must decide if the different parts of the test are to have equal weight or some proportional weight. Should a 20-minute multiple-choice portion weigh as much as a 90-minute essay portion in determining the final score? Half as much? One-sixth as much? As always, the numbers will serve the people who understand how to use them.

Yet an additional burden accompanies receiving the numbers from multiple-choice tests: relating the numbers to decisions about the students. The numbers will not say who fails a proficiency requirement or who should be placed in a remedial class. Only informed teachers can make that decision after reviewing everything relevant to the test, including the numbers. It is tempting to imagine that the numbers, or the people who report them, can make that decision, but such a reliance on numbers avoids responsibility. Finally, test results turn out to be only data, to be used well or badly. The most important responsibility of administrators of testing programs is to use the data well.

EVALUATION AND USE

Reporting Test Results

There is a wide gulf between the message intended by most tests and the message conveyed by the test scores. This sad fact is true in classrooms, where students are ever ready to read grades and teacher comments on their work as judgments of their personality or their relationship to the teacher. Many studies have documented the gap between what professors say or think they are saying in their commentaries on papers and what students actually perceive. Large-scale testing programs suffer the same distortions in score reporting, only, of course, on a much larger scale.

The desire to obtain simple answers to complex questions leads to misunderstanding and distortion of test results. Schools may receive test reports designed to help them assess their programs but use the information solely to argue that they are more (or less) effective than other schools and hence more deserving of funds. Writing tests at the upper-division college level, designed to warn juniors who are poor writers to develop their skills, turn into barriers for seniors who have met all other degree requirements. The full range of information provided by some national college entrance tests is always in danger of being read by students and admissions officers as a simple pass-fail cutting score. Public school administrators, looking for an easy way to combine economy with the appearance of high standards, mandate particular scores on the National Teachers Examination (an entry-level test for credential candidates) for experienced classroom teachers looking for raises in salary. Multitest programs, such as the College Board Admission Testing Program or the College-Level Examination Program, merge in many instances into a single conflated score or a hazily understood single test. Even college administrators will talk about a student's "CLEP score," without awareness that more than 40 tests exist in that program, about a half dozen in English alone.

Since the principal pitfall in reporting test results, whether in individual classrooms or in schoolwide, statewide, or nationwide programs, is the misunderstanding and misuse of scores, institutions must pay particular attention to proper reading and interpretation of scores. Sometimes this means the development of graphs as well as numbers, presentation of several kinds of comparative or normative data, reminders of just what the examination is or is not testing, and other similar efforts. A number of writing tests with essay portions include the essay score in a total score and then, in addition, give the essay raw score, the sum, perhaps, of two readings on a given scale. This useful separate report for the essay portion allows educators receiving the score to understand how that particular score was reached and to use it separately if they wish. But the danger here is that some audiences are so likely to misuse an essay score if they get one that it may be more responsible for test reports to bury that score in a composite score.

Finally, a testing program must provide some machinery for students who want to review the test and their performance on it. It would be irresponsible for a classroom teacher to give a test and to refuse to hold office hours afterward; it is just as irresponsible (as new legislation has made clear) for users of tests to refuse to allow students to challenge test questions or test results. Even some large campus testing programs include in the test fee a charge for advising after the test. Despite what the public and legislators may think, tests are not devised solely for the purpose of failing students, and the best programs consider carefully how to make information from a test clear and useful.

Follow-up Studies

Tests and testing programs must themselves be tested. If they do not pass the test, they should be failed and discontinued. Again, the classroom can serve as a model: if a test does not "work," it is abandoned and replaced by a better one. Large-scale tests require large-scale evaluations, but the same principle holds.

The differing purposes of tests require different kinds of evaluations. A college entrance test, for example, must be evaluated by discovering its "predictive" validity: most students who pass the test should succeed in college. A college placement test, on the other hand, should be evaluated by discovering the accuracy of the placement, through such means as surveying the faculty to discover obvious misplacements. Predictive validity is a tempting but disastrous method of evaluating a placement test, since a placement test is designed to *change* predictions; weak students are placed in a program to help them succeed, and their success will lower the predictive validity of the test, whose prediction of failure the curriculum attempts to forestall. Thus anyone using predictive validity to evaluate a placement testing program is using the success of the program as a way to document the supposed failure of the test. A placement testing program has different goals from an admissions testing program and should be evaluated differently.

Proficiency testing and equivalency testing require follow-up studies, sometimes over many years, for evaluation. We want to find out what happens to students who receive credit by examination for freshman English as they move through their college years. If the credit is too easily earned, we would expect these students to perform less well than similar students who had the benefit of the freshman English course. If the test is appropriately encouraging to the best students, we might expect to find them taking more English courses, at a higher level, than their counterparts, and doing better. The only way to know for sure is to design a follow-up study to trace the group through college and to compare them with a group of similar ability.

A proficiency test calls for a different kind of follow-up study. Students identified as not proficient on a writing test had better not be publishing articles and books or editing newspapers; proficient writers, according to the test, should also be proficient writers according to other measures, such as their grades in writing-related courses and their success in professions calling for writing skill. A recent court case in Florida has also required the public schools to show that they are in fact teaching the skills on their proficiency tests. Similar cases in relation to various professions have called attention to the appropriateness of tests for the job skills actually involved in the profession for which the test is given.

Committee members and administrators evaluating tests and testing programs ought not to be the people who devised the tests or who have demonstrable commitments to them. At the same time, evaluators who have little knowledge of the purpose or setting of the program bring their own assumptions and biases to bear upon programs they do not understand, despite the claims of objectivity made by "goal-free" evaluators. Developers of testing programs must seek out evaluators who are in fact neutral and uninvolved as well as informed. Since the lack of evaluation (or an insufficiently rigorous or negative evaluation) is likely to signal the end of the program, test developers should not take the selection of evaluators and the evaluation design lightly.

Political Pitfalls

Finally, it is important to remember that the teaching and testing of English are, in a large sense, political acts. People who devise tests for the public schools are not likely to forget this fact, faced as they are with vocal parents, elected school boards, and public financing. College faculties, however, are more likely to imagine that the tests they choose or create deal only with academic matters. That may be so for an individual instructor, who often claims that academic freedom (which protects the scholar's right to speak freely without professional punishment) should extend to a right to grade students without interference from others. But testing programs are inevitably political, and college-level tests are sometimes attended by high political stakes.

Political matters exist at all phases of the testing program, from the planning of goals statements (which require general assent) to test development and scoring (which require funding and general participation) to evaluation (which is often prepared for the use of public funding agencies). Power over testing programs often resides with administrators or others controlling funds, and these people may well have goals that differ from those of the developers of the tests. Sometimes, unfortunately, the political needs of these administrators or even their personal career goals lead them to assume control over testing programs and to change them radically. It is easy (as I can attest from some sad experience) for administrators of successful testing programs to neglect these perennial issues and to find that power over dollars overwhelms academic concerns, academic due process, and even academic courtesy.

Finally, testing is power, and power is a root political issue. In our classrooms, we need to use that power with decency and humanity, and proper testing practice helps us to use power wisely. In large programs, that power remains at our backs and over our shoulders, always to be reckoned with. Administrators who ignore the politics of testing may well find themselves replaced by better politicians, and even those alert to the power pressures and power drives of administrative and political figures or of the public may wind up defeated by forces with little concern for academic matters. No one should imagine a test to be above politics or a testing program to be outside the political arena.

Thus, in the long run, the pitfalls that await writing assessment programs do not differ significantly from those that await any major educational program. At every stage, from initial planning through reporting and evaluation, opportunities for confusion of purpose, improper action, and unprofessional influence offer themselves to the unwary. Fewer such dangers are open to classroom teachers, although it would be quite wrong to imagine that this difference in scope is a difference in kind. Classroom abuses of testing are no less to be condemned than public ones and, since they are usually less readily rectified, may even be more heinous. As the extent of a program grows, so does the chance of encountering (or, more usually, failing to avoid) one of the many problems I have addressed. The surprise is not that pitfalls occur in the testing of writing; the wonder is that, given the general lack of understanding of these issues and the general lack of communicating among people involved in evaluation, so much testing goes on so competently and intelligently at large and small institutions throughout the country.

NOTE

1. I am indebted to Professor James Popham of UCLA, whose conversation about norm and criterion referencing is reflected in this discussion.

REFERENCES

Fish, Stanley E. *Is There a Text in This class? The Authority of Interpretive Communities.* Cambridge, Mass.: Harvard UP, 1980.
White, Edward M., and Leon L. Thomas. "Racial Minorities and Writing Skills Assessment in the California State University and Colleges." *College English* 43 (1981): 276–83.

6

Writing Samples and Virtues

DANIEL FADER

"I've got her exam book on my desk," I tell him. "Would you like to hear a couple of sentences from it?"

I take his silence on the telephone as agreement. I read a two-sentence paragraph to him, trying with my voice to be fair to the text of the student writer, his daughter, and to the perceptions of the two faculty readers, my colleagues, who have agreed that she must take our tutorial (basic skills) course. When I finish reading, I hear only more of his silence. I am about to ask if he's still there when I hear the explosion of his breath, followed by the almost quiet words, "That's really awful."

That's a fact. His daughter has written so badly in her entrance exam that her chances of success in the college without special help are small. She is one of about 400 new students (8 percent of our first-year and transfer students) who have been told that they must complete at least one intensive tutorial writing course before they can enroll in Introductory Composition. She has mostly sobbed her way through two interviews with faculty members of the English Composition Board (ECB), and now her father has mostly shouted his way to this point in our telephone conversation. After I read part of his daughter's exam paper to him, he does not shout anymore.

The first and best virtue of a writing sample as a means of assessment is that *you have it, it's substantial, it's there*; and if it's an hour-long piece of writing on a topic broadly within the writer's knowledge and interest, it is almost certain to represent at least the writer's minimum competence at that time. The one category of exceptions we have found in six years of administering our writing assessment to more than 30,000 undergraduate students at the University of Michigan is composed of students for whom English is a relatively recent or uncertain acquisition. Sometimes the reverberations of the test and its environment can so shake their confidence that it shatters their competence. However, we are satisfied that the test almost always gives an accurate account of a native speaker's minimum writing skills.

That, in our opinion, is the greatest virtue of an extensive writing sample developed and administered by a school's faculty for its own incoming students.

Not only does it test actual student writing rather than some correlative thereof, but also it is done where much more writing will be done and is assessed by teachers who will be teaching those students—as they have taught their predecessors—in some part of the school's curriculum. Out of that constellation of virtues all else arises.

What arises first is the propaganda value of giving a home-bred, home-grown assessment whose nature is writing itself. From the legislature that sometimes sends us money to the rural school district that sometimes sends us a single student, we have had the kind of response that virtue always deserves but seldom receives: praise, support, and emulation that have gone some way toward easing the pain of more than 5000 essays a year, each of which must be read by at least two readers at the rate of about 115 a day on 45 days—including all Sundays—between mid-June and mid-August. On those eight Sundays, especially, we try to think a lot about praise and support.

More tangible than either is the improvement we think we have seen in the writing of our entering students during the past two years. About three-quarters of our students come from Michigan; during the first four years of our new composition program, which is built on the writing sample, we gave half-day or full-day faculty seminars on the campuses of more than 200 high schools and community colleges throughout the state. The subject was always the teaching of writing, which we intended, and the writing sample, which at first we did not. We did not have to be quick learners, however, to discover that the sample—our bridge to every school that sends us even a single one of its graduates—was of immediate and intense interest to English teachers, administrators, and parents of students who might come to the University of Michigan.

What happened, of course (we say "of course" now, but we did not then understand how inevitable it was), was that "the feeder schools in our catchment area," as our admissions office puts it, began to direct an increasing amount of their teaching to the test. Unlike the process of directing one's teaching to an SAT or ACT, the only way to teach to a writing test is to teach—assign, evaluate, discuss, revise—more writing. If you can't be certain who will take the test and who won't, the best way to teach to it is to increase the amount of writing and rewriting done throughout the school. This is what has happened in many of Michigan's high schools and two-year colleges since 1979.

Another virtue of this pervasive teaching to a test has been the continuous flow of evaluation and criticism from our colleagues in the state that has shaped both our program and our writing sample. In addition to more than 200 seminars on other campuses, we have held eight workshops—from one day to two weeks in duration—on our own campus for more than 1200 writing teachers from throughout Michigan. One of the effects of this massive exchange of ideas, practices, and opinions and of actions based on the exchange is that many of our colleagues from other schools have a proprietary interest in our program and especially in our writing sample. Because it affects what and how we all teach, we all want it to be as good as it can be. This strong common interest goes some way toward forming a network of writing teachers and an articulated writing program across the state.

If our writing sample has had a salutary effect on the teaching of writing in our catchment area, it has had an even more powerful effect on that teaching in our own school. Some of this effect could be foreseen, and was, but we were surprised by at least one of its dimensions: the amount of writing required in courses that have no formal connection to the writing program has increased markedly, and treatment of that writing by experienced teachers has changed significantly. Before the advent of the writing sample and the program, a great many faculty members believed that writing should be taught but that it should be taught by someone else. Now such teachers form a small, quiet minority in our faculty.

A year after our faculty had voted for the writing sample, a colleague and I offered to faculty and graduate students a workshop from 4 to 6 P.M. on five Tuesdays in October, advertised as "How to Write and How to Teach Writing Better Than You Do Now." We thought a dozen of our friends and students might come. On the first Tuesday, 106 people came, about 80 of them faculty members; we never had less than 75, with 60 of them our faculty colleagues. During the five workshops we spoke individually to nearly all attendees, our primary purpose being to ask what had brought them and what they hoped to take away with them. The predominant answer to the second question, "some sort of apparatus for editing," has greatly influenced a book on the rhetoric of revision that I have been working on. The most frequent answer to the first question, "the writing assessment that our students are taking," has led us to a deeper appreciation of how rich a symbol of concern and commitment a writing sample can be.

The sample as symbol as well as test has led us to discover another of its virtues: hundreds of students have found some way to tell us that they were impressed with the importance of writing well at Michigan because we, the college faculty, take it so seriously. When asked for evidence of our seriousness, they cite repeatedly the summer reading ("you guys actually do this all summer") and the immediate—within the day—evaluation as well as equally rapid placement in the program. This sort of comment has often been made by students who have come to discuss their writing samples with us because they are unhappy with their tutorial placement or their failure to be among those exempted from Introductory Composition. Very few, we note with interest, are unhappy with the test; even fewer dislike the idea of a writing sample as the basis for a writing program.

Perhaps the happiest discovery we have made is a kind of distributive oddity: the writing sample is most valued by some of our least competent undergraduate writers and by some of our best graduate students. An attractive, if unrepresentative, member of the first group is the entering athlete worried about his readiness for collegiate work. Far exceeding his own expectations, he is assigned to

Introductory Composition rather than a tutorial course after writing the assessment sample. Not only has he exceeded his expectations, but he has actually disappointed them, as we discover when he asks to be assigned to a tutorial section *in spite of* the quality of his writing. His argument is that he wrote better this time than he knows how, that he needs a lot more help and practice before he tries "Introcomp," and that he has heard about how much the ECB tutorials have helped other athletes. Could he please have a place in one of them? We find his appeal hard to deny.

The graduate students who value the writing sample so highly are those who teach the Introcomp course. For these instructors, the single greatest problem in the course was always the combination of their inexperience with the diversity of preparation and range of problems brought to it by their students. Now, however, the writing of every student in their classes has passed through analysis and classification made possible by the writing sample, and the course has been designed to meet the relatively narrow range of writing problems between tutorial work and unusual competence. Because graduate instructors find themselves more able to cope, undergraduate students now appear to write significantly better after taking Introcomp, and they like the course much more than they did.

Perhaps the greatest institutional value of the writing sample is the intense inquiry into the nature and definition of both good writing and bad that it engenders. Careful administration of a writing sample virtually guarantees both the discovery and the dissemination of institutional value for literacy that may otherwise remain hidden or, worse, be wrongly understood. This guarantee is nearly absolute because no writing sample can have an extended life within an institution unless it is both designed to incorporate and perceived to support those values.

After 17 faculty members from many disciplines at Michigan had spent two years examining all possibilities for a writing program that they could discover or conceive, they agreed on only three indispensable elements: a survey of the faculty's values for writing and subsequent interviews with representative respondents; a proprietary writing test, administered after students are admitted and before they attend their first class; and at least two required writing courses for adequately prepared students, one in either of the first two undergraduate years and one in the junior or senior year—preferably in the student's area of concentration.

We began with the broad survey, to be followed by selective interviews, and had our first astonishment: in all three divisions of the college—natural sciences, social sciences, and humanities—a very large number of faculty respondents valued competent organization and argument far more than command of diction and convention in their students' papers. This seemed so contrary to what we'd heard and what we thought we knew of our colleagues (especially the natural scientists, who had frequently characterized themselves, in collegiate discussions of the need for a writing program, as formal sticklers) that we pursued the question through a number of personal interviews. Pursue it however we wished, the answers remained substantially the same: we are primarily concerned with our students' ability to organize and argue their materials, our colleagues told us, and these are the two qualities you should emphasize in your reading of the sample, in your tutorial teaching and workshop instruction, and in your responsibility for introductory composition.

Such advice was enormously valuable to us in constructing and evaluating the writing sample. Whereas our colleagues made clear their dislike of what they called "mechanical" errors, referring generally to convention and diction in that order, they had no hesitation in telling us that the most appropriate tutorial students *might* be mechanically aberrant writers but that the *certain* tutorial candidates were writers who organized and argued their materials badly.

This attitude has had a profound effect not only on the nature and legitimacy of the sample but also on the shape of the entire program. What it has allowed us to do in designing the program is to use the faculty's own observations to convince its members of our argument for the teaching of writing in all disciplines by senior members of each discipline. We have been able to say—with the force of familiarity, especially to those who used similar language to us—that we can and do read the sample primarily for what it reveals about the writer's rhetorical command, and we do concentrate on the teaching of organization and argument in our tutorial classes. What we all know, however, is that intensive remediation of writing deficiencies is more successful with failures of form than of thought. We will work very hard at getting them to think better, we say, but we can only guarantee that they will not get through sample, tutorial, or Introcomp without attaining a satisfactory level of formal competence. You, however, experts in the organization and argument of materials that constitute your areas of study, must ultimately be the ones who teach that disciplinary rhetoric.

This approach to the meaning of the writing sample and the division of teaching responsibilities that derives from that meaning has freed the sample from its most deleterious possible effects on students who write it, teachers who read or teach to it, and curricula that harbor it: *no one*—not a single student or teacher—views it as trivial. This is not meant as a comment on its classifying effect on its various constituencies, although that effect is important to us all. Instead, this is intended to reflect everyone's sense that the writing assessment is to be taken seriously because its first purpose is to determine quality of thought rather than precision of form. As our students, our readers, and our network of cooperating teachers have told us, it matters because it tries to test something that matters so much.

If writing samples are possessed of so many virtues, why are they so infrequently used in our colleges and universities? More particularly, if they serve as such strong propaganda for writing in a catchment area as well as in a curriculum, why are they not in use at least in those schools that take the majority of their students from a relatively small geographic area? The answer seems to be composed of real ignorance and apparent cost, in about equal proportions.

The real ignorance characterizes teachers and administrators who still believe that testing *components* of writing is the same as or significantly like the testing of writing itself. The failure of so-called objective tests to test their implied correlatives, especially where those correlatives are subjective and discursive, is manifest in the superior test results of inferior writers; that failure is also well known to teachers of both the most and the least accomplished students. An instructive difference lies in the comparative cost of failure for these two groups of students.

The most accomplished of our students, numbering as one of their many attainments the taking of tests, approach college entrance with long experience of test taking and very little experience of writing itself. Part of their experience of test taking has been the testing of writing through its imputed correlates in the narrow range of diction and convention that lends itself to objective testing. Apt learners of lessons both explicit and implicit, they know when they come to enter college at least that writing that is correct in its form (writing that corresponds in some of its parts to the good examples and right answers of their objective tests) is likely to be assessed as satisfactory and even praiseworthy in its performance, that appropriate diction and convention are not only necessary but usually sufficient constituents of successful writing, that well-shaped emptiness is preferable to ill-shaped fullness, and that inspiration is more appropriate to breathing than to writing.

Although confirming this knowledge for them is as unnecessary as defining success, confirm it we do when we offer them yet another *objective* opportunity to demonstrate their mastery of one of the most *subjective* of human skills. Where we ask for answers to questions about writing instead of asking for writing itself, and our questions are asked in the context of college curricula, one of the clear implications for good students is that writing is regarded by us primarily as a technology of expression rather than as an art of the intellect. So regarded by us and accepted by them, writing too easily and too often becomes merely a recording device instead of a means of discovery.

The cost of this restricted definition of writing can be extreme for good students. It leads to the reasonable yet destructive conclusion that mastery of the parts of this technology—as no technology by its nature can be greater than the sum of its parts—is precisely the same as mastery of the whole. That this belief leads repeatedly to triviality (no matter how well formed) can hardly be perceived by convinced technologists as reason to discard the belief; instead, they devitalize the technology, avoiding its use whenever possible in matters that require significant discovery.

If the effect of treating writing as a technology is to teach good students that it is inappropriate to acts of discovery, the effect of such treatment on poor students is different and more devastating. Whereas good students lose one significant aspect of their means for knowing, poor students lose that *and* a part of their means for communicating what they know. Where writing is represented to unskilled students as an exact technology to be mastered rather than an inexact art to be practiced, those students learn to avoid the pain of failed mastery by avoiding the technology. In so doing, they make of writing not only a technique unavailing for them but a resource unavailable to them.

These parallel losses to both groups of students are the price of ignoring the effect on them of the explicit lessons taught by using objective tests of diction and convention to measure their writing skills. Where the cost of these losses is either not perceived or not understood, writing samples are often unused because the apparent expense of their administration is so great when compared to other kinds of tests. Careful consideration of that expense is likely to make it not only acceptable but even attractive for its contribution to learning and teaching.

All other costs of a writing sample are or can be small when compared to the human and financial expenditure necessary to assess that sample. Development, administration (excluding assessment), and even placement can be controlled for expense in ways that evaluation either cannot or should not be. Where expense of administration including assessment is given as the chief or sole reason for not using the sample to evaluate student writing, it is often the case that benefits purchased by that expenditure are not well understood. Where assessment is the responsibility of those who will teach students whose writing they evaluate and whom they will place at an appropriate level in a writing program, those benefits can be extensive.

Foremost among benefits is the salutary effect of a relationship between performance and placement that is clear to instructor and student alike. Here the several implications of "clear" are (1) that the teacher, acting as assessor, has based an evaluation on criteria enunciated by faculty members who will determine the student's success; (2) that teaching is aimed at helping the student to produce writing that satisfies those criteria *as the student's writing sample demonstrably both did and did not*; (3) that the sample can be used to illustrate the student's strengths and weaknesses in writing rather than in taking tests (about writing); and (4) that both teaching and learning in the program occupy definable *individual* spaces between attainments of the sample and requirements of the criteria.

These four kinds of clarity are especially valuable for investing with significance both the aims and the accomplishments of work done between students and teachers in a program based on institutional criteria and writing samples rather than on agency criteria and objective tests. Because this significance can infuse an entire curriculum so that writing becomes an occasion for discovery as well as a means of communication for many students, the cost of obtaining that significance is justifiable.

If justifiable, it is nonetheless large by any standard except value. A few writing samples can be evaluated in any brief period and their authors appropriately placed in any academic program by a single experienced and well-trained reader whose reliability deteriorates rapidly over number and time. Both research and experience support the conclusion that two primary readers for each paper are several times better than a single reader in terms of consistent and valid results. This conclusion is no less true of the difference in reader reliability between a smaller and larger number of essays and a limited or lengthy extent of reading days.

By using *consistent* and *valid* to refer to the standards for measuring success, I mean to invoke the two most difficult criteria of assessment, which, unmet, rapidly destroy the value of a program based on writing samples. In our experience at Michigan, validity has proved more important and consistency more difficult to obtain than we had at first anticipated.

Validity in this context refers to the relationship between placement and instruction in our writing program. The governing question for us here is one of fit: Do the needs of any student whom we may place at one of the various levels of underclass writing instruction match the content of the course and the competences of the instructor? The answer to this question is vital because we have made explicit promises to three different groups of participants in the program.

The first and most important of our promises is to our entering students, who give us an hour's sample of their writing: we tell them that they will not be sent unprepared as writers into the college's curriculum. On the basis of their performance in the initial essay, we will, where necessary, improve their present skills or teach them new ones required for success in our institution. This undertaking to the students is the basis for the promise we make to the faculty: You will have no conventionally unprepared writers in your junior and senior classes. All students who come to you in their last two undergraduate years, including all transfer students, will have been instructed in our underclass program or tested out of it. You may assume at least sufficient competence in the technique of their writing.

Our third promise, where the question of fit is most critical, is to the two very different groups of instructors who do the basic skills introductory composition work in our program. One group, which teaches students in need of remedial help, consists of experienced teachers with records of proven success in helping such students. Each has been competitively selected for the position primarily on the basis of superior qualifications as a teacher of students whose writing is inadequate to their own needs. By contrast, the second group is composed of instructors in introductory composition who have been chosen competitively as graduate students, primarily in English, with very little teaching experience. Both groups receive the same promise: the reliability (consistency and validity) of our testing procedure will provide you with students whose writing problems fit your capacities as teachers and the content of your courses. Fulfilling this promise is significant to the success of both groups, but it is vital to the work of the second. *Given a relatively narrow range of problems in their students' writing,* then prepared to meet those specific problems and supervised by experienced teachers, graduate students become instructors adequate to most of their students' needs as writers.

If matching students to teachers is the key to validity, matching readers to essays is the key to consistency. Whereas "matching" in the first clause has to do with a process of carefully defined selection, in the second it has to do with preparation that is virtually limitless in its demands, for the matching process between reader and essay is unending, requiring training before, during, and after the actual reading so that rational standards, well understood by every reader in a similar way, are applied consistently by all readers to each essay. No one could deny that the employment and training of people capable of such reading, and the teaching that develops from it, is a costly process no matter how its cost is measured. Only value received makes such a cost worthwhile.

If writing samples are virtuous and their cost is handsomely repaid by their effect on both students and teachers of writing (and other subjects as well), what significant choices must be made by a school convinced of their desirability and contemplating their use? This question may be more profitable when preceded by another: What response is the requirement of a writing sample meant to elicit? Several answers suggest themselves.

For purposes of assessment alone, the sample must be sufficient only in length. Except for extremes of competence and inadequacy, a brief sample can be an ambiguous and sometimes misleading index to the skills of its author. (I shall explain this later.) However, since assessment is coupled with placement by the assessors in institutional systems that appear to work best, samples in such systems must not only be extensive enough to represent their authors' command of convention, organization, and argument but must also be able to reflect the ability of those authors to respond to directions in an assignment and to cues in a stimulus. These requirements go a considerable way toward determining the choices that test designers must make.

One of the earliest choices must be between fullness and brevity in the instrument itself. Typical of the short form are the College Board's invitations to 20 minutes of writing for high school juniors and seniors, such as the following, which is quoted here (line numbers added) from the test given in December 1978:

ENGLISH COMPOSITION TEST

PART A

Time—20 minutes

1 *Directions*: You will have 20 minutes to plan and write the
2 essay assigned below. You are expected to express your
3 thoughts carefully, naturally, and effectively. Be specific.
4 Remember that how well you write is much more important than
5 how much you write. DO NOT WRITE ON A TOPIC OTHER THAN THE

6 ONE ASSIGNED BELOW. AN ESSAY ON A TOPIC OF YOUR OWN CHOICE
7 WILL RECEIVE NO CREDIT.

8 You must fit your essay on the answer sheet provided. You will
9 receive no other paper on which to write. You will find that
10 you have enough space if you write on every line, avoid wide
11 margins, and keep your handwriting to a reasonable size.

12 First, consider carefully the following quotation. Then, read
13 and follow the directions that are given in the *assignment* that
14 follows the quotation.

15 "We have met the enemy and he is us."

16 *Assignment*: What does this quotation imply about human
17 beings? Do you agree or disagree with its implications?
18 Support your position with examples from your reading,
19 observation, or experience.

20 DO NOT WRITE IN YOUR TEST BOOK. You will receive credit
21 only for what you write on your answer sheet.

22 BEGIN WRITING YOUR ESSAY ON THE ANSWER SHEET.

A year earlier, the College Board had reintroduced the English Composition Test with Essay with the following quotation and assignment surrounded by the same directions as those above (but for use of "statement" where "quotation" appears in lines 12 and 14):

15 "We must live in the present. If we dwell on the past, we will lose
16 the present."
17 *Assignment*: To what extent and in what ways do you agree or
18 disagree with this statement? Explain and illustrate your answer
19 from history, literature, observation, or experience.

By contrast, the English Composition Board at Michigan attempts to provoke an hour of writing from entering students with longer instruments such as this (line numbers added):

1 Write an essay that represents your position on the death pen-
2 alty. Your audience is a group of young people who will soon
3 have the opportunity to vote for or against abolition of
4 the death penalty.

5 Begin your essay with the following sentence (which you should
6 copy into your bluebook):

7 Interpretation of current laws often allows con-
8 victed murderers back on the streets within a short

  9 period of time.

10 Select *one* of the following as your next sentence and copy it
11 into your bluebook.

    12 A. Although we must denounce crime and sometimes demand
    13   more severe penalties, we must also temper justice
    14   with mercy.

    15 B. Capital punishment, dismissed by many as an inhu-
    16   mane deterrent, keeps convicted murderers from
    17   murdering again.

    18 C. Punishment is not an effective way to treat criminals;
    19   they need, instead, a rehabilitation program that
    20   turns them away from crime.

21 Now complete an essay which develops your position. Do your
22 best to make your argument convincing to your audience.

Although both instruments contain 22 lines, apparently negating the claim that the ECT and ECB examples are "short" and "longer" stimuli, respectively, in fact the latter has a much fuller explication of the assignment than the former. Whereas only five of the lines (15–19) in the ECT are devoted to content, the other 17 being given to directions, the proportion is exactly reversed in the ECB test, where 17 lines contain content and only five (5–6, 10–11, and 21) offer directions. This reversal is possible because the ECB test is given in a context provided by the following instructions, which are read aloud to students just before they write their prose samples:

> *The test you are about to take will require you to write an essay on an assigned topic. The topics have been chosen because of their general significance, because they are controversial, and because they will give you the opportunity to construct an argument either for or against a position. It is important to find out now just how effectively you can do this kind of writing because you will be asked to write persuasively in limited periods of time throughout your career at Michigan.*
>
> *Your essay will be read and judged independently by two experienced teachers of writing. Their primary interest will be in the organization and support you give your argument. They will expect you to express your own point of view and support it with good reasons.*
>
> *This examination will be used to place you at an appropriate level in our writing program. Some of you will take a special seven-week class where writing skills needed for success at Michigan are taught in small classes by experienced teachers of writing. Others will be placed in an introductory composition class; and a very few will be exempted from either of these classes. Your placement is a commentary upon your writing skills, not an indication of your intellectual competence. It is the College's way of providing each of you with the experience you need to respond successfully to writing assignments in your classes here at Michigan.*

In comparing these two invitations, one from the College Board and the other from the English Composition Board, one must remember that the CB has a single purpose in its English Composition Test, while the ECB has three. The CB must elicit only enough writing to enable experienced readers to evaluate the sample of a scale of 1 to 4 where the criteria for evaluation derive solely from the quality of the essays relative to one another. By contrast, using similar readers and the same scale, the ECB must elicit writing that falls within the external and formal constraints of most of the writing done by undergraduates in the college—50-minute hours of persuasive writing in monitored classrooms— and that lends itself readily to evaluation on a scale derived from faculty-defined criteria as well as to placement in a teaching program with four separate levels of instruction.

Conscious of those three purposes—evaluation, placement, and propaganda—the ECB first chose forms that seemed best able to fulfill them: an hour's argumentative essay on a provocative, familiar topic written in a classroom with other students after admission to the college and before registration for any class. (All students placed at the basic skills level must take at least one tutorial writing class in their first semester. They cannot take Introductory Composition until they have written the sample again at the end of a seven-week tutorial cycle and have been judged ready by two readers, neither of whom is their tutorial teacher.)

The last two sentences are enclosed in parentheses because their substance does not strictly pertain to forms chosen by the ECB but rather to the products of their use as that use affects all three of their purposes, especially propagandizing for writing. The ECB had, and has, no doubt that evaluation and placement can be accomplished nearly as well by a one- or two-line provocation to write for 20 minutes embedded in negative imperatives as by a longer and more circumstantial provocation to write for 50 minutes, free of negative instructions. What the ECB also has no doubt about is that the forms the CB has chosen for its English Composition Test with Essay promote two seriously mistaken beliefs about writing.

The most significant misconception invited by a short sample coupled with a longer objective test (ECT with Essay: 20-minute essay and 40-minute objective test) is that error-free writing is good writing. This is a proposition containing a paradox that is apparent only: error-free writing is not necessarily good writing, but good writing is often error-free. For students at all levels of secondary and collegiate instruction in our schools, the paradox is only apparent because it has insufficient reality to create a problem. Who among them does not *know*—as the result of most teaching procedures and virtually all tests in their experience— that error-free writing is good writing? Nothing about the College Board's definition of what the English Composition Test measures would even surprise them, much less cause them the distress that it should:

> The basic assumption of the test is that students who recognize problems in the writing of others are likely not to have those problems in their own essays, an

assumption confirmed by careful research. Most of the multiple choice questions in the ECT, therefore, ask the students either to locate problems in sentences or to resolve problems that they have identified.

The empty essay, often error-free and frequently written by students rated "good" against all standard measures, is a more likely product of the belief that error-free writing is good writing than of any other belief but that writing is a technology of expression. Both beliefs receive strong support from stimuli like "We have met the enemy and he is us"—stimuli meant to provoke 20 minutes of writing in the context of a test that has 40 minutes of multiple-choice questions about writing. The rhetoric of such a test is as clear to student writers as the hollow sounds of their essays are to us.

Having chosen fullness rather than brevity, what shall compose it? Two characters of fullness suggest themselves, both relevant to obtaining the most useful samples of student writing. One of those characters depends on instructions and cues for its identity; the other derives its nature from prescribed concepts and language. A significant difference between the two is that the former is of speculative value in obtaining representative student writing, while the value of the latter is more certain.

What is speculative is that extensive cuing is of clear value in eliciting writing responsive to the cues. Having found arguments for cuing persuasive and still finding them persuasive even though the evidence remains ambiguous, the ECB builds a number of potential cues into all its stimuli. The most extensive usage of intended cuing is in the four carefully varied sentence forms of the prescribed opening statement (lines 7–9) and its three alternative second sentences (A, B, C). Each is a different rhetorical type, and each contains both convention and diction chosen to invite imitation.

For example, both the common opening sentence and alternative C use colloquial metaphors—"back on the streets" and "turns them away" instead of "to return to society" and "keep them from," respectively—to elicit varied diction from student respondents. For a similar purpose, alternatives A and B have the strong verbs "denounce," "demand," and "dismissed," and B uses the forceful repetition of "murderers from murdering again." The common opening as well as A and B rely on alliteration for emphasis, while several different uses of internal punctuation are meant to emphasize the rhetorical range of the three alternative second sentences.

Another kind of cuing is represented by the repetition of "your position" and "your audience" from lines 1 and 2 in lines 21 and 22. The first is intended to invite the writer to have or to formulate more clearly a position not consciously or clearly held before, and the latter is meant to remind the writer of the readers defined in the opening paragraph of the assignment.

If the cause-and-effect relationship between using a variety of cues and receiving richer texts from respondents is ambiguous, the second character of fullness—prescribed concepts and language—has no such ambiguity in the effects it creates. More than any single aspect of the writing sample other than the fact of its existence, it is the *extent* of the student writer's response that supports all three of an assessment's possible purposes. Evaluation, placement, and propaganda are all served by more rather than less writing, but it is the latter two that profit most from an extensive sample.

The ECB has found that providing its student writers with a prescribed first sentence and choice of one of three second sentences has the dual effect of creating a small amount of resentment about loss of freedom and the like (almost entirely abated now, after six years, by the force of widespread expectation) and a very large amount of writing from almost every student. Simply to begin physically the act of writing is an important step toward engaging the intellect in that act, as all teachers who have used writing journals in their teaching and not forbidden copying know.

Length serves placement at all three customary levels of any writing program by affording experienced readers an expanded opportunity to confirm or alter their original impressions and support their conclusions. This opportunity is of small significance, perhaps, in the case of agency evaluations that will neither be discussed by readers with distant writers nor result in placement of writers by those same readers; it is, however, of far greater importance in the case of institutional evaluation, which can be examined and discussed by local writers to whom readers are easily available. This generalization applies most specifically to the work of poorer writers placed in basic skills portions of any program.

Finally, length serves the propaganda function of a writing sample, especially as that function is manifest beyond the walls of the testing institution. Many teachers, representing numerous schools in our area, have told us that the most significant dimension of our assessment for their writing programs, after the fact of its existence and its placement between admission and course registration, is its length. That students who come here must be prepared to write *for an hour* and are penalized if they cannot do so successfully has sometimes reduced composition class size as well as number of students and classes per teacher and has increased the amount of writing required in curricula of secondary schools and community colleges that send us their graduates.

These virtues turn us once again to the title of this chapter, "Writing Samples and Virtues," which was intended not only as a brief summary of meaning but also as an early warning of bias. The source of that bias lies in our experience of writing samples rather than in an unfounded notion of their worth. Having built a writing program upon them, we are now very glad that we have done so.

7

Beginning a Testing Program: Making Lemonade

KENNETH A. BRUFFEE

Most testing programs begin in a political context. Programmatic testing is itself a political act.

I use the word *political* in these two dogmatic opening sentences as a descriptive term, not as an honorific or pejorative one. It's simply a matter of fact. A "testing program" has little in common with the midterm or final that individual teachers might require students to take in their own classes. That kind of test is course-specific. It is controlled by the course syllabus, the individual teacher's aims, and the teacher's estimate of student abilities in that particular course during that particular semester. A testing program is an institutional affair. It tests large numbers of students regardless of course or teacher. It does not (because it cannot) take into consideration the particularities of teachers' individual course syllabi, abilities of students aggregated into classes, teachers' individual aims and interests, or, for that matter, students' individual aims or interests. Furthermore, because a testing program applies to large numbers (perhaps even all) of the students in a given educational institution, it proclaims the goals and limitations of that institution—more clearly, conspicuously, and honestly than the college catalogue and the president's proclamations.

A testing program speaks clearly for the institution's goals and limitations because it turns into unequivocal action the needs, aims, and abilities of the college faculty, the community of educated people who make up that institution. It is at this level that the beginnings of a testing program are so evidently political. Decisions about how an institution will educate its students must be made at least by vote (and at best by consensus) among the members of the community. To have a testing program (and to determine what it shall be like) is one of those decisions. It may be the decision that will have the greatest direct impact on students' intellectual life and college career. Everyone has an interest in what that impact will be.

Sometimes, of course, testing programs begin in even more obviously political contexts. Fortunate is the college that can decide for itself to institute a testing program. More than one public college or university has created a testing program mandated by law, a law written not by educators but by members of a state or municipal legislature.

The fact that testing programs begin in a political context has many implications for the people charged with the responsibility of actually creating the test to be given. What people so charged may do is both constrained and, in some respects, freed by that political context. Those so charged must therefore be as aware as possible of the principles of the politics of testing. Only through awareness of those principles can they work intelligently within the constraints that a political context imposes. Perhaps more important, only through awareness of those principles can they take fullest advantage of the freedom that those political principles also provide.

The first principle of the politics of testing is that the people who decide testing must be done are almost never the people who actually choose or design the test and administer it. In most cases, the people who decide that a school must have a testing program are people in authority. The dean or the president decides, the faculty council decides, the alumni or local business community (de facto) decides, or the legislature may decide. The people who actually choose or design the test and administer it are, in most cases, faculty members appointed willy-nilly to a committee.

The second principle of the politics of testing is that in most cases neither the people who decide that testing must be done nor the people who actually choose or design the test and administer it know much about testing. Nor does either group have much of a notion of the size of the job, if the job is to be done right.

The third principle of the politics of testing is that in many cases the true purpose, and hence the implications and potential of the test, is not clear to those who decide it must be done, nor is it likely to be clear at first to those who must choose or design and administer it. The purpose of the testing program in most cases emerges as the test is chosen or designed. It emerges as those who choose or design it learn what their options really are and as they become more fully aware of the political constraints they are working under. It may also emerge as those who choose or design the test begin to become aware of the new freedom (and thus new power) with which their task invests them. If a testing program proclaims an institution's goals and limitations, the people responsible for the test find themselves in the interesting position of writing that proclamation. They may discover, set, and perhaps even make significant changes in the institution's goals. They may also contribute significantly to overcoming or aggravating the institution's limitations.

These principles may not apply everywhere and to the same degree. But they certainly applied in my experience at my institution. The body that decided that all City University of New York students should be tested for basic proficiency was the New York City Board of Higher Education (now called the Board of

Trustees of the City University of New York). This board is appointed by the mayor of New York City and the governor of New York State. Its members are local business, professional, and political leaders. They are not CUNY faculty. The board made the decision to test CUNY students in response to pressure brought to bear by the business and professional community, by university faculty and administration, and by the general public.

The people who undertook to determine the nature of the test, however, were university faculty. One committee decided that there should be not one test but three—in reading, writing, and math. The same committee decided when in each students' college career the test should be given. This committee in turn recommended the appointment of three more faculty committees, one for each of the tests that had been decided on.

This is where I came in. I was appointed to a committee called the Chancellor's Task Force on Writing. I worked with a wonderful group of people masterfully led by the committee's chair, Professor Robert Lyons of Queens College. All of us were seasoned writing teachers. All of us understood the conditions prevailing in the city and the university from long experience with both. We represented a wide variety of campus situations, from a near-idyllic liberal arts campus to the shattered campus of an inner-city college, from graduate study to community college courses staged in local department stores. And with the exception of the one "test expert" on the committee, we knew very little about testing. None of us knew a thing about testing 180,000 students a year in writing.

We found, as we began our work, that we agreed on a great deal. We agreed that we were starting from scratch, not only with regard to our own limitations but with regard to the purpose, implications, and potential of the test. What the board had in mind was clear. Responding to community pressure, the board wanted to enhance the reputation of the university, reeling after six years of open admissions. The testing program was a way to shore up our damaged academic reputation and to ensure that students who entered upper-division courses were prepared for them.

It was only when the faculty got into the act that the larger implications of the testing program began to emerge. Take, for instance, implications of the test for teaching and the curriculum. The faculty committee appointed to determine the general nature of the testing program—the one that decided that there were to be three tests, in reading, writing, and math—decided also that the battery should be given to students as they entered the university rather than halfway through their college career. This was a humane gesture, to be sure. The idea was to give students who failed the tests two years to pass them before reaching their junior year. It provided those who needed it two years of grace. But besides being humane, it was also a politically judicious decision. It is a fact that every test tests not only the person tested but, indirectly, the people who taught that person. Tests can expose the strengths and weaknesses of teachers and curricula as well as the strengths and weaknesses of students. By placing tests at college entrance that were not to take effect until midcareer, this faculty committee decided that if teachers and curricula were to be tested by this testing program, what would be tested would not be college teachers or college curricula. CUNY faculty would not yet have taught students tested as they entered college. Their hands would remain clean. The teachers who would have taught students just entering the university would be New York City high school teachers. The decision *when* to give the test therefore set the stage for an evaluation of New York City high school education and, potentially, provided the university with a tool for affecting the quality of that education.

It also made one of the jobs of the testmaking committees a good deal easier. The Chancellor's Task Force on Writing had as its direct constituency the faculties of 17 markedly different colleges. Whatever we did needed the board's and the chancellor's approval. Much more to the point, it needed the approval of our colleagues throughout the university, whom we represented. Being able to point out that the test in no direct way threatened them enormously simplified our task of persuading them of the value of our work.

As it made that part of the job easier, it made another part of the job a good deal more interesting. At least some of us had begun the task of testmaking by thinking that what we were to do was a dull and mechanical matter, a necessary evil perpetrated on the faculty by an uncomprehending and perhaps educationally obtuse administration. As we realized the larger implications of what we were doing, however—that we had an opportunity to revise or at least directly affect the revision of the whole New York City postprimary educational system with regard to writing in particular and perhaps to "language arts" in general—everything we did became charged with excitement.

I am revealing all this not by way of exposé. There were no devious motives, no hidden agendas. We were just a dozen or so intelligent people feeling our way along. We began with little knowledge and nothing but closed doors before us. As our knowledge increased, and as we opened each of the doors one by one, new horizons spread out before us. Being basically scholars and curious people, energetic, and professionally committed, we followed our natural bent. Issued a lemon, or so it seemed to at least some of us, we had found ourselves able, as our esteemed midwestern colleague Joe Trimmer put it, to make lemonade.

I offer this sketch of one institution's experience in developing a testing program from scratch to illustrate the political principles of testing with which I began this chapter. I should like to end by drawing a few inferences from that sketch that may possibly influence the thinking of people who find themselves beginning a testing program at any level, deciding to institute one, designing the program, or administering it. As for those who are responsible for deciding whether or not to undertake a testing program, those who must make the inital decision, I think it is safe to say that the issues as they appear are quite enough on which to base such a decision. It is not helpful—indeed, at this level it is impossible—to look deeply into the implications of the decision to begin or not to begin a testing program. If the consensus, inside or outside the institution, seems to be to have one, have one, If not, don't.

If the decision is made to have one, quickly, with no further instruction than "Do it," turn the whole matter over to the institution's faculty. Faculty members are trained to deal with ignorance, their own as well as others'. That is presumably what scholarship is all about: not what we know but what we don't know. A spirited, committed faculty will find its own way to fulfill the mandate, and the way it finds will more likely be one that satisfies most interested people in most respects.

I warn the faculty that undertakes fulfilling the mandate that complaints will be many, and often legitimate. No test is perfect. No test will suit every situation. If anyone says, "Use our test because it works for us at our place," say, "Thanks, but no thanks." Every place is different; tests must be tailored to their own particular clientele, both faculty and students.

Finally, no test tells "the truth." No test does anything more than approximate. Every test doesn't do some of the things that some people think are important. No test does perfectly all—perhaps any—of the things almost everyone thinks are important. A test is a bludgeon in a profession that advances, if it advances at all, only by strokes and pats.

8

Testing Black Student Writers

ROSCOE C. BROWN, JR.

The effort to devise fair and accurate means of measuring ability, monitoring achievement, and predicting performance has challenged both the ingenuity and the integrity of professionals concerned with education for nearly a half century. While the education community can boast of some progress toward that effort, many longstanding criticisms lodged against assessment are as yet unsatisfied. Although some criticism of testing is based in a suspicion of the futility of any attempt to "render measurable that which is not," most criticism has focused on the content of tests and the application of test results and has been directed toward the elimination of unfair tests and discriminatory application of such tests. The issue of testing must, of course, be viewed in the larger context of equal educational opportunity, a multifront war wherein the battles over affirmative action, desegregation, and federal support of public education have been fought. In that context, our criticism should represent steps toward compensation for past injustices and prevention of future inequities.

We must, however, avoid the pitfalls of broad-brush rejection of testing as a tool of measurement, monitoring, and prediction. Standardized tests do have some value; at some point decisions about entrance into college, graduate, or professional schools must be made, and some kind of procedure will be used. The task before us is to persist in our evaluations of the test instruments, to insist on the coupling of tests with other criteria whenever appropriate, and to accelerate the recent trends toward the creative use of testing as a facilitator and not a roadblock. Moreover, we should strive to improve the quality of education experienced by blacks and other minorities so that they will have a better chance to perform well on tests.

TEST FAIRNESS

Fairness in measurement is primarily a question of whether selection measures are free from bias with respect to their content, the accuracy of the predictions based on the measurement, and the way the measures are used for students. In addition, fairness involves general social equity. The issue of fairness raises an important question: To what extent should society members who have been previously disadvantaged through economic and social circumstances continue to be disadvantaged by the use of selection and other procedures that more or less condemn them to second-class status? The movement in higher education toward a realignment of priorities so as better to meet the needs of students and their communities will undoubtedly continue to collide with countermovements toward what we have come to term the "meritocracy." Political developments during the past few years and major cuts in the federal education budget and entitlement programs are evidence of such countermovements and promise to impede further the progress of disadvantaged minorities in higher education.

In the more favorable climate of the 1960s and early 1970s, when opportunity replaced merit as the dominant social ideal, decisions such as *Griggs v. Duke Power*, establishing the standard that employment tests must be job-related, were welcome steps toward curbing discriminatory uses of tests. In addition, in *Larry P. v. Riles*, a California federal district court barred school officials from using standardized intelligence tests to place children in classes for the mentally retarded, ruling that the tests did not measure native intelligence and were culturally biased. Later in the 1970s, an effective consumer rights campaign was launched against the testing establishment in the form of "truth-in-testing" legislation, which subjected standardized tests to public scrutiny for the first time in this nation's history.

The atmosphere of crisis concerning tests prompted the National Association for the Advancement of Colored People (NAACP) to pass a resolution at its national convention in 1974 for a moratorium on the use of standardized tests as a means of measuring the aptitude and achievement of black students wherever such tests had not been corrected for cultural bias. In 1978 the controversial case pitting the Regents of the University of California against Allan Bakke exacerbated the sense of crisis, focusing national attention on the selection process for admissions to professional schools. In a split decision, the Supreme Court at once reinforced the legitimacy of testing as a predictor of future performance and supported the use of race as one criterion meriting consideration in the selection process. The impact of the ruling, despite its reinforcement of the principle of affirmative action, was to fuel a growing public conviction that colleges and universities had gone too far in their attempts to compensate for past discrimination (Tollett).

As educators continue to examine the principle of assessment, we should ensure that conflicts over specific techniques of testing do not obscure the need to place increased emphasis on basic skills. The acquisition of basic skills is not merely desirable; it is essential. Support for reinforcement of basic skills and for the use of tests to chart progress and achievement must, of course, be qualified in light of continued abuses and the potential for abuse. We must maintain a constant vigilance and must be prepared to examine each testing program carefully in terms of the merits of the tests and the uses to which they are put. The factors requiring continued monitoring are by now familiar but are nonetheless worthy of some attention here. They include three types of test bias—bias due to content factors, bias due to norms, and bias due to the testing situation itself (Green and Griffore 240). Of the content factors that should continue to concern us—bias resulting from regional differences, urban-rural differences, and racial and ethnic differences—I wish in this discussion to focus on the last.

Although some residue of the Jensen-Shockley "campaign" regarding genetic determinism of intelligence resurfaces periodically, most serious discussion of possible racial bias in testing allows that the differences in performance are primarily attributable to socioeconomic factors. In that blacks are dispro-portionately represented in the lower rungs of the economic ladder, it follows that any bias owing to economic status would have a greater impact on blacks. Warren Willingham, Hunter Breland, Richard Ferrin, and Mary Fruen summa-rize the issue thus:

> Since blacks and other minorities tend too often to have scores below the average of other groups on admissions tests, the question of whether content of such tests is biased against minorities, naturally, arises. In a sense that the tests may reflect the biased social order, the answer is clearly yes. (138–39)

There are many definitions of cultural bias in testing. The following definition by T. A. Cleary is generally accepted by psychologists and educational researchers:

> [A] test is biased for members of a subgroup of the population if, in the prediction of a criterion for which the test was designed, consistent nonzero errors of prediction are made for members of the subgroup. In other words, the test is biased if the criterion score predicted from the common regression line is consistently too high or too low for members of the subgroup. With this definition of bias, there may be a connotation of "unfair" particularly if the use of the test produces a prediction that is too low. (115)

Otherwise stated, "unfairness in the test itself, or test bias, is present when a test does not measure the same dimension(s) of achievement across different groups" (Green).

VARIABLES AFFECTING TEST RESULTS

Variables in testing situations—the level of speed required to take the test, the experience of the test taker, and the test taker's level of anxiety—can affect disadvantaged students more adversely than others. Although the data are not entirely clear regarding the effect of the time allowed for testing, Franklin Evans and Richard Reilly report that reducing the time restrictions on standardized tests does produce higher scores (123). Other studies have found that inexperienced test takers score significantly better under unspeeded conditions; since disadvantaged youth may be particularly inexperienced test takers, the time limits, especially as applied to early achievement tests, could be unfair to them (Knapp 22). There is still some discussion as to whether another potentially biased variable, test wiseness, can be minimized by teaching test-taking skills or even coaching for specific tests (Evans and Pike).

Another issue voiced frequently is concern for test anxiety and its impact on minorities. Bloxom points to a survey by the Educational Testing Service, which found that more than 80 percent of students taking the SAT experienced a degree of test anxiety. To the extent that anxiety acts as a debilitating factor, test performance is motivated by fear of failure, which might result in lower test performance. Performance on the SAT has been found to be very susceptible to examinees' anxiety. To a substantial extent, SAT scores may indicate more about examinees' state of debilitating test anxiety than about their ability to perform in college. Since the SAT and other aptitude tests may in fact measure anxiety, content bias may be inherent in these tests. This bias is all the more a problem in that test anxiety appears to be inversely related to social class and prevalent among minority examinees. We might then expect the performance of minority students on aptitude tests to be disproportionately and unfairly affected by test anxiety (Kirkland 303).

MINIMUM COMPETENCY TESTS

Minimum competency testing programs now offered in at least 40 states have received mixed reactions among educators concerned with the testing of black students. The main features of minimum competency testing are (1) the focus on pupil performance in the basic skills of writing, reading, and computation; (2) the establishment of statewide standards of achievement in a defined geographic area; (3) the assignment to remedial programs of students who do not demonstrate adequate achievement; and (4) the requirement in some states that demonstration of proficiency at a certain level be requisite for the award of a regular high school diploma. The uproar over statewide competency testing programs has led to several court challenges. *Debra P. v. Turlington* in 1979, which challenged denial of standard high school diplomas under Florida's statewide testing program, resulted in a decision that delayed the application of a diploma sanction until the 1982–83 school year. In the *Debra P.* decision, Judge George C. Carr recognized that the immediate imposition of a diploma sanction would have an adverse effect on minority students who had been exposed to segregated and inferior education throughout the years prior to taking the competency tests. Judge Carr also challenged the validity of the test to define functional literacy in a way that was consistent with generally accepted definitions. In addition, the *Debra P.* case raised questions concerning the adequacy of remedial instruction, the extent to which remedial classes required of students failing the exam represented a form of resegregation, and the exemption of private schools from this regulation. Clearly, the *Debra P.* case is a forerunner of many other legal challenges to the misapplication of the principle of minimum competency. Hugh Scott criticizes minimum competency tests as being the most poorly conceived of all achievement tests and cautions against tendencies inherent in the tests to mislabel students, to justify homogeneous grouping, and to arouse racial prejudice by documenting underachievement of minorities.

Yet despite the consequences of testing programs that may be flawed or biased, the concept of minimum competency is nonetheless sound. The principle behind minimum competency tests is that students should be assessed periodically to determine the extent to which they demonstrate mastery of basic skills in reading, computation, and writing. Although one might wonder what kinds of basic skills students actually need in an age of televised communication and pocket computers, any serious examination of today's job market will show that reading and mathematics skills are necessary for advancement in a society that is becoming increasingly verbal and computational. Banks, department stores, and insurance companies in our big cities have recently begun to participate in the upgrading of the skills level of high school graduates to enable them to perform simple clerical and computational tasks. There is a clear need for improvement in performance of basic skills. As with many educational issues concerning minorities, the resolution is not simple. On the one hand, tests may not be valid and may be used in discriminatory fashion; on the other hand, there is a clear need to establish objective data on performance of students for use in evaluating their progress and in establishing instructional programs. Appropriate use of the data from competency tests can not only significantly improve the performance of black and other minority group students but also can be used to assist in improving instruction.

A basic principle underlying minimum competency tests is frequently that the skills being tested are those that are included in the curriculum and that can be stated as specific behavioral objectives. Competency tests designed in such a way can assist in identification of areas of instruction where students require additional attention or training, and improving instruction is the key to improving the quality of student performance. On the basis of my experience with the New Jersey Minimum Basic Skills program, I believe that competency tests following this model are useful in assessing basic skills and in determining the relationship of achievement to characteristics of school districts. Insufficient attention, however, has been directed to using the results of various competency testing programs to improve instructional programs.

TESTING BLACK STUDENTS' WRITING

The decline in literacy among American students brought the following comment from Christopher Lasch:

> *People increasingly find themselves unable to use language with ease and precision, to recall the basic facts of their country's history, to make logical deductions, to understand any but the most rudimentary written texts, or even to grasp their constitutional rights. . . . Standards of teaching decline, victims of poor teaching come to share the experts' low opinion of their capacities, and the teaching profession complains of unteachable students. (128)*

Much of the debate on the decline in test scores centers on the role of minority students. This decline is not entirely a function of the increased number of minority students. The fact that, in recent years, 50 to 60 percent of the students at the University of California are required to enroll in remedial English is testimony to the universality of the problem. Only one-fourth of the 1975 entering class at Stanford University was able to pass that university's English placement test (despite high SATs). A survey of colleges and universities nationwide conducted by Lederman, Ribaudo, and Ryzewic for the City University of New York's Office of Academic Affairs in spring 1981 found that 31 percent of the entering freshmen required assistance in basic writing (12).

In his debate with Samuel Livingston over the issue of testing for competency, Robert Ebel makes the point that "when we are attempting to impart or assess knowledge, the main burden of communication must be carried by words" (3). It is clear that writing competency is key to student success, perhaps all the more challenging in the case of black students. When designing tests for minority students, Paul Ramsey suggests that "students be allowed to choose among topics in different modes. In addition, testing should be linked to the goals of instruction: if students write expository prose in their courses, then it is fair to test them in this mode."

Researchers who study black students' writing usually find differences between black and white students. For example, Delsey Noonan-Wagner reports on a study in which six judges evaluated 20 randomly selected essays from a basic writing program at the University of Houston that showed that black students demonstrate different writing patterns from those of white students. The essays were examined for the following writing features: free associations; redundancy; quotations and misquotes; sermonizing and moralistic tone; biblical references; word choice; use of metaphor; and use of proverbs, maxims, aphorisms, and clichés. These features figured far more prominently in the essays prepared by black students; the averages were 56.5 features per black student and 13.8 per white student—a ratio of greater than four to one. The study suggests that teachers should be alert to various stylistic features of black writers that require modification in order to develop a writing style that meets the demands of college writing.

Commenting on the Florida college-level testing program designed to follow the statewide high school testing program, Steven Rubin highlights again the problem of testing writing of blacks and Hispanics:

> *Among the many uncertainties surrounding the future of CLASP (College-Level Academic Skills Project) is the issue of the program's impact on minorities. There is concern that black and Hispanic students will possibly have more difficulty than dominant culture students with the writing portion of the test.(6)*

Testmakers continue to search for ways in which tests for writers can be used without creating adverse effects on minorities. Paul Ramsey makes the following observation:

> *While we must trust essay tests, we need to be concerned about how they are scored. Most essay tests are read holistically, to get a general impression. Some critics of holistic scoring say it merely assesses "scribal fluency," and if that is so, dialect features will influence the general impression left with the reader. An interesting area for research is whether primary trait analysis of holistically scored tests would change the scores of minority students.*

Kenneth B. Clark addressed the issue in the following manner:

> *Valid and effective writing tests must test one's ability to communicate ideas. Tests of writing are inherently tests of social interaction. One writes in an attempt to communicate one's perceptions and understanding of reality to others and to share feelings and values. . . . By helping students understand how language facilitates the ability to cope and grapple with ideas and feelings, the students will gain a sense of confidence, achievement and security.*

One of the intended benefits of tests is the development of sufficient data for more effective analysis of learning styles, blocks, and facilitators so that test results can be used to enhance learning rather than merely to classify or label. When we test the writing of minority students, it is crucial that the tests assess accurately the characteristics of writing that affect their performance. Benjamin Bloom advocates a shift from emphasis on testing assumed intelligence and aptitude as indices of performance to assessment of what he calls cognitive entry characteristics:

> *Quite in contrast to intelligence and aptitude indices are cognitive entry characteristics. These are the special knowledge, abilities, or skills that are the essential prerequisites for the learning of a particular school subject or a particular learning task.*
>
> *Cognitive entry characteristics are highly alterable because they represent particular content and skills which may be learned if they are absent. Much of the variation in school learning is directly determined by the variation in students' cognitive entry characteristics. (341)*

CUNY ASSESSMENT TESTS AS TEACHING TOOLS

The City University of New York pioneered the use of minimum competency tests in 1978. Students take the Freshman Skills Assessment Tests in reading, writing, and math shortly after being admitted but before matriculation, and the results are used for placement decisions. All students are required to pass all skills courses before entering their junior year. The City University of New York's Freshman Skills Assessment Program used the principle of cognitive entry characteristics as part of the rationale in establishing its test procedures:

> Our mandate was to devise a test that would demonstrate the "minimal readiness" of students entering the City University to work effectively and survive in an average entry-level freshman composition course anywhere in the University. (Bruffee 4)

Responding to the position shared by the distinguished panel of educators responsible for the recent report on American higher education, the CUNY Writing Task Force has taken steps in the right direction. In altering existing systems of assessment, the Study Group on the Conditions of Excellence in American Higher Education urged administrators and faculty to "insure that the instruments and methods used are appropriate for the knowledge, capacities, and skills addressed and the stated objectives of undergraduate education at their institutions" (45). Furthermore, the panel recommended that faculty "participate in the development, adoption, administration, and scoring of the instruments and procedures used in student assessment as a teaching tool" (45). The CUNY task force attempted to address both of these recommendations in the design and administration of the Writing Assessment Test. A clear standard was defined as requiring that, upon entering the university, "students should already understand the basic form of academic, professional, and business discourse" and "be able to formulate and state a position in reasonably correct standard written English" (Bruffee 4).

The test provides a choice of topics so as to accommodate best the diversity of backgrounds and experiences of CUNY students and suggests where writing coursework should begin, the direction it should take, and where it should end. Robert Lyons points out that as for faculty participation, 9 of the 10 faculty members responsible for development of the test were currently teaching freshman-level writing courses (the tenth being a test and measurement expert). Faculty readers were selected at each campus and were trained in the methods and standards recommended by the task force. Each reader was given a booklet of sample essays illustrating each point on the evaluation and explaining the scores (25).

The CUNY Writing Assessment Testing program does not rely on standardized tests but rather uses assessment as a teaching tool, acknowledges the value of faculty involvement, and assumes responsibility for clarification of expectations of students performance. These are all aspects of a program moving in the right direction. With respect to minority students in the university with poor writing skills, there is still work to be done. Some faculty members have, for example, raised the issue of speededness as a testing bias, arguing that the 50-minute time restriction places bidialectical and bilingual students at a disadvantage (Ruiz and Diaz). Others have pointed out certain sociological biases in topic options:

> *Undebatable is the fact that students are asked to write within a framework defined by the largely middle-class identity of teachers. So one topic states that "success is measured to a very large extent in terms of money," and asks students if they agree or not with the validity of that statement. We submit that only people who are not financially desperate can respond to that question in good faith, and their response is a foregone conclusion. (Brick 32)*

Still others caution that though we trust essay tests, we need to be concerned about how they are scored. Recall Paul Ramsey's call for research into the question of whether primary trait analysis of holistically scored essay tests would change the scores of minority students, suggesting that holistic scoring may merely assess "scribal fluency" and, if that is so, that dialect features would influence the general impression left with the reader. Ramsey added the further caution that although tests can be used to assess the best methods of instruction, they can also be used to exclude or segregate minority students.

CONCLUSION

In determining the benefits of testing, particularly in the area of prediction, selection, and diagnosis, tests and testing procedures must be carefully examined lest the negative effects outweigh the positive ones. Edward Fiske stated the issue very succinctly: "Tests don't judge people; people judge people" (158). Because people do judge people, an analysis of the social benefits of testing must include a concern for the value system implicit in the results of the tests. The many Americans who feel that they have been unjustly excluded from the benefits or opportunities in our society because of tests are carefully observing administrators, testmakers, admissions officers, and academicians to see if they can meet the challenge. Those seeking to test the writing of black students must be ever mindful of this responsibility and able to extend their efforts beyond services to the majority to do justice to the minority.

Challenges to testing per se will not cause major breakthroughs in education. Improvement of instruction will. Our focus should be on making the colleges more effective for minority students by emphasizing quality education and quality teaching. We should use every tool at our disposal, including tests, and use our professional judgment and positions to ensure that all students receive a quality education, for it is through quality education that we will move toward closing the educational and socioeconomic gap between the majority and minority group populations.

REFERENCES

Bloom, Benjamin S. "The New Direction in Educational Research: Alterable Variables." *Journal of Negro Education* 49.3 (1980): 337–49.

Bloxom, Bruce. "Research Bulletin on Test Anxiety and Performance." *Educational Testing Research Bulletin* 68–30 (1968).

Brick, Allan. "The CUNY Writing Assessment Test and the Teaching of Writing." *Writing Program Administration* 4.1 (1980): 28–34.

Bruffee, Kenneth. "Some Curricular Implications of the CUNY Writing Assessment Test." *Notes from the National Testing Network in Writing* Jan. 1983: 4–5.

Clark, Kenneth B. "Testing Writing: For What?" *Notes from the National Testing Network in Writing* Dec. 1983: 2.

Cleary, T. A. "Test Bias: Prediction of Grades of Negro and White Students in Integrated Colleges." *Journal of Educational Measurement* 5 (Summer 1968): 115–24.

Debra P. v. Turlington. 474 F.Supp. 244 (U.S.D.C.) 1979.

Ebel, Robert L., and Samuel A. Livingston. "Issues in Testing for Competency." *NCME* 12.2 (1981): 1–6.

Evans, Franklin R., and L. W. Pike. "The Effects of Instruction for Three Item Formats." *Journal of Educational Measurement* 10 (1973): 257–72.

Evans, Franklin R., and Richard R. Reilly. "A Study of Speededness as a Source of Test Bias." *Journal of Educational Measurement* 9 (1972): 123–31.

Fiske, Edward B. "Finding Fault with the Testers." *New York Times Magazine* 18 Nov. 1979: 152–62.

Green, Donald R. "What Does It Mean to Say a Test Is Biased?" Meeting, American Educational Research Association. Washington, D.C., Mar. 1975.

Green, Robert, and Robert Griffore. "The Impact of Standardized Testing on Minority Students." *Journal of Negro Education* 49.3 (1980): 238–52.

Griggs v. Duke Power Co. 292 F.Supp. 243 (D.C.N.C. 1968), *reversed in part*, 420 F. 2d. 1227 (4th Cir. 1970), *reversed*, 401 U.S. 424 (1971).

Kirkland, Marjorie C. "The Effects of Tests on Students and Schools." *Review of Educational Research* 41 (1971): 303–50.

Knapp, R. R. "The Effects of Time Limits on the Intelligence Test Performance of Mexican and American Subjects." *Journal of Educational Psychology* 33 (1963): 22–30.

Larry P. v. Riles. 343 F.Supp. 1306 (D.C.N.D. Calif. 1972), *affirmed*, 502 F. 2d. 963 (9th Cir. 1974).

Lasch, Christopher. *The Culture of Narcissism: American Life in an Age of Diminishing Expectations.* New York: Norton, 1977.

Lederman, Marie Jean, Michael Ribaudo, and Susan Ryzewic. "A National Survey on the Assessment and Improvement of the Academic Skills of Entering Freshmen: Some Implications for Writing Program Administrators." *Writing Program Administration* 7.3 (1984): 11–16.

Lyons, Robert. "The City University of New York Writing Assessment Test: A Faculty-generated Model." *Writing Program Administration* 4.1 (1980): 23–27.

Noonan-Wagner, Delsey. "Black Writers in the Classroom: A Question of Language Experience, Not Grammar." *ERIC Clearinghouse on Tests, Measurement, and Education* (1980).

Ramsey, Paul A. "Writing Assessment and Minorities." *Notes from the National Testing Network in Writing* Dec. 1983: 14.

Regents of the University of California v. Allan Bakke. 438 U.S. 265 (1978).

Rubin, Steven J. "The Florida College-Level Academic Skills Project: Testing Communication Skills Statewide." *Notes from the National Testing Network in Writing* Oct. 1982: 6, 18.

Ruiz, Aida and Diana Diaz. "Writing Assessment and ESL Students." *Notes from the National Testing Network in Writing* Dec. 1983: 5.

Scott, Hugh J. "Minimum Competency Testing: The Newest Obstruction to the Education of Black and Other Disadvantaged Americans." *ERIC Clearinghouse on Tests, Measurement, and Evaluation* (1979).

Study Group on the Conditions of Excellence in American Higher Education. "Involvement in Learning: Realizing the Potential of American Higher Education." *Chronicle of Higher Education* 24 Oct. 1984: 35–49.

Tollett, K. S. "What Led to *Bakke*." *Center Magazine* Jan.–Feb. 1978: 2–10.

Willingham, Warren W., and Hunter M. Breland, in association with Richard I. Ferrin and Mary Fruen. "Use and Limitations of Selective Measures." *Selective Admissions in Higher Education*. Report issued by Carnegie Council on Policy Studies in Higher Education. San Francisco: Jossey-Bass, 1977.

9

"Objective" Measures of Writing Ability

GERTRUDE CONLAN

In the measurement of writing ability, certain assumptions are made about multiple-choice questions and tests. Some of these assumptions form the basis for multiple-choice testing; for example, at the very heart of some multiple-choice testing is the assumption that test takers who recognize the error in a test question are unlikely to make the same error in their own writing. Quite rightly, the validation of this basic assumption has been the purpose of several research studies, and such studies will continue to be conducted as long as multiple-choice tests are developed to measure writing ability. We should pay attention, however, to some other commonly held assumptions that, although they deal with more peripheral matters, strongly affect attitudes toward multiple-choice tests of writing ability and the interpretation and use of scores derived from such tests. These assumptions—whether they cause people who hold them to favor multiple-choice testing or to condemn it—are seldom discussed, either because their falseness seems self-evident to anyone familiar with multiple-choice testing or because the effects of these assumptions are simply overlooked. Whatever the reason for their not receiving intensive examination, the assumptions do exist and do have considerable power in determining methods of testing to be used to measure writing ability and the value to be attributed to scores achieved on various kinds of tests.

The most important of the assumptions, in terms of their effect on attitudes toward measures of writing ability, are briefly stated as follows:

1. A multiple-choice test is an objective test.
2. The choice for the testmaker is either multiple-choice questions or essay questions, not both.
3. Any essay test is a better measure of writing ability than a multiple-choice test.

4. All multiple-choice questions in tests of writing ability look alike and do the same thing (i.e., they all ask test takers to find errors).

THE "OBJECTIVE" TEST

In the educational world, there is a tendency to refer to multiple-choice tests as "objective" tests. For some people, the term immediately suggests that other kinds of tests are "subjective" and do not measure, as it is thought any "objective" test must do, with the wonderful dispassion of true justice. With the term *objective*, too, comes the connotation of scientific accuracy and precision. One need only look at the various kinds of data associated with the examination of multiple-choice tests by statisticians to understand where this idea comes from. What is forgotten in all these associations and misconceptions is that *objective* refers to the method of scoring, not to the test itself.

An objective test is simply one that can be scored by a machine or by people who need make no judgment about the acceptability or unacceptability of a response. The rightness or wrongness of an answer has been decided by the test developer. The test itself is not objective; it does not function as an ideal criterion against which all and everything in a subject can be measured. It fulfills a certain purpose and only that purpose. Most important, it was designed and put together by human beings who, like all other human beings, have faults and have opinions. Those opinions inform what is measured by the test they have developed and how what is to be measured is measured. A test of writing ability, for example, that includes questions on spelling is certainly not objective in the conception of writing it presents. The developers of any "objective" test are sending a clear message about the relationship between spelling and writing to students, to teachers, and to the world.

When one considers that all testing is merely a matter of sampling a particular universe of skills or knowledge, any emphasis placed on a particular facet of writing—either by the number of questions assigned to the measurement of a particular skill or bit of knowledge or by the kinds of questions used and the types of writing problems tested—helps the testmaker make a clear statement about writing. Schools and teachers should consider the test developers' assumptions about the nature of writing and the writing process that they are accepting when they purchase or commission a test. Too often, an "objective" test is ordered and administered without anyone's examining the test and its questions beforehand in order to determine not only what students are being asked to do to show their ability but also what message about writing is being sent to them.

A test that requires actual writing is sending a clear message to the students, teachers, parents, and the general public that writing should be taught and tested by having students write. Although it may be that a test that includes a writing sample will gain little in psychometric terms over an all-multiple-choice test, the educational gains may be enormous. The English Composition Test, administered as part of the College Board Achievement Tests, contains one 20-minute essay section in the December administration only. At that administration approximately 85,000 students write in response to a set topic, and each of the 85,000 papers must be scored twice. That scoring may cost in the neighborhood of $500,000. The increase in predictive validity for the test is minimal. Admissions officers and others who use the scores are probably not seeing a dramatic increase in the usefulness of scores despite the expenditure of the half million dollars. However, thousands of English teachers in the United States consider the money well spent. The political clout that a writing sample provides for teaching writing and for emphasizing writing across the curriculum has no monetary equivalent. Teachers do not need to defend themselves for assigning compositions instead of doing the kinds of grammar and usage drills that some parents and school administrators, by false analogy, have reasoned will prepare students for the multiple-choice test the College Board offers. They have the support they need, however obliquely it may be derived, for emphasizing actual writing in the English curriculum. That this support from a test should be unnecessary and irrelevant goes without saying; that it is necessary and relevant in many schools is a fact of educational life.

Like the test developer who includes an essay, the testmaker who includes questions on spelling in a test of writing ability is sending a message about how writing should be taught. Regardless of the reasons for including questions on spelling in a test of writing ability, that test developer has provided that test with face validity for users—and all other interested parties—who believe spelling to be of great importance in the teaching of writing.

A writing test may have four kinds of validity:

1. Predictive validity—the ability to predict success in a particular writing course
2. Concurrent validity—the ability to predict success on other tests that measure the same skills
3. Construct validity—the ability to measure the essential skills and abilities that comprise writing competence
4. Face validity—the ability to measure the skills that writing teachers consider to be important

Lack of face validity is the reason many people reject the multiple-choice test of writing ability: a test that does not require any writing does not look as though it is measuring writing ability. The face validity of an essay test leads many people to consider it not only the best possible way to measure writing ability but also the only possible way. Face validity, however, deals only with how things look, not what they are; it cannot substitute for the other types of validity.

AN ESSAY IS NOT ALWAYS BETTER

At one time, it was fashionable for programs assessing basic skills, usually at the ninth-grade level, to include a writing assignment that asked students to write a letter of application, usually in response to an advertisement printed in the test booklet. The assignment seemed to please everyone: it was a practical writing task, something done in the "real" world; it provided students with a purpose and an audience for their writing; and it gave students the chance to write. What more could be asked of a test question aimed at assessing writing ability? A great deal.

Looking below the surface of the assignment into the realities of the educational world and the job market, one instantly recognizes that the letter of application is not at all a valid measure of the writing ability of 13-, 14-, and 15-year-olds. Only rare students in the eighth and ninth grade can look at themselves and discover marketable skills and then can sell themselves as the most appropriate applicants for jobs. Indeed, few ninth graders have ever heard of a letter of application, and fewer still have ever been taught to write one. In the usual high school English curriculum, only a few seniors who may one day have the need to write letters of application are taught to do so. Letters of application are for their future, not their present. High school students applying for the job open at the local fast-food restaurant appear at the restaurant in person and fill out applications. They are interviewed on the spot by the manager or other person doing the hiring. The manager will probably decide which applicant is best suited for the job on the basis of whether hands and fingernails are clean and whether the person is willing to smile. The manager probably cares little about whether the applicant can use the English language in writing with style and correctness. As a matter of fact, in this age of telephones and fast transportation, the letter of application, except in a few professions, is rapidly becoming passé.

Thus the mere inclusion of a writing task in a test does not make it a valid test of writing ability. In measurement, two distinct and important terms are validity and reliability. Both must be present in order to provide the kind of measurement that is appropriate to the kinds of choices and decisions the information from the test will be used to make. Validity concerns the degree to which a test measures what it is intended to measure. Reliability concerns the degree to which the same results are achieved each time the measuring instrument is used. If we have a yardstick measuring 37 inches and use that yardstick repeatedly to measure a yard, we have an exceedingly reliable measuring instrument in that we get the same results every time we use it: it always measures 37 inches. It is not a valid instrument, however, since our goal is to measure a yard, which is 36 inches. A 37-inch yardstick is not measuring what it is supposed to be measuring.

When a test includes a writing sample, that test, to be valid, must ask test takers to perform a task that suits not only the purposes of the test but also the skills and knowledge expected of test takers at the age level being tested. A writing test that requires students to write on a subject about which they know nothing is not a valid test of writing ability because any writer finds it extraordinarily difficult to write without thinking and without knowing. Even when students are required to write on a single topic that is appropriate to their skills and knowledge, the essay test may not be a valid measure of writing ability either. Testing, as we have said, is a matter of sampling a particular universe of knowledge or skills.

Of the universe of skills or knowledge to be measured, the test can deal with only a small portion. It is to be hoped that this portion will include important matters taken from that original universe, but whether they are or are not, they will still only sample the universe, not duplicate it. Therefore, it is reasonable that the more parts of the universe included in the test—the greater the number of different relevant tasks assigned to the student—the more accurate the sampling is likely to be. The more chances students have to show what they can do or what they know about a particular subject, the more accurate the measurement is likely to be.

To make a judgment about writing ability on the basis of one sample produced under one set of conditions is to make a judgment about behavior that may not be very stable. Whether a sample takes five minutes or three hours to produce, it is still only one sample from a large universe. It may lack both validity and reliability. Scores from writing task to writing task may show a tremendous lack of consistency. Depending on the nature of the task assigned, the one-writing-sample assessment may have face validity but little else. Belief in the accuracy of the measurement obtained will be belief in the illusions of measurement, not in its realities.

Furthermore, even if a test includes several writing samples, the test may be unreliable and therefore invalid if the scoring of the essays is divergent from scorer to scorer or if all essays are not scored on the same standard because there is no guarantee that nearly the same scores will result if the same papers were scored again. Since reliability is a necessary ingredient for validity, scores that are unreliable have no hope of being valid.

Multiple-choice tests have in their favor the fact that they are scored reliably. The fiftieth scoring of the same answer sheet is, under ordinary circumstances, consistent with the first scoring. In addition, because they offer in the testing time allotted more chances for the student to show what he or she knows or can do than essay tests offer, multiple-choice tests usually have greater reliability than essay tests. However, reliability is not in and of itself a virtue. As the 37-inch yardstick demonstrates, reliability must always be accompanied by validity. The multiple-choice questions used must measure what they are intended to measure.

Because, in view of some test users, an aura of scientific accuracy and objectivity surrounds the multiple-choice test, it is common for people who are using standardized multiple-choice tests in the classroom to accept these tests unquestioningly. They may use a test that has been reported as valid and reliable by the testmaker without considering whether the multiple-choice test they are using is valid for their purposes, for their goals, for their curriculum, or for their students. It may be, for example, that the multiple-choice test they select deals with spelling, capitalization, and punctuation but that these skills have not been emphasized or even discussed in the particular writing class in which the test will be used. Perhaps the test selected does not include questions on sentence fragments or subject-verb agreement, when these problems have been at the core of the instruction given to students in the class to be tested. Or the test may ask students to distinguish between *who* and *whom*, but the entire English department in the school administering the test considers the distinction between these pronouns too trivial to be worth any classroom time. Further, it may be that the very nature of the test undermines what instruction in a particular classroom has been all about. For example, the test may present the problem of *who* and *whom* in the context of conversation (as in "*Who, Whom* did you say was calling?"), inevitably confusing students who have learned from their teachers the differences in levels of usage and to distinguish between the language of the written text and the language of conversation. Because each test, no matter how it is scored, is a subjective creation, it is important for the test user to examine what the test is testing and what message the test is conveying to students and their teachers.

When we consider validity and reliability, we must understand that their value and importance may differ, depending on the purpose of the measurement. If a test is to be used to determine whether the wheels will stay on an automobile when the speed of the automobile exceeds 50 miles per hour, we would want that test to have absolute validity and absolute reliability for each and every automobile. When it comes to the spelling test that the fourth graders take every Friday morning, the validity or the reliability of that test is not a major consideration. There is nothing crucial about the test. First of all, the grade received on it is only one of the many grades that each fourth grader will receive throughout the course of the marking period. Second, the tradition of the Friday morning spelling test may, in the opinion of some educators and parents, bring with it bonuses that have nothing to do with the measurement being done. Perhaps that routine spelling test fosters such things as self-discipline in study and teaches students the need to study in order to learn. In such a context, the measurement characteristics of the test are unimportant.

In the normal course of testing large groups of people for such purposes as admission to college or placement in a college English course, however, the measurement characteristics of the test are important. The instrument that is being used to make decisions about individuals must have sufficient reliability and validity. It will not have absolute reliability, nor will it have absolute validity. No test (even the one for automobile wheels) is perfect. Every test score carries a degree of error; the degree of error that can be tolerated is determined by the kind of decision the information provided by the test will be used to make. The decision to admit or not to admit a student is, for example, of tremendous significance. If the student is not admitted to a college, the results of the test can never be corrected if they are in error, for the student will never appear on the college campus. If a student is to be placed in an English class once that student arrives on campus, however, a test that is used to help in determining appropriate placement need not be either so reliable or so valid as the admissions test. Because the student is on campus, any decision made on the basis of the test score can be amended. The student will have opportunities to appeal the decision and through classroom assignments can demonstrate that the test score is inaccurate, if it is. Any error in the placement test score is not so crucial as to affect the person's entire education.

Any test that provides information to be used in making a crucial decision must have both high reliability and high validity. Since there is error in the test and in every method of assessment, the test score should be used in conjunction with as much other information about the individual student as it is possible to acquire. Of course, that information should also be reliable and valid.

Multiple-choice questions are often described as "efficient." What that adjective means in testing is essentially that a great many valid questions can be presented to the student and responded to in the limited amount of testing time available. In a 30-minute time period, for example, the student can probably respond to only one essay question. In the same 30-minute period, the student can respond to up to 50 multiple-choice questions, depending on their difficulty and complexity. The degree of sampling has increased dramatically. Providing the student with that many more chances to prove what he or she knows or can do increases the reliability of the measure.

Further, multiple-choice questions lend themselves to a variety of statistical analyses that essay questions do not. It is difficult to set a precise numerical figure to describe the difficulty of an essay test in comparison with other essay tests administered to the same group. Each essay topic presents a unique writing problem. A topic like "Describe the trees you saw on the way to school this morning" is a very different topic from "Describe the cars you saw on the way to school this morning." The knowledge each student brings to the topic is different, the affective response of the student to the topic is different, and the vocabulary and diction used to describe the objects will be different. For some students, the first topic will be easier; for others, the second. Though the change in relative difficulty may be apparent in individual cases, no numerical figure has yet been derived that will indicate to the initiated evaluator the relative difficulty of the topic in relation to other topics given to the same group of individuals. Such figures have been derived for multiple-choice questions, however. Because the answers to multiple-choice questions are predetermined to be either correct or incorrect and because the scoring need not take into account degrees of correctness, as essay scoring does, the percentage of individuals answering a question correctly in the test-taking population can be calculated exactly. This figure can be compared with the kinds of responses given to other questions by the same group of test takers, and the relative difficulty of the question in relation to all other questions taken by the same group can be determined. Further, through the process of score equating, which frequently involves administering in a new test a subset of questions from an earlier test, the relative difficulty of the whole multiple-choice test can be compared with that of another multiple-choice test administered at a different time. Scaled (standard) scores can be derived that will indicate—allowing, of course, for errors in measurement—the same level of measured ability from test to test and from year to year. New tests can be developed at exactly the same level of difficulty if they are wanted. The comparability of scores that multiple-choice tests provides is not always necessary, but it does give a sense of security to all who must make crucial decisions about the relative abilities of a particular student who took the test in March and one who took a different form of the test in May.

MULTIPLE-CHOICE, ESSAY, OR BOTH

If we had but money enough and time, we would measure writing ability by collecting, over a period of several months, a number of samples of a student's writing, produced in reaction to various stimuli and written under various conditions—some impromptu exercises strictly timed and some untimed essays done at home, for example. This collection would then be evaluated by as many different trained evaluators as we could manage, and the score achieved might then provide, if all goes well, an extremely accurate picture of that student's writing ability. But since we have neither enough money nor enough time to do that kind of extended evaluation, we usually compromise. Sometimes the compromise means that a student's skill will be evaluated on the basis of only one piece of writing. Sometimes the student's skill will be measured on the basis of only one piece of writing and the answers to some multiple-choice questions. Sometimes the evaluation will involve only the responses to multiple-choice questions. Which sort of compromise is best? The answer lies in our priorities, our concerns, and, sad to say, our budgets.

Too often, multiple-choice questions and essay questions are thought of as antithetical. They are better described as partners. A summary of some qualities of both methods of assessment that are important to the testmaker follows.

One of the greatest wastes of the essay question is to use it to measure purely factual knowledge. Multiple-choice tests can do that efficiently and cheaply; they can also measure whether students have learned the rules for the comma and the colon or the rules of subject-verb agreement and pronoun case. Though testing factual knowledge is not the limit of what the multiple-choice questions can do, it is something the multiple-choice test does well.

Essay and Multiple-Choice Questions in Tests of Writing Ability

	Essay	*Multiple-Choice*
Method of measurement	Direct—candidate asked to perform task to be measured.	Indirect—measurement relies on correlation between test performance and actual task performance.
Skills measured	Unlimited—candidate must compose, organize, marshal evidence, spell, punctuate, etc.	Limited—certain aspects of writing cannot be measured (e.g., ability to marshal evidence, ability to set proper tone).
	Total—all aspects of writing can be measured simultaneously. Permits use of complete essay.	Fractionated—writing skill must be separated into parts to be measured independently. Relies mostly on aspects of writing that can be measured in the sentence.
Time required	Depends on kind of writing required; not less than 20 minutes per question.	Depends on item types used; can require as little as 30 seconds per item.
Sampling done	Limited by time—no more than 3 samples per hour; best to have fewer. Candidate who misinterprets or does not understand question misses major part of test.	As many as 100 items per hour. Candidate who misses one question is not in serious jeopardy.
Method of scoring	Individually, by trained readers.	Can be machine scored.
Validity	Increases face validity by providing direct measure. By requiring actual task, extends what can be measured; thus increases validity. Because sampling is limited, validity of essay used alone is less than that of essay used with multiple-choice.	High correlation between scores on multiple-choice and essay tests.

(continued)

(*continued*)

	Essay	Multiple-Choice
Reliability of scoring	Reliance on subjective judgment reduces reliability.	Same as other machine-scored tests.
Test reliabiliy	Limited by scoring reliability; length of test.	Can be above .90; a one-hour test can be 100 items long.
Cost	Increases for scoring (housing and paying readers, etc.) and special procedures (new answer sheet, new systems design, etc.).	Same as regular machine scoring.
Time for scoring	Readers can read 20-minute essays at rate of 38 per hour; reading day about 6 hours.	Same as regular machine scoring.
Reaction of English faculty	Approval	Hostility and distrust. Many believe (1) multiple-choice tests are so limited in what they measure that they reduce writing to level of subject-verb agreement, (2) tests are exercises in error-hunting, and (3) the way to measure writing is to have people write.
Influence on curriculum	Thought to encourage requirement of actual writing in schools.	Thought to encourage exercises in error detection as method of teaching writing rather than encouraging writing of compositions.

When the writing skills of large numbers of students are to be tested, a multiple-choice test can be used as a screening device to separate out those at the top and at the bottom who will probably not need to have their scores verified by an essay. The procedure reduces the number of essays to be scored and thus saves time and money, and it allows the essay to make its important contribution. In another situation—the selection of an honors class, for instance—the use of a multiple-choice test to select the best students might be advisable, with the essay used both to verify the multiple-choice scores and to add one further bit of information to make the decisions required.

If one of the purposes of the test is to make comparisons over time, the inclusion of a multiple-choice section with the essay might be the only answer. The comparability of scores provided by the multiple-choice test will help to reduce the effects of differences in the level of difficulty of different topics and to ascertain, if results should differ over time, whether the test has changed, whether the population has changed, or whether something else needs investigation.

Sometimes, too, the multiple-choice section of a test is the only way to guarantee fairness to the students. The College Board English Composition Test, for example, administers only essay topics that have been tried out or pretested by having students respond to them before they are put in the test. Even a topic that students deal with appropriately when it is being pretested does not always produce desirable results when 85,000 students from across the nation respond to it. Responses to topics are affected by news, local problems, television programs, and all sorts of events that change the view students have of the world. Especially when such changes affect students' writing adversely or when some unforeseen misinterpretation of the topic surfaces in thousands of essays, the multiple-choice section provides security against the problems inherent in the assignment. One cannot foresee in June, when the test is set, that, for example, a disaster on the order of Three Mile Island will be on everyone's mind the following spring and that, regardless of the topic assigned, students will express their ideas on a life-threatening situation that immediately concerns them. The examiners who chose the topic did not have an inkling from the trial testing that the following quotation used to stimulate the students' response would be a serious problem for students: "The trouble with being open-minded is that your brains may fall out." No one expected what happened. Students by the score, instead of interpreting the quotation figuratively, vividly described brains scattered about a variety of surfaces.

Such failures with pilot-tested essay questions are, fortunately, rare. Much more basic reasons than protection against the failure of the topic underlie the use of multiple-choice questions with an essay. Because multiple-choice questions increase reliability by increasing the amount of sampling done, they increase the validity of a test containing an essay section. They enhance what the essay has to contribute, not detract from it. And, important always when any decision is to be made on the basis of test scores, they increase the amount of information on which to base the decision.

NOT ALL MULTIPLE-CHOICE QUESTIONS ARE ALIKE

Multiple-choice questions have often been criticized for asking the student to do nothing more than find the error. Indeed, questions of this type are the most familiar, but they are by no means the only kinds of questions available. Examples of a variety of multiple-choice questions follow, to illustrate various ways of measuring writing ability.

Multiple-choice questions have often been criticized because they deal only with the sentence. Items can, of course, be constructed so that they involve a greater context and require the student to deal with such problems as organization and transition. Items involving connected discourse, however, must be used with care, for inevitably they require careful reading. A test made up of such items may provide a better indication of a student's reading ability than writing ability. Because all verbal skills are closely related, demanding a high degree of reading ability in the writing student is appropriate. What is not appropriate, however, is administering a writing test to students that does not yield one iota more information than a reading test they have taken.

Ways of measuring aspects of writing ability through the use of multiple-choice questions are illustrated below. None of them asks the test taker to find an error.

Example 1

Directions: For each of the following, choose the one phrasing that makes the intended meaning clear, that is, the one that avoids ambiguity, that does not leave the actual meaning open to question, or that does not leave the reader guessing about what is intended.

A. That new hybrid corn is growing well.
B. That new hybrid corn is worthless.
C. That corn is hybrid, new, and for the birds.
D. That new corn was a hybrid; it is for the birds.
E. That hybrid corn is new; it is also for the birds.

This item type is intended to measure the student's ability to recognize the aspects of language that interfere with communication because they suggest more meanings than the writer intends or because the writer has failed to clarify the meaning intended. Originally designed only to deal with the ambiguity that results when modifiers are inappropriately placed or when the antecedent for a pronoun is not clear, the item type was expanded to include the identification of inherently ambiguous phrasing. The item type is meant to discover the student's ability to recognize a failure to communicate exactly, for exact communication is a necessary distinguishing feature of the written word, which cannot rely on tone, gesture, or immediate amplification in response to the listener's query to specify the meaning intended.

Example 2

Directions: For each of these sentences, select the answer that, when inserted in the blank in the original sentence, produces the best sentence. Pay attention to meaning and choice of words.

The next time I go to Philadelphia, I _____ in the same hotel.

A. have a longing to stay

B. am desirous of staying
C. want to stay
D. care to stay
E. aspire to stay

This item type might be called an exercise in seeking the *mot juste*. It asks the student to find the phrasing that best fits the intended meaning of the sentence. The item type is meant to measure the student's sensitivity to idiom and ability to choose the apt word.

Example 3

Directions: For each of these questions, you are to choose the version of the underlined sentence or part of the sentence that not only has the same or nearly the same meaning as the original but follows the requirements of standard written English. That is, in selecting the version that matches the underlined part in meaning, pay attention to grammar, choice of words, sentence structure, and punctuation. The answer you select should, when inserted in the original sentence, produce an effective sentence—clear and exact, without awkwardness or ambiguity.

<u>Sometimes we wonder when we should take action</u>, not what action to take.

A. Sometimes the question is when to take action
B. Sometimes the question is in the nature of when action is taken
C. The question sometimes relates to the time to take action
D. The question sometimes is of when action is taken
E. Sometimes the question is the time of taking action

In this item type, the student is presented with underlined words that, although they are acceptable as they stand, can be reworded to provide the kind of variation in structure or in vocabulary that writers sometimes seek. The item type often deals with matters of subordination and coordination, parallelism, conciseness of expression, and clarity of modification.

Example 4

Directions: In this group of questions, two or three underlined sentences are followed by a question or statement about them. Read each group of sentences. Then choose the best answer to the question or the best completion of the statement.

<u>Dan is very disorganized.</u>

<u>The bills in his wallet are arranged by denomination.</u>

What does the second sentence do?

A. It gives a cause.
B. It gives an example.

C. It makes an exception.
D. It makes a generalization.
E. It confirms the first statement.

This item type presents sentences, and the student must determine the relationship between those sentences. The item type is an attempt to measure the student's ability to recognize principles of organization—cause and effect, arrangement according to size or time, comparison or contrast, and illustration or example supporting generalization, to name a few.

Examples 5 and 6
Directions: Each of the questions or incomplete statements below is followed by five suggested answers or completions. Select the one that is best in each case, and blacken the corresponding space on the answer sheet.

"Reading is very relaxing. If you feel tense at the end of the day, sit down with any book for two hours and you will feel better."

The speaker assumes that all people

A. need help to relax
B. try to avoid straining their eyes
C. can relax in the same way
D. are tense at the end of the day
E. have been taught to read well

What conclusion about reading or books must we accept if we accept the speaker's statement?

A. Reading for more than two hours can make one tense.
B. All books have the same effect on the reader.
C. Reading in the morning serves no useful purpose.
D. One must read only books that are designed to relax the reader.
E. Reading is useless unless one is tense.

This item type presents a statement of opinion, and the questions following the statement ask about the speaker's assumptions and biases and about flaws in the speaker's argument. The item type is meant to discover the student's sensitivity to the way language can be used to manipulate and the ability to see through verbiage to underlying illogicality and ill-supported generalization.

Example 7
Directions: Revise each of the following sentences according to the directions that follow it. Although the directions may at times require you to change the relationship between parts of the sentence or to make slight changes in other ways, make only the changes that the directions require.

Below each sentence and its directions are listed words or phrases that may occur in your revised sentence. When you have thought out a good sentence, choose from A to E for the word or entire phrase that is included in your revised sentence.

Sentence: Coming to the city as a young man, he found a job as a newspaper reporter.

Directions: Substitute He came for Coming.

    A. and so he found
    B. and found
    C. and there he had found
    D. and then finding
    E. and had found

This item type requires the manipulation of structures mentally, approximating the writer's task of finding alternative ways of saying the same thing as he or she edits a piece of writing. The item type presents the student with a sentence that is acceptable as it stands; however, the revised sentence is meant to be an improvement on the original or, at least, no worse than the original.

This item type is appropriate for testing the student's ability to move from coordination to subordination, to change emphasis within a sentence, to maintain parallel structure, to express ideas clearly by placing modifiers appropriately, to make a shift in part of the sentence and to match that shift with an appropriate change elsewhere in the sentence (keeping verb in agreement with subject, for example), and to use language idiomatically.

These variations in item type by no means exhaust the possibilities. They are meant only to illustrate some of the different kinds of questions available to the testmaker. Even the often criticized item types that require students to find errors long ago went beyond asking students to decide whether "It is I" or "It is me" is correct. The points tested by multiple-choice questions often deal with more than just the surface features of writing, and no amount of mere drill in pronoun case and the principal parts of a verb will prepare the student to respond to them correctly.

The two items that follow illustrate the kinds of problems of logic and clarity that multiple-choice questions can be written to test.

Example 8

If your car is parked in this lot while not eating in
A   B   C

the restaurant, the car will be towed away. No error
                                    D   E

The error in this sentence is, obviously, in the writer's failure to provide some reasonable indication of who is not eating in the restaurant. The basic problem is not in such matters as subject-verb agreement or punctuation but in the absolute nonsense that the words of the sentence produce. The sentence can be corrected by changing C to something like *even though you are not eating in*, but it cannot be corrected by simply changing an inflection.

Example 9

Harry grew more vegetables <u>than his neighbor's garden</u>.

A. than his neighbor's garden
B. than in the neighboring garden
C. than his neighbor, having a garden also
D. in his garden than his neighbor
E. in his garden than his neighbor did in his

The ideas in this sentence do not fit together logically. Clarity of communication is lost. To make the written text clear, the brief, elliptical nature of the original statement must be expanded, as in E, or reduced to eliminate the mention of the garden, an option this multiple-choice question does not allow. In any case, the sentence is corrected by establishing a clear and logical relationship between the ideas in the sentence.

No matter how sophisticated the multiple-choice question, however, the multiple-choice format is limiting. No multiple-choice question can be used to discover how well students can express their own ideas in their own words, how well they can marshal evidence to support their arguments, or how well they can adjust to the need to communicate for a particular purpose and to a particular audience. Nor can multiple-choice questions even indicate whether what the student writes will be interesting to read. All multiple-choice questions can do is provide by indirect means an estimate of how likely it is that the writing the test taker does for such practical purposes as writing business letters or answering essay questions on history tests will be judged competent. The multiple-choice test is never suitable for assessing skill in imaginative writing.

The limits of the multiple-choice test in assessing writing ability make it eminently desirable to enhance the results of multiple-choice testing with an examination of the student's actual writing whenever possible. As is the case in all measurement, the more reliable and valid information available for use, the more accurate and fair the judgments and decisions made on the basis of that information will be.

SUMMARY

In any assessment of writing ability, the major concern should be the use of valid and reliable instruments. These instruments must be appropriate in terms of the tasks set before the test taker and the use that the tasks make of testing time.

These tasks should be suitable to the skills and knowledge of the student, to the curriculum, and to the purposes of the test. The information needed should be secured in the most efficient manner possible and should not be redundant with information obtained from another test administered to the same students.

No test provides perfect measurement. The test developer's responsibility is to reduce in every way possible and as much as possible the error inherent in a test score. One way of improving the accuracy of an assessment of writing skills is to use the advantages of multiple-choice questions and the advantages of essay questions by incorporating both methods for assessing writing.

10

Testing ESL Student Writers

SYBIL CARLSON AND BRENT BRIDGEMAN

English as a second language (ESL) students bring to our attention problems that force educators and evaluators to reappraise existing definitions of competence in written communication in English. These students, both United States citizens and internationals, because they use different organizational structures for representing ideas and different ways of expressing concepts, offer new insights into the diversity and complexity of written prose. As the writing competence of ESL students is evaluated, the traditional standards for evaluating compositions should be reexamined as well, not for the sake of relaxing standards for ESL students but for purposes of investigating the relevance of some of these standards. Professionals in the the field of writing instruction and evaluation continue to look at the writing process and attempt to answer numerous questions. In this context, particularly for the ESL student, measures of writing competence must be designed and evaluated carefully, and caution must be exercised in relying on results from measures that are themselves open to question.

The evaluation of ESL writing ability should incorporate insights now emerging from the field of writing assessment in general. With the development of competence in basic communication skills (writing, speaking, listening, and reading) as a primary goal for education and with the recognition that many students pass through our educational system with inadequate English-language competence, educators are reappraising their methods and redefining their objectives. Writing competence, in particular, is being addressed as a skill that is integral to effective communication. Therefore, the development of measures of writing ability is essential to the educational process. In the past, the assessment of competence in writing previously focused on indirect measures, often in a multiple-choice format. Although such indirect measures provide some indicators of written language skills, educators now recognize that the skills they assess represent a limited definition of writing competence. Direct measures of writing —actual writing samples—now serve as the preferred means for assessing writing performance because they more nearly approximate real discourse. Writing samples permit the evaluation of writing skills—such as organization, coherence, and the elaboration of ideas—that are not measured satisfactorily with existing indirect measures. Further, the writing sample requires the students to produce an essay; it thereby permits testing of the student's ability to *apply* knowledge about the conventions of writing rather than simply to recognize a correct answer when given several choices.

The evaluation of writing samples must be approached systematically, however. Richard Lloyd-Jones criticizes both indirect and direct measures of writing that are currently in use, warning that they may understate the competence of many candidates who might be successful writers in other contexts. These tests need not be abolished, but they must be interpreted in light of their limitations. Although writing samples most nearly approximate real discourse, numerous problems are associated with them; Lloyd-Jones admonishes, "A writing sample is not real writing" (3). He recognizes, on the other hand, that objective (indirect) measures are based on limited, discrete elements of language. The evaluation of separate elements of writing skills, he believes, is not equivalent to the evaluation of actual discourse, since good writing consists of a blend of skills, not of a sum of these skills viewed separately.

Since evaluation serves as a tool to facilitate various forms of educational decision making, the valid, objective measurement of writing performance must be perceived as a fundamental key to attaining educational objectives. The quality of this measurement directly influences the quality of the educational process throughout—in preliminary assessment or placement, as indicators of writing development and the effectiveness of educational intervention on that development, or as assurance that a student has achieved a designated level of competence. Especially today, as professionals seek to gain new insights about the writing process and new approaches to writing instruction, good measurement will provide information about the writing process as it is reflected in its products.

In this chapter we discuss a program of research on ESL writing assessment that responds to some of the important issues we have just cited. The research we are describing, which focuses on direct measures of writing performance, is an attempt to apply measurement concerns to the evaluation of ESL writing.

MEASUREMENT ISSUES IN THE ESL ASSESSMENT OF WRITING

A Definition of Writing Competence

The scoring of the writing sample, as opposed to the objective scoring of indirect measures, introduces myriad measurement concerns. Because human judgment is exercised in evaluating writing samples, numerous factors contribute to the validity and reliability of these measures. Although psychometric theory and practice contribute to making educated assumptions about the scoring of writing samples, research on the writing process and the evaluation of its products does not offer explicit formulas or definitive guidelines. However, the factors that contribute to instrument validity and reliability can provide considerable guidance.

It is essential to examine closely the standards that are applied to the writing ability of ESL students and will be reflected in the scoring of the writing assessment instruments. Current standards may reflect the views of English composition instructors, whose referents may be the population of native speakers of English; observed differences between native speakers and ESL students may exist, but these differences may not evidence poor or undeveloped writing ability. Evaluators of measures of writing need to be aware of these cross-cultural differences, particularly those that may contribute to writing skills within an expanded definition of writing competence. Some of these differences are discussed in the section concerned with writing assessment parameters.

The prevailing standards may also reflect traditional views of the writing process and the teaching of English composition skills; these views may not be appropriate for ESL students, especially in the light of recent research findings concerning the writing process. Although some instructors may give lip service to the new approaches to and concepts of the writing process, the traditional views may still unconsciously influence their judgments about evidenced writing skill. Richard Quintanilla, in his brief review of conditions that exist in ESL programs in New York City high schools, notes that goals for ESL instruction are just beginning to focus on writing for functional purposes. Most writing curricula are grammar-based, but the influence of new textbooks and of competency testing for functional skills has directed classroom instruction toward more communicative-oriented approaches. David Eskey describes this "swing of the pendulum" in second-language teaching as a movement away from the fundamentally formalist position, which teaches language as a closed set of forms with emphasis on formal accuracy, to an activist position, which approaches language as an open-ended series of communicative functions, with emphasis on functional fluency. Eskey warns, however, that fluency in language is no guarantee of formal accuracy. Inaccurate language is not acceptable just because it communicates; students need to acquire the ability to produce correct forms as well. The new techniques will need to balance form and function.

Although theory and research point to the need for new methodologies in writing instruction, such new methodologies are in their infancy. We are still exploring techniques that may or may not "work" with respect to promoting the development of writing skills. Another aspect of the approaches used to teach writing skills is that speakers of languages other than English, particularly international students, may have received writing instruction that communicated a variety of standards defining the elements that contribute to a "good" piece of writing. Margaret Lindstrom, in her report of research on the reactions of native speakers to stylistic errors in writing, recommends that errors be studied to determine which errors affect communication to the greatest extent (error gravity). Research data provide very little information about the perception and evaluation of errors by native speakers of English in the communication of ESL students. As Lindstrom points out, no single measure of "correctness" exists; linguistic research has been limited to reactions to and perceptions of grammaticality. In fact, J. Richards discusses the existence of a range of rhetorical and communicative norms for speech acts, particularly for ESL students. The range of norms and linguistic rules that are applied vary with the situation. Error gravity in situational contexts needs further examination.

A related consideration that deserves emphasis is the question of which standards might confound the assessment of ESL writing ability. Again, we do not suggest a relaxation of standards but instead recommend the necessary awareness that ESL writers may not be prepared to meet the same standards that are applied to the writing of native speakers of English. When the issue of standards is addressed from the standpoint of functional communicative competences that are essential to writers in academic settings, attention becomes focused on the more realistic standards that all students need to attain in order to be "successful" in the English-speaking educational environment. An objective appraisal of writing-task demands and of writing activities with which the students will be confronted can provide a framework for designing or selecting appropriate writing assessment measures. The research we recently conducted, which we will discuss shortly, is one example of an attempt to define and assess writing ability in terms of the specific purposes and expectations that are the basis for one particular assessment program.

THE ASSESSMENT OF ACADEMIC WRITING SKILLS

Since our research is being conducted for a testing program[1] that provides an early indicator of readiness to participate in an English-based curriculum at the undergraduate and graduate levels, we approached our initial research task from the standpoint of functional communicative competency.

Functionally Based Communicative Competence

Linguists who have investigated the dimensions of second-language teaching and testing (Canale and Swain; Munby; Walz) stress a functionally based communicative approach, as opposed to a grammatically based communicative approach. Briefly defined, it entails the ability to use language to communicate effectively within the specific context in which the communication takes place; it is "functional" in that it "works," serving to convey what the person intended and resulting in appropriate receptive behavior (thought or action) from the recipient of the communication. One justification for this emphasis is the face validity of the materials and syllabus on which the second-language learning is based. From the standpoint of the learner, Canale and Swain provided two "subjective reasons" for their point of view: (1) the more positive consequences for learner motivation resulted from less emphasis on "communicative incompetence" and more emphasis on the communicative purpose of language and (2) what is achieved is the "more natural integration of knowledge of the second language culture, knowledge of the second language, and knowledge of the language in general" (60). Such functional approaches to second-language learners underscore the discrepancies that have been observed between knowledge of grammar and actual written production in present measures of language skills. With regard to the testing of communication in a second language, the important distinction between communicative competence and performance made by Canale and Swain, among others, can be summarized as follows:

- Performance, which can be assessed in various ways, serves as an indirect means for evaluating language proficiency. The kind and degree of language proficiency being measured by a specific task are determined by the nature of that task.
- In order to evaluate performance on a task, the specific dimensions of that task, which condition the performance that is elicited, must be specified clearly. This clarification of situational task demands should contribute significantly to the interpretation of task perfomance.

With regard to the interpretation of test results, the Canale and Swain framework suggests that two important factors influence testing outcomes:

1. Performance is a result of the relative contributions of language proficiency and general cognitive proficiency; hence linguistic demands should not be confused with the cognitive demands of a task.
2. Performance on a task is also influenced by socialization and acculturation; the testing situation is a social event.

As Canale concludes, "it is important to keep in mind that language proficiency is only one of many complex and little understood cognitive systems that interact in performance of any language tasks" (342).

Writing Task Demands within Functional Contexts

The foregoing arguments stress the importance of more precisely identifying written communication performance that is demanded within functional contexts in order to arrive at a more accurate description of the kinds of writing tasks that are required of undergraduate and graduate second-language students. Recently a number of researchers have attempted to identify some of these tasks, with a focus on improving instruction by more directly addressing students' communicative needs through instruction. Barbara Kroll surveyed a small number of students in freshman English courses for international students and in comparable courses for native speakers of English at the University of Southern

California. Responses to her questionnaire indicated that the profiles of past writing experiences and current writing needs of foreign and American students were predictable and similar, justifying the requirement that foreign students take the English writing course because they expect to write in English in order to fulfill academic requirements. These foreign students had past experience with written English and also expected to use written English in the future. The writing task demands that Kroll identified resulted in her recommendation that students be provided opportunities to gain experience with modes of discourse they will be called on to use. Thus, for example, the personal essay was found to be less important than business letters of persuasion, reports, and other writing tasks.

Surveying the academic needs for advanced ESL students, also at the University of Southern California, Shirley Ostler reported a clear distinction between the academic skills needed by graduate and undergraduate students; some of these skills were specific to major fields. Ann Johns ("Necessary English") surveyed randomly selected faculty members from all departments at San Diego State University to determine which academic skills (reading, writing, speaking, listening) were most essential to the success of nonnative speakers of English in their university classes. All departments rated the receptive skills (reading and listening) as most important, suggesting that writing was a skill that should be taught as secondary to the receptive skills. Although most of the faculty agreed that general English was of more benefit to the students, the engineering faculty preferred special-purpose English over general English.

In contrast to Johns's result with engineering departments, Barbara Weaver found that "faculty from many disciplines expressed similar values about writing." Her approach involved studying the standards of writing competency used by faculty readers of writing samples. In general, these faculty members defined competency in terms of careful and logical organization of ideas, placing less emphasis on errors; the readers, however, tended to seek errors in poorly developed essays and to ignore errors in well-organized prose. Sarah Freedman used a similar approach to studying features of writing that are valued in compositions by comparing the holistic ratings of trained evaluators. College students' expository essays were rewritten to be stronger or weaker in four areas: content, organization, sentence structure, and mechanics. Ratings were most affected by content and organization, with smaller effects attributed to mechanics and sentence structure. However, the features of mechanics and sentence structure were found to interact and to have a significant influence on ratings of organization.

Field-specific Writing Task Demands

Other researchers have focused their research in academic writing task demands on field-specific requirements, with emphasis on English for special purposes (ESP). For example, Gregory West and Patricia Byrd surveyed 25 engineering faculty members at the University of Florida to identify the kinds of writing assigned to graduate students during one academic year (1979–80). They determined that examinations, quantitative problems, and research and technical reports were required most frequently; homework and papers, less frequently; and progress reports and proposals, least frequently. West also surveyed 33 engineering faculty members during the same year, asking them to rate American and foreign students on eight writing dimensions. These faculty members ranked the performance of all foreign graduate students lower on the writing dimensions than that of American students on the same writing dimensions, except for quality of content. Making pairwise comparisons on the eight dimensions of foreign student writing, West ordered the dimensions from weakest to strongest as follows:

1. Correctness of punctuation
2. Quality of sentence structure
3. Vocabulary size
4. Correctness of vocabulary usage
5. Quality of paragraph organization
6. Quality of overall paper organization
7. Quality of content
8. Overall writing ability

In particular, his results indicated that ESL graduate engineering students needed help with sentence-level writing skills.

In another study that typifies research in writing for academic purposes, Ann Johns ("Cohesion") focused on the cohesive elements in written business discourse. Three types of written discourse were coded for cohesive elements. Johns was able to identify "constellations" as cohesive elements in the types of discourse but concluded that generalizations about cohesive factors in broad classes of discourses could not be made. Lexical cohesion, for example, was the most common category in all three discourse types but varied considerably among them. In addition, Johns noted that other features of written discourse in English of business and economics (EBE) need to be distinguished. Susan Hill, Betty Soppelsa, and Gregory West, stressing the academic need for ESL students to learn to write experimental-research papers, outlined an instructional approach that similarly aims at functional discourse. Pointing to the growing interest in English for specific purposes (ESP) and in English for academic purposes (EAP), these researchers identified experimental-research papers as important to academic and professional success in the sciences and social sciences. Their instructional method explicates the rhetorical divisions of this type of paper, to enable ESL students to understand the principles of organization that are required.

Another ESL instructional approach recently described by Ruth Spack and Catherine Sadow emphasizes the composing process and writing assignments that students will face in academic and professional situations. They use student-teacher working journals to facilitate expressive writing (with informal, loosely structured language), which, they believe, will encourage transactional writing (writing to inform, instruct, or persuade).

Contrastive Rhetoric

Another area of research that has explored the academic task demands on nonnative speakers of English has been termed "contrastive rhetoric." Rhetorical patterns across cultures are identified and compared.[2] The results of studies of contrastive rhetoric provide somewhat mixed evidence, some rejecting and others supporting the underlying assumption that the structural differences between the native language and the foreign language may interfere with the learning of the foreign language.

Thomas Buckingham described the operational levels of instruction in the teaching of composition, providing a description of skills at each level (I–III). Particularly at level III, the "advanced" level, students should be prepared to write for a variety of communicative purposes, and sociolinguistic factors of language use in the academic setting should be emphasized. Buckingham circumscribed this level of communication competence as a point in which students learn flexibility in reaching a specific audience to influence the "mental or physical behaviors in the reader" (246). He distinguished between the "conceptual paragraph" and the physical (mechanical) aspects of paragraphing; ESL students need to recognize that the elements of a paragraph become united by a single theme through the logical sequencing of ideas. Significantly, nonnative speakers of English tend to organize their writing in the manner in which they organize writing in their first language—in "un-English discourse" (250). Thus cultural differences in logical development emerge. In English, for instance, we employ logical proof, culturally defined levels of formality, and cultural referents; in other languages, different syntactic choices and kinds of proof that are selected and valued by particular cultures are more predominant. Similarly, Fraida Dubin and Elite Olshtain stressed the difference in rhetorical patterns from one culture to another, patterns that influence cohesion and communicative purposes. The form of organization of written text is influenced by a particular communicative purpose. To achieve that purpose, different languages use different overt and covert signals to express relationships to achieve cohesion. "Thus in English it is quite common to find that the referential pronoun *this* in the first sentences of a new paragraph refers . . . to the whole earlier paragraph. In Hebrew, however, one could not do this. It would be necessary to use a phrase such as 'all the facts mentioned above' or 'everything that was said until now'" (356). They emphasized the importance of reading in English for ESL students, a task that will expose them to the elements of English prose style that can be transferred to written composition.

Margaret Lindstrom also underscored the pedagogical implications of contrastive analyses, viewed from the standpoint of error gravity, the extent to which errors influence communication. The judgments of educators and evaluators of writing tasks may be influenced by their idiosyncratic experiences and language backgrounds; the perception of errors varies with the situation. In academic writing, when errors substantially affect rhetorical patterns, logical and coherent communication is affected as well.

According to Christine Pearson, the academic skills needed by ESL students at entry level in degree programs are further hampered by the students' problems with handling the concepts that underlie these skills. Many of these concepts reflect a culture-bound way of thinking that is unfamiliar and illogical to foreign students, such as distinguishing between points that would be considered relevant and irrelevant in Western thought; they require considerable practice to be grasped, even by American students. Pearson recommended that the skills that are basic to the communication skills (reading, writing, listening, speaking)—skills that cannot be developed without conceptual structures to support them— be transmitted to students beginning in the lowest-level ESL classes. Concepts such as paraphrasing and summarizing, the general-specific dimension, and the relevance-irrelevance dimension should be presented to ESL students within a functional communicative approach rather than through the traditional order of presentation of discrete basic skills, without any logical bases. ESL specialists (Blanton; Taylor, *Teaching ESL*) have suggested that the linguistic and cognitive approaches to academic learning situations need to be identified so that ESL teachers can more effectively help students to meet communication expectations. In particular, Blanton noted that ESL students need to learn to communicate in modes that will meet future academic requirements. Unfortunately, ESL students who receive early instruction in personalized, narrative-based writing may not be aware that these narrative writing tasks cannot be applied to all academic writing; thus their writing fails to meet the academic expectations of impersonal, formal exposition.

In juxtaposition to the contrastive rhetoric position, some researchers suggest that implicit "universals" in scientific and technical languages, or common rhetorical or grammatical processes, may (or may not) exist. Larry Selinker, Mary Todd-Trimble, and Louis Trimble, for example, investigated rhetorical function shifts in English for science and technology (EST) discourse within a single paragraph. Their results indicated that EST students typically confuse rhetorical levels in the elementary stage of second-language learning and that rhetorical process development is only one form of EST paragraph development. They recommended research to investigate the rhetorical and grammatical processes of international scientific and technical languages, acknowledging the possibility that "universal modes of thought and practice" (Widdowson 40) may be explained by the fact that a great deal of the scientific and rhetorical information of the world is coded in English.

Survey of Academic Writing Skills

Our review of the literature cited and of many other sources enabled us to determine the more significant dimensions of the functional communicative demands in writing that feasibly might be imposed on entry-level nonnative speakers of English. These writing task demands can be described as general academic skill and assignment requirements and as field-specific competences, placed within the situational contexts that include academic settings and the culturally based expectations and perceptions of evaluators of student writing.

This analysis of the literature served as the basis for the design of a research project that would provide a definition of writing task demands in postsecondary academic settings. The primary objective of this project (Bridgeman and Carlson) was to identify and describe the expectations of writing competence required of nonnative speakers of English at the beginning of their educational experiences in institutions of higher education in the United States and Canada. The information we gathered took into account the various factors that should be considered in defining communicative competence in writing—the functional task demands for which students are expected to be prepared as well as the perceptions, sometimes culturally influenced, of the people who evaluate them. The informal interviews and the literature review provided the basis for the design of a survey instrument that incorporated the full range of expectations of writing competence. The writing task demands, features of writing tasks, and types of writing-sample topics were expressed in terminology that would communicate clearly to individuals in various disciplines. Subsequently, a representative sample of departments within institutions responded to the questionnaire.

From our perspective, in which the TOEFL is used as an admissions instrument, we could assume, at least, that writing assessment at the point of admission takes place in undergraduate and graduate institutions in order to evaluate the competence of students to undertake the kinds of writing tasks that will be required of them academically. Ultimately, the goals of postsecondary academic education in the area of writing skills are twofold: (1) to assist students to develop writing competence as a tool to facilitate performance in courses, both English and major-specific, and (2) to prepare students to function in the world of work after graduation and, possibly, in their personal lives as well. These competences, which need to be developed in the course of academic instruction, must be defined in terms of the actual writing activities that take place and the expectations that are held, both for native and nonnative speakers of English. Before we inferred the specific purposes of writing tasks in the academic context, the survey we conducted asked representatives of various departments to respond on the basis of their perceptions; these perceptions may not match perfectly with actual practices, but their responses served as a more efficient means for gathering representative data than did on-site observations of classroom activities. These perceptions, at least, do influence how faculty members perceive student writing in their classrooms.

Summary of Survey Results

The survey questionnaire was completed by faculty members in 190 academic departments at 34 universities in the United States and Canada with high foreign student enrollments. Undergraduate English departments were chosen to document the skills needed by undergraduate students. At the graduate level, six academic disciplines with relatively high numbers of nonnative students were surveyed: business administration, civil engineering, electrical engineering, psychology, chemistry, and computer science.

The major findings are summarized as follows:

- Although writing skill was rated as important to success in graduate training, it was consistently rated as even more important to success after graduation.
- Even disciplines with relatively light writing requirements (e.g., electrical engineering) reported that some writing is required of first-year students. Lab reports and brief article summaries are common writing assignments in engineering and the sciences. Longer research papers are commonly assigned to undergraduates and to graduate students in business administration, civil engineering, and psychology programs.
- Descriptive skills (e.g., describing apparatus or procedures) are considered important in engineering, computer science, and psychology. In contrast, skill in arguing in favor of one point of view in contrast to another is seen as very important for undergraduates, business administration students, and psychology majors but of very limited importance in engineering, computer science, and chemistry.
- Faculty members reported that in their evaluation of student writing, they rely more on discourse-level characteristics (e.g., paper organization, quality of content) than on word- or sentence-level characteristics (e.g., punctuation, spelling, sentence structure, vocabulary size).
- Discourse-level writing skills of natives and nonnatives are perceived as fairly similar, but significant differences between natives and nonnatives were reported for sentence- and word-level skills and for overall writing. A majority of departments reportedly use the same standards for evaluating the writing of native and nonnative students, although nearly a third of the departments reportedly use different standards.
- Respondents were asked to rate types of writing-sample topics, to indicate their preference for topics that would most likely elicit evidence of the writing skills that would facilitate performance in academic contexts. (Two examples of each type were provided.) The 10 topic types represented a range of writing assignments: (A) personal essay, (B) sequential or chronological description, (C) spatial or functional description, (D) comparison and contrast, (E) comparison and contrast plus taking a position, (F) extrapolation, (G) argumentation with audience designation, (H) description and interpretation of a graph or chart, (I) summarizing a passage, and (J) summarizing a passage and analyzing or assessing the point of view. The clear favorite among the engineering and science departments was type H. However, this topic was perceived as inappropriate by a majority of the undergraduate English faculty. Type G was the favorite among business

administration programs; type E also was evaluated positively by these programs and was the favorite among undergraduate English faculty members.

- To obtain a summary picture of the relationships among topic types both within and between academic disciplines, the acceptability ratings were analyzed using a multidimensional scaling approach that accommodates differences between raters. Within each discipline, the pattern of responses to each topic type was compared to the pattern of responses for every other topic type. The positions of the topic types, as rated by the respondents, reflect the perceptions of the similarities and differences among the topic types. The multidimensional scaling suggested that the respondents reacted to the topic types as having two dimensions, one determined by the complexity of the task demanded by the topic type, the other by the degree of personal involvement required. Type H can then be seen as a relatively simple and impersonal task. Type E is a little above average on the complexity dimension and is a task requiring a relatively high degree of personal involvement in the topic.

Thus the faculty members surveyed appear to view student writing skills from the standpoint of functional communicative competences. For example, the written products prepared by students in different disciplines may be considered competent to the extent that they meet the task demands—particularly kinds of writing assignments and certain skills—that are specific to a discipline. In addition, faculty members reported that written assignments are evaluated on the basis of discourse-level rather than word- or sentence-level characteristics and that they perceived the discourse-level writing skills of natives and nonnatives to be fairly similar. Grammatical competence, however, tends to influence evaluations of student writing to some extent, in that respondents reported that nonnative speakers of English are more deficient in word- and sentence-level skills than are native speakers.

Although some important common elements among the different departments were reported, the survey data distinctly indicate that different disciplines disagree on the writing task demands and on a single preferred mode of discourse for evaluating entering undergraduate and graduate students. The extent to which essays written in different discourse modes produce different rankings of the evaluations of the same students remains to be seen.

DESIGNING MEASURES TO ASSESS ESL WRITING PERFORMANCE

Our present research (Carlson, Bridgman, Camp, and Waanders) builds on the information obtained in the survey of academic writing tasks summarized to this point in the chapter. The current project is investigating whether scores from a current Test of English as a Foreign Language (TOEFL) and the Graduate Record Examinations (GRE) General test scores, as well as indirect measures of writing ability, are predictive of writing skills on the kinds of tasks that are faced by first-year graduate students. Although our survey of writing tasks indicated that no single essay topic was universally accepted by all the academic disciplines surveyed, two topic types were selected as most representative for the writing samples to be obtained in this study. Graduate departments in engineering and science generally favored a type of topic that asked the student to describe and interpret a graph or chart (arbitrarily labeled type H), and undergraduate English departments favored a type of topic that asked the student to compare and contrast plus take a position (type E). Graduate business departments also rated type E highly. Although type H was viewed as unacceptable by many undergraduate English departments, it was the most highly favored type of topic among all graduate departments in the sample. In the multidimensional scaling, types H and E were farther apart than any other pair of types, suggesting that they were perceived as distinctly different tasks. Thus topic type E was selected as an effective contrast to topic type H; the fact that departments perceived these two types as distinctly different may imply that writing samples on types H and E elicited different writing skills as well.

For the current project, two essays of type H and two essays of type E were written by each subject, who were allowed 30 minutes to respond to each question. The four topics were developed during an extensive process that involved pilot testing of approximately 30 topics and pretesting of 8 topics. This procedure will be discussed more fully later in this chapter.

Because it is possible that results might differ across language groups, three major language groups with large numbers of TOEFL candidates were studied: Spanish, Arabic, and Chinese. The sample of foreign students with TOEFL scores who completed four writing samples was 542, consisting of 138 Arabic-language, 230 Chinese-language, and 174 Spanish-language candidates. The sample also included 43 native-English-speaking students with GRE scores who were candidates for graduate admission to U.S. institutions and who completed four writing samples as well as an indirect measure of writing ability.

The results of the data analyses are presented at the end of this chapter. The value of these results would have been significantly diminished without careful planning that took into account the numerous parameters that might influence the assessment of the writing ability of ESL students.

WRITING ASSESSMENT PARAMETERS

The design of a writing assessment program is influenced by practical considerations such as costs and staffing; whatever the limitations imposed for the sake of efficiency, the interpretation of the results of any writing assessment must be conditioned by the factors that may have contributed to them. Some of these parameters of a writing assessment program can be controlled, or accounted for, by good advance planning; others that cannot be controlled should at least be recognized as exerting possible effects on the outcomes of the assessment. The parameters discussed briefly here consist of task, administration, scoring, psychometric, and interpretation factors.

Task Factors

The writing stimulus—the verbal statement that elicits the specific writing performance being targeted—requires careful development and pretesting. In addition to considering the definition of writing performance that is to be demonstrated and in order to reflect the purposes of the assessment, we must determine the content of the writing stimulus and other design features of the test. The writing stimulus might be composed of elements such as the topic specification, a cartoon, a map, or instructions to the writer.

Determination of Content.   Particularly with ESL students, the experiences that writers bring to the assignment may significantly alter their ability to produce a representative piece. The content implied by the topic must be as fair as possible, not favoring a specific set of personal or cultural experiences. Cultural bias can be very subtle. For example, topics that suggest a set of potentially controversial social norms (family size may imply family planning), technological advances (home computers), or social systems (the U.S. secondary school) can present a writing situation that creates an emotional reaction or a dilemma about what is expected by the writer of the topic. Likewise, the topic should not convey the impression of a cultural perspective that the writer is expected to share, such as a strictly U.S. or middle-class point of view.

Vocabulary and concepts that are embedded in the writing stimulus also may be culture-bound; they should reflect instead a difficulty level that does not penalize the nonnative speaker, since the objective of the writing sample is not to test vocabulary or reading ability.

Furthermore, in determining the content of the stimulus, topics that may evoke heavily emotion-laden responses should be avoided, particularly if the mode of discourse is not a personal essay. For example, one topic that we pretested for our study and rejected concerned the advantages and disadvantages of the use of chemicals by mankind. Several samples written in response to this topic, however, exhibited highly charged reactions, such as anger that wealthy nations use their power to control less affluent nations. The papers were perceived by some readers as diatribes that obstructed the writers from demonstrating their ability to write a comparison-and-contrast paper and also interfered with an objective evaluation from the standpoint of academic writing competence.

Finally, the topic developer must recognize that writing involves a "bi-directional movement between content and written form" (Taylor, "Content and Written Form" 5); the assignment must be sufficiently compelling to stimulate the writer's willingness to communicate ideas. From the standpoint of the readers who will evaluate numerous writing samples on one topic, the stimulus should encourage some divergence in ideational expression; otherwise, the tedium of the readings will influence scoring accuracy.

As we initially selected the topics to be pilot-tested for our research study, we recognized the limitations that are imposed in attempting to develop stimuli for students from diverse cultures and regions of the world. Thus our first set of topics, cast in the two type formats (comparison and contrast, graph or chart), resulted in relatively universal subjects (e.g., area and population of continents; changes in farming, travel, and reading; the exploration of outer space). In addition to pilot-testing these topics, we also asked students at a local English language institute to react to the topics on a questionnaire. The questionnaire included, for each of 22 topics, a rating of the students' perceptions of the difficulty level as well as their choices of topics about which they would most like to write. For topics that were rated as difficult, they were asked to indicate reasons for this rating: grammar, ideas, or vocabulary. In instances where a considerable number of students indicated that the *ideas* they would have to produce for a topic would pose problems, we chose not to pretest the topics further. On the basis of the samples we obtained and the responses to the questionnaire, we were able to reduce the number of potentially usable topics. The pilot testing yielded other interesting reactions from students and ESL faculty with regard to content. For example, a topic that included pie charts of the areas and population of the world continents may have imposed difficulty for international students who are not accustomed to this type of representation of data. To avoid this obstacle, the topic stimulus now includes tables that summarize the information that appears in the pie charts. Other topics did not warrant further pretesting for several reasons; four of these were that they did not elicit a broad enough range of responses or ideas, they encouraged the relating of personal experiences or a personal essay, they were misunderstood, and students did not have sufficient background or vocabulary from which to draw in order to communicate their ideas.

Development of the Stimulus Material.   Other parameters of the writing stimulus must also be considered carefully: length and specificity of the task, communication of expectations, mode of discourse, specification of audience and purpose, number of samples to be written by one individual, and whether or not individuals should be given a set of topics from which to choose.

The length of the stimulus is related to the expectations, or task demands, that are conveyed by the stimulus. Regarding the communication of task demands, task specificity possibly depends on the interactions of the particular kind of topic, topic content, individuals being tested, and other factors. Studies that control for a number of such possible variables need to be conducted. Clearly the task should not present a stimulus that imposes a lengthy reading exercise, which may heighten anxiety and introduce the variable of reading ability.

However, depending on the objectives of the writing-sample assessment, the stimulus should describe the demands of the particular writing task, but as succinctly as possible. At the extreme is a stimulus that consists of a terse phrase or one sentence; it may lack sufficient specificity, leading to a wide range of responses from writers. Ideally, the range of responses should be sufficiently broad, yet not so broad that the responses are too divergent to compare on an evaluative scale, nor so narrow that the writers are limited in demonstrating their abilities to deal with the assignment. Topic specificity must communicate the expectations that are held, reflecting at least briefly the criteria that will influence the evaluation of the response to the topic. Individual writers, however, may react differentially to the instructions; some individuals may pay little heed to detail because of anxiety or inexperience (Greenberg) and approach the task with a different response set than others. Not all students may perceive the requirements of a task in the same way as the writer of the topic (Odell).

The mode of discourse or type of writing assignment that the task presents (personal essay, persuasive argument, etc.) must be considered carefully. We cannot be assured that "good writing is good writing" regardless of the kind of task that is assigned (Quellmalz, Capell, and Chou). Although personal essays permit the writer to draw from experiences that are common to all, they require a mode of communication that may not transfer to other forms of writing (Blanton). When determining the purpose of the writing sample, the kind of writing that is elicited should be anticipated; if the writing is expected to provide a sample of how well students will perform in the classroom, the stimulus should be representative of that type of writing. In our survey of academic writing tasks, respondents indicated that different types of writing are valued in different disciplines. Although personal and creative writing received high ratings of importance by respondents in English departments, this kind of writing was not rated as highly by respondents in other disciplines.

Specification of the purpose of the writing sample is determined by the ways in which it will affect the writer. Most writing assessment authorities, including Odell, strongly recommend that both purpose and audience be specified. Typically, students in academic settings are accustomed to writing to an audience of one, the instructor who grades the assignment. Clearly, knowing the purpose of the piece as well as to whom it should be directed will explicate the task to the student as well as influence the structure, tone, and style of the composition that is produced.

One writing sample is, in measurement terms, the equivalent of a one-item test. From the standpoint of validity and reliability, inferences and generalizations drawn from this limited performance sample are severely restricted. Ideally, a writing assessment should be composed of more than one item. To date, research has not provided sufficient information to assist us in equating one topic with another with regard to ability of the topics to elicit equivalent performance. Even topics that superficially appear parallel, within the same mode of discourse, cannot be considered equal. When students whose essays will be compared in the same assessments are given the opportunity to select from a menu of topics, differential performance in response to different topics confounds the scoring and interpretation of the results, thereby invalidating the assessment. Frances Swineford noted, in fact, that students appear to be unable to select topics on which they will exhibit their best writing; in her research, better students tended to select more difficult topics, receiving lower scores because of the difficulty level. Again, more research is needed to provide more concrete guidelines on topic and mode equivalence.

In our current research, subjects wrote on four different topics, in each of two different modes of discourse, to determine whether performance differences result when the same individual responds to a topic within the same mode of discourse or across different modes of discourse.

Pretesting of Writing Stimuli. For the present study, we collected representative writing samples on eight topics, four of each type, in order to select the four topics that might yield the most dependable data. We conducted a holistic scoring session of these pretest data that focused on two objectives: (1) selecting four topics on the basis of criteria that were agreed on by the readers and would be used during the scoring of our larger sample of data and (2) determining whether a six-point scale could be applied to ESL papers and would provide sufficient discrimination among papers. Discussions following the reading of essays on each topic indicated that our 30-minute time limits appeared to be reasonable and assisted us in selecting the four topics for our full-scale research study, in redesigning the topic stimuli, and in evaluating our scoring procedures. The readings also indicated that the six-point scale worked well in differentiating among papers. This pretesting session convinced us that the pretesting of topics is essential.

Administration Factors

Factors pertaining to test administration also contribute to the outcomes of writing-sample assessment: physical layout of the writing stimulus, time limits and other testing conditions, and the physical conditions of the room in which the testing takes place. Significantly, the assignment of a writing sample as a measure of writing ability under testing conditions is an artificial situation. The testing conditions do not parallel conditions in which the student is likely to write more naturally. The time limits that are allowed for writing are determined by practical considerations such as the amount of time available during admissions testing or during one class period. Time limits place students under pressure, possibly simulating conditions in which students may be placed when being tested in academic coursework. In addition to the anxiety that some students may experience, time limits restrict prewriting activities and prevent any major reorganization or revision. It may be possible that some students do well under such "first draft" conditions, whereas others, who might be equally good writers, do not. Nancy Lay's composing-aloud studies revealed that adult ESL learners may require more composing time to allow for native-language switches. Second-language students tend to translate key words into the first language as they deal with the organization of ideas; in Lay's research, they produced better-quality essays when more native-language switches were made. Thus the pretesting of the topics, with close observation and feedback from the writers, should indicate the reasonable time limits for a given topic.

Scoring Method

Selection of an appropriate scoring method for an ESL writing sample depends on the purposes of the assessment. A holistic evaluation (a single score representing the overall impression created by the sample) may be more efficient for making selection or placement decisions, whereas a more analytic framework (separate scores for a number of organizational and grammatical features of the sample) may be more useful for providing diagnostic information to teachers. Although other methods (e.g., t-unit analysis) may yield more objective scores as a rough index of second-language proficiency, they may be poor indicators of functional communicative competence.

Holistic scoring is impressionistic, but it is not haphazard. Considerable care must go into selecting sample essays (range finders) that represent each point on the score scale, and thorough training of the readers is necessary. Such training involves discussion among the readers to reach consensus on the criteria. During a reading session, continual checks must be made to ensure that no reader is straying from the standard originally set. Since scorers' judgments are subjective, each essay should receive at least two independent readings. The scores from the two raters are typically added together to form the single holistic score.

Holistic evaluations may be influenced by a number of characteristics of an essay, including content, organization, sentence structure, and mechanics. As mentioned earlier, a study by Freedman, in which essays were rewritten so that they exhibited strengths or weaknesses on each of these four traits, indicated that content and organization had the greatest influence on holistic scores. Mechanics and sentence structure influenced scores only if the essay was well organized. However, generalizing from studies based on essays written by native speakers to essays written by ESL students may be unwarranted. Hunter Breland and Robert Jones used a set of 20 scores classified as discourse, syntactic, or lexicographic characteristics to predict holistic scores that had been independently assigned. Paralleling Freedman's findings, they found that the discourse characteristics were the best predictors of holistic scores. However, unlike Freedman, Breland and Jones included a group of essays written by Hispanic ESL students. In this group, syntactic and lexicographic scores were relatively much more important. Subject-verb agreement and range of vocabulary were particularly strong correlates of holistic scores in the Hispanic group. This finding may simply reflect the greater range of syntactic and lexicographic skill found in this ESL population. Regardless of the reason for the differences in the ESL group, this study serves as a useful reminder that even well-established "facts" concerning the scoring of writing samples may have to be modified for ESL populations.

For native speakers, for example, organizational skills usually parallel mechanical skills, and it is unusual to find a highly organized essay written by a student with very poor grammatical skills. With students for whom English is a second language, it would not be unreasonable to expect a greater disparity between organizational skills and mechanical competence in English.

If a single holistic score is to be used, the raters must agree on how to score essays that present a large discrepancy between organizational and mechanical skill. They must also agree on which mechanical errors are most serious. This judgment of error gravity may stem from a strictly functional communication point of view (Does this error interfere with what the author is trying to say?), or it may also penalize errors that are stylistically undesirable (e.g., redundancy, run-on sentences). In addition, raters must agree on how to evaluate essays in which writers attempt complex sentence structures but make errors in doing so versus essays that use only simple sentences but contain few errors. In her research, Greenberg noted that ability to avoid errors predicted teachers' quality ratings better than the writer's ability to manage complex syntactic structures. She found that one major problem consisted of word form errors. Mina Shaughnessy in fact recognized that word form errors exemplify "advanced errors." Such errors indicate attempts to acquire formal academic vocabulary, in spite of the risk of error. Thus more competent writers may commit more errors, yet may be penalized by raters who focus on freedom from errors as a predominant feature of good writing. During the training for holistic scoring, discussion about errors should be limited in order not to interfere with the process of reading for total impression and to ensure that particular features of writing do not unduly influence that total impression.

Despite the most rigorous procedures in the training of scorers, holistic scoring schemes inevitably require some degree of subjective judgment, and these subjective judgments may be particularly difficult when the writer and reader (scorer) do not share a common set of cultural conventions and expectations. These conventions go far beyond mere differences in grammatical rules. Robert Kaplan's "Cultural Thought Patterns in Inter-cultural Education" clearly demonstrated cultural differences in patterns of logic used to order ideas within paragraphs. For example, Kaplan suggests that Anglo-European expository essays typically follow a linear development. In contrast, paragraph development in Semitic languages is based on a complex series of parallel constructions of coordinate rather than subordinate clauses. Oriental essays use an indirect approach; the reader is told how things are not, rather than how they are. In French and Spanish essays, Kaplan noted more digression and introduction of extraneous material than would be considered acceptable in an English essay. Karen Thompson-Panos and Marie Thomas-Ruzic recently noted certain contrasting features of English and written Arabic that may contribute to perceived weaknesses in the writing of Arab ESL students. For example, paragraph development in Arabic languages consists of a series of parallel constructions connected by coordinating conjunctions, thus lacking the use of subordination that is valued in English paragraph organization.

ESL teachers who are aware of distinct cultural patterns may assign essay ratings that differ significantly from ratings of English teachers with no ESL experience. On the other hand, if the criterion for competence is success in a standard course in a United States university, the "insensitive" ratings may be better at predicting academic performance than the culturally sensitive ratings. In our work, we compared ratings by ESL readers with ratings by readers whose predominant experience is with native speakers of English. In addition, we compared these ratings to ratings given by faculty members in engineering and in the social sciences. The classic research of Paul Diederich, John French, and Sydell Carlton suggests that even among native speakers, different "schools of thought" exist among readers and that certain professions are more likely to emphasize a particular characteristic. For example, lawyers appear to focus more on organization, whereas editors tend to focus on style and wording. In our study, the essay readers also completed a questionnaire intended to identify the features they attend to when evaluating a composition in order to determine if the criteria applied by ESL and English readers differed substantially, as well as the extent to which the training during the reading sessions diverged from the standards they apply in practice.

Because analytic scoring yields more scores than holistic scoring, it is potentially more valuable for prescribing educational interventions for individual students. One scoring scheme that has been used extensively with ESL students provides separate scores for content, organization, vocabulary, language usage, and mechanics (Jacobs, Zinkgraf, Wormuth, Hartfiel, and Hughey). Other analytic scoring schemes provide for even finer-grained analysis. However, the apparent advantage of several separate scores is frequently an illusion; the reader's general impression is likely to influence ratings on each of the "separate" aspects being evaluated. In addition, analytic ratings are very time-consuming. Stephen Wiseman found that four general-impression markings were equivalent in time and effort to one analytic marking. Further research is needed to determine the best compromise between a single score and a complex analytic scoring scheme, as well as which kinds of scores are more appropriate to specific situational contexts.

The ultimate means for the objective scoring of essays may eventually be achieved by computer software such as Bell Labs' *Writer's Workbench* (Cherry, Fox, Frase, Gingrich, Keenan, and MacDonald; Kiefer and Smith). This sophisticated word processing tool can identify such features as spelling errors, overuse of a particular word, and sentences that are consistently too long or too short. Analysis of these structural features might help some writers to improve their writing. However, this kind of computer program cannot judge how well a piece of writing accomplishes its main purpose of communicating with its intended audience, nor can it evaluate features such as development and organization. For our research, representative subsamples of the writing samples written in response to each of the four topics were scored with *Writer's Workbench* to obtain information regarding the specific features of the papers.

Psychometric and Interpretation Factors

Reliability, or consistency, of essay scores can be assessed in a number of ways (intrarater, interrater, across topics within genre, across genre). Intrarater reliability indicates how consistent a single rater is in scoring the same set of essays twice with a specified time interval between the first and second scoring. Interrater reliability estimates the extent to which two or more raters agree on the score that should be assigned to an essay. When essays and raters represent different cultural perspectives, interrater reliability is likely to be lower than when both essays and raters come from a homogeneous group. But even if *interrater* reliability is perfect, the claim cannot be made that the essay test is perfectly reliable. Other factors such as variations over time, from one topic to another, and from one sample of students to another also must be considered.

Intertopic reliability assesses the extent to which the ranking of student scores depends on the topic. Scores will vary from one topic to another even within the same general topic type. A relatively small intertopic variation in a group representing a single cultural group may become quite pronounced in a culturally diverse sample if one of the topics is particularly salient for students from one culture. For example, a topic comparing life in a democracy to life in a dictatorship may represent an abstract academic exercise for North American students but may stimulate an intense personal reaction from students from Central America. In addition, variations from one topic type to another (e.g., narrative versus persuasive mode) may be even more influenced by cultural factors.

High reliability does not provide sufficient evidence that a test is valid. Instead, the test may be measuring a variable consistently that is not the primary criterion of interest. Thus a 30-minute writing sample might be judged to be reliable by the various criteria discussed, but it still might not serve as a valid indicator of the student's ability to write a long paper without limitations on time and with an opportunity to make extensive revisions and drafts.

As Lee Cronbach has noted, it is not tests that are validated but interpretations of data from tests used in specific contexts. Scores from an essay test that may be valid for one purpose may be invalid for another purpose. For instance, a test that serves as a valid indicator of skill in writing a narrative essay may have little value in predicting a student's ability to meet the writing demands in a graduate engineering program. Furthermore, a test that is considered a valid predictor of success in meeting the writing demands of undergraduate study for native speakers may or may not predict with comparable validity for ESL students.

Optimally, validity should be determined by establishing that a test is measuring the same performance objective that a good external criterion is also measuring. When the parameters that condition a measure of writing skills are taken into account, the external appearance of a writing-sample topic, or its face validity, is not sufficient to ensure the validity of the performance that is intended to be measured. An objective means for determining the validity of scores on a writing sample can be achieved by correlating these scores with scores on other measures that have been demonstrated to predict well for the same criterion. This criterion, likewise, must have evidenced validity and reliability. One frequently used criterion of academic success, such as the grade point average, may not meet consistently the constraints of validity and reliability. Instead, valid and reliable scores on an established test that has been shown to predict for the criterion may serve as a more objective indicator for validating writing-sample scores. The validity of scores for writing samples that are included in standardized tests, for example, is established by demonstrating that the scores are highly correlated with scores on indirect measures of writing ability.

Ideally, however, scores on direct and indirect measures would not be perfectly correlated. Since a writing sample requires the production of a composition, in contrast to the recognition of correct responses on a multiple-choice test of writing ability, we would not expect the two types of tests to assess identical skills. Instead, they would be highly correlated because some of the skills they are measuring overlap and reflect a form of "general" writing ability. In addition, writing samples would be expected to contribute additional information about writing performance that is not yielded by an objective test, thus explaining an imperfect correlation.

In our study, we chose topics carefully and investigated interrater reliability and intertopic reliability both within a single topic type and across topic types. To fulfill the purposes of our investigation, we attempted to validate scores on the writing samples by comparing them to external criteria such as the TOEFL examination and the GRE General test scores, including indirect measures of writing ability.

SUMMARY OF RESULTS AND CONCLUSIONS

This research generated a considerable amount of information contributing to the validity of measures of English-language proficiency—writing samples, the TOEFL, and the GRE General test. The complex results, considerably abbreviated, are summarized as follows:

- The two scoring methods for the writing samples, holistic and discourse- or sentence-level, yielded essentially the same mean levels of performance, indicating that the two-score method does not provide any advantage over the one-score method.

- The estimates of reliability of holistic scores assigned to the same paper by different readers were consistently high (.80–.85, according to Spearman-Brown corrections based on summing the judgments of two raters), indicating that they were in close agreement regarding the criteria that influence general impressions of writing skills.
- When the holistic scores were correlated within and across topic types, the correlations were no higher within topic types than across topic types. This finding supports the notion that at least for these topics, there were no systematic differences in the ranking of student scores for papers written in response to different topics.
- The high estimates of reader reliabilities assigned by different readers indicate that the readers were able to reach considerable agreement on the relative quality of the papers they were judging, but they do not indicate whether readers are evaluating the same features of writing or are attending to different features when making decisions to assign a specific score to writing samples that require different approaches to the task (e.g., comparison and contrast versus chart or graph). In fact, the readers did report that the overall writing performance of candidates on the chart or graph topics was not as high in quality as performance on the comparison-and-contrast topics.
- The means of the writing-sample scores reflected consistent level differences for the three language groups for whom English is not the primary language. For every writing-sample score, the means were lowest for the Arabic sample, in the middle for the Chinese sample, and highest for the Spanish sample.
- A principal-axes factor analysis with varimax rotations of holistic scores and TOEFL section scores resulted in a two-factor solution. The two factors appear to be method factors, one consisting of scores on the three sections of TOEFL and the other of holistic scores on papers written in response to the four topics. One interpretation of the two factors suggests that performance on measures of English-language proficiency becomes more differentiated when these measures require a candidate to respond by applying different cognitive processes—recognition versus production.
- The holistic ratings assigned by subject matter professors to subsamples of the papers were highly correlated (.82–.92) with the holistic scores assigned during the regular scoring session. This outcome supports the assumption that general agreement exists, even when not formally identified and verbalized, concerning standards for academic writing competence.
- A comparison of the relationships of writing-sample and TOEFL mean scores showed that the pattern of means across the three language groups is highly consistent. The correlations between the holistic score total and the TOEFL total suggest that the two measures are evaluating English proficiency to a very high degree but that the overlap is not perfect. Thus the writing samples contribute additional information concerning the English proficiency of

candidates. In addition, the relationships of the writing-sample score with other sections of the TOEFL are consistent with the degree of relationship among the TOEFL sections.

- When the holistic writing-sample scores, averaged over four topics, were related to scores on item types within the sections of the GRE General test, the pattern of correlations observed was consistent with relationships reported in other GRE studies. Specifically, the analytical reasoning and logical reasoning scores were not highly correlated (.24), and the analytical reasoning items were more highly correlated with the quantitative items (.35–.50) than were the logical reasoning items (low, insignificant correlations). On the other hand, the logical reasoning items were more highly correlated with the verbal items (.59–.67) than were the analytical reasoning items (.17–.24). The holistic scores were more highly correlated (.64) with the logical reasoning items than with the analytical reasoning items (.23) and had relatively high correlations (.67–.70) with the verbal items. This last result indicates that the holistic scores, as expected, reflect verbal ability.

Overall, the results of the study indicated that with careful topic selection and adequate training of raters, the writing performance of nonnative speakers of English can be evaluated reliably. The writing sample scores are substantially related to other measures of language proficiency, such as the TOEFL or GRE verbal scores, but they also measure some separate ability that is not tapped by the recognition measures. Writing performance clearly differed across language groups, just as TOEFL performance differs across language groups. However, there is no evidence that writing samples discriminate unfairly against any group.

Ultimately, the utility of writing samples as a complement of the TOEFL will not be established until it is demonstrated that scores on the samples are related to other indicators of readiness to handle the writing tasks actually assigned in American postsecondary institutions. This longer-range goal will be a task for future research. We recommend a series of validation studies to determine the representatives of writing samples as predictors of performance on writing tasks in different academic contexts. Alternative predictor measures, for example, may be more appropriate to, and require particular writing skills in, certain specific academic situations but not others.

Research on the development of the writing process and the evaluation of the products of that process is in a period of discovery. Well-designed studies will eventually yield more substantive information about how the various parameters we have described influence writing and its assessment and how these factors might affect ESL students differentially. Until we can design writing assessment tools with more confidence, all individuals who apply writing measures to decisions regarding ESL students should be cognizant of the numerous variables that condition the interpretation of their results. Although comparable considerations are taken into account for both ESL students and students for whom English is the primary language, the writing of ESL students contributes an additional dimension to the developing definition and evaluation of writing competence.

NOTES

1. The study described in this section was funded by the Test of English as a Foreign Language (TOEFL) program at Educational Testing Service. The subsequent and current research described in later sections has been funded jointly by the TOEFL program and by the Graduate Record Examinations (GRE) Board.
2. See the following works by Robert B. Kaplan: "The Anatomy of Rhetoric," "Contrastive Rhetoric: Some Hypotheses," "Contrastive Rhetoric: Some Implications," and "A Further Note on Contrastive Rhetoric."

REFERENCES

Blanton, Linda Lanon. "ESP: Benefits for All of ESL." *English for Special Purposes* 64 (1982): 6–7.
Breland, Hunter M., and Robert J. Jones. *Perceptions of Writing Skill.* ETS RR No. 82–47. Princeton, N.J.: Educational Testing Service, 1982.
Bridgeman, Brent, and Sybil Carlson. *Survey of Academic Writing Tasks Required of Graduate and Undergraduate Foreign Students.* ETS RR No. 83–18. Princeton, N.J.: Educational Testing Service, 1983.
Buckingham, Thomas. "The Goals of Advanced Composition Instruction." *TESOL Quarterly* 13 (1979): 241–54.
Canale, Michael, and Merrill Swain. *Communicative Approaches to Second Language Teaching and Testing.* Ontario: Ontario Ministry of Education, 1979.
Carlson, Sybil, Brent Bridgeman, Roberta Camp, and Janet Waanders. *Relationship of Admissions Test Scores to Writing Performance of Native and Nonnative Speakers of English.* TOEFL Research Report No. 19. Princeton, N.J.: Educational Testing Service, 1985.
Cherry, Lorinda L., Mary L. Fox, Lawrence T. Frase, Patricia S. Gingrich, Stacy A. Keenan, and Nina H. MacDonald. "Computer Aids for Test Analysis." *Bell Laboratories Record* May-June 1983.
Cronbach, Lee J. "Test Validation." *Educational Measurement.* Ed. Robert L. Thorndike. Washington, D.C.: American Council on Education, 1971. 443–507.
Diederich, Pual B., John W. French, and Sydell T. Carlton. *Factors in Judgments of Writing Ability.* ETS RB No. 61–15. Princeton, N.J.: Educational Testing Service, 1961.
Dubin, Fraida, and Elite Olshtain. "The Interface of Writing and Reading." *TESOL Quarterly* 14 (1980): 353–63.
Eskey, David E. "Meanwhile, Back in the Real World . . . : Accuracy and Fluency in Second Language Teaching." *TESOL Quarterly* 17 (1983): 315–23.
Freedman, Sarah Warschauer. "How Characteristics of Student Essays Influence Teachers' Evaluations." *Journal of Educational Psychology* 71 (1979): 328–38.

Greenberg, Karen L. "Some Relationships between Writing Tasks and Students' Writing Performance." *The Writing Instructor* 2 (1982): 7–14.

Hill, Susan S., Betty F. Soppelsa, and Gregory K. West. "Teaching ESL Students to Read and Write Experimental-Research Papers." *TESOL Quarterly* 16 (1982): 333–47.

Jacobs, Holly L., Stephen A. Zinkgraf, Deanna R. Wormuth, V. Faye Hartfiel, and Jane B. Hughey. *Testing ESL Composition: A Practical Approach.* Rowley, Mass.: Newbury House, 1981.

Johns, Ann M. "Cohesion in Written Business Discourse: Some Contrasts." *ESP Journal* 1 (1980): 35–44.

———. "Necessary English: A Faculty Survey." *TESOL Quarterly* 15 (1981): 51–57.

Kaplan, Robert B. "The Anatomy of Rhetoric: Prolegomena to a Functional Theory of Rhetoric." *Language and the Teacher: A Series in Applied Linguistics.* Philadelphia: Center for Curriculum Development, 1972. Vol. 8.

———. "Contrastive Rhetoric: Some Hypotheses." *ITL* 39–40 (1977): 61–72.

———. "Contrastive Rhetoric: Some Implications for the Writing Process." *Learning to Write: First Language, Second Language.* Ed. Ian Pringle, Aviva Freedman, and Janice Yalden. London: Longman, 1982. 139–61.

———. "Cultural Thought Patterns in Inter-cultural Education." *Language Learning* 16 (1966): 1–20.

———. "A Further Note on Contrastive Rhetoric." *Communication Quarterly* 14.2 (1976): 12–19.

Kiefer, Kathleen E., and Charles R. Smith. "Textual Analysis with Computers: Tests of Bell Laboratories' Computer Software." *Research in the Teaching of English* 17 (1983): 201–14.

Kroll, Barbara. "A Survey of the Writing Needs of Foreign and American College Freshmen." *English Language Teaching Journal* 33 (1979): 219–26.

Lay, Nancy Duke S. "Composing Processes of Adult ESL Learners: A Case Study." *TESOL Quarterly* 16 (1982): 406.

Lindstrom, Margaret W. "Native Speaker Reactions to Stylistic Errors in Writing: An Error Evaluation." Diss. Colorado State, 1981.

Lloyd-Jones, Richard. "Skepticism about Test Scores." *Notes from the National Testing Network in Writing* Oct. 1982: 3, 9.

Munby, John. *Communicative Syllabus Design.* Cambridge, Eng.: Cambridge UP, 1978.

Odell, Lee. "Defining and Assessing Competence in Writing." *The Nature and Measurement of Competency in English.* Ed. Charles R. Cooper. Urbana, Ill.: National Council of Teachers of English, 1981. 95–138.

Ostler, Shirley E. "A Survey of Academic Skills in the Low-Level ESL Class." *TESOL Quarterly* 14 (1981): 489–502.

Pearson, Christine R. "Advanced Academic Skills in the Low-Level ESL Class." *TESOL Quarterly* 15 (1981): 413–23.

Quellmalz, Edys S., Frank J. Capell, and Chih-ping Chou. "Effects of Discourse Mode and Response Mode on the Measurement of Writing Competence." *Journal of Educational Measurement* 19 (1982): 241–58.

Quintanilla, Richard. "Articulating ESL Instruction in New York City High Schools and CUNY." *Selected Papers from the 1982 Conference "New York Writes."* Ed. Barry Kwalick, Marcia Silver, and Virginia Slaughter. New York: City U of New York Instructional Resource Center, 1983.

Richards, J. "Rhetorical and Communicative Styles in the New Varieties of English." *Language Learning* 29 (1979): 1–26.

Selinker, Larry, Mary Todd-Trimble, and Louis Trimble. "Rhetorical Function-Shifts in EST Discourse." *TESOL Quarterly* 12 (1978): 311–20.

Shaughnessy, Mina P. *Errors and Expectations.* New York: Oxford UP, 1977.

Spack, Ruth, and Catherine Sadow. "Student-Teacher Working Journals in ESL Freshman Composition." *TESOL Quarterly* 17 (1983): 575–93.

Swineford, Frances. "Test Analysis, Advanced Placement Examination in American History, Form MBP." ETS SR No. 53. Princeton, N.J.: Educational Testing Service, 1964.

Taylor, Barry P. "Content and Written Form: A Two-Way Street." *TESOL Quarterly* 15: (1981): 5–13.

———. "Teaching ESL: A Communicative, Student-centered Approach: Student Initiative in the ESL Class." 16th annual ESL convention. Honolulu, May 1982.

Thompson-Panos, Karyn, and Marie Thomas-Ruzic. "The Least You Should Know about Arabic: Implications for the ESL Writing Instructor." *TESOL Quarterly* 17 (1983): 609–23.

Walz, Joel C. *Error Correction Techniques for the Foreign Language Classroom.* Washington, D.C.: Center for Applied Linguistics, 1982.

Weaver, Barbara T. "Contemporary Testing and Writing Program Development." *Notes from the National Testing Network in Writing* Oct. 1982: 13.

West, Gregory K. "Engineering Faculty Evaluations of Foreign Graduate Student Writing." Gainesville, Fla.: U of Florida, ms.

———, and Patricia Byrd. "Technical Writing Required of Graduate Engineering Students." *Journal of Technical Writing and Communication* 12 (1982): 1–6.

Widdowson, H. G. "An Approach to Teaching Scientific English Discourse." *RELC Journal* 5.1 (1974): 27–40.

Wiseman, Stephen. "The Marking of English Composition in Grammar School Selection." *British Journal of Educational Psychology* 19 (1949): 200–09.

11

How Do We Judge What They Write?

ROSEMARY HAKE

INTRODUCTION

With the "process, not product" focus of current research in written expression, little attention has been given to audience process. Why is the receiver component of the classical rhetorical trivium (sender ⟷ message ⟷ receiver) so neglected? We know too little about the perceptions of the receiver; we have paid too little attention to what the audience does when it not only receives the message but also evaluates it.

That "what" depends on one of the most pervasive but elusive phenomena in our lives: judgment. Although judgment is obviously important, we know very little about it. Much research is needed (Einhorn 88) to deal with important questions like these: Can judges reproduce their own judgments? Are they consistent in using a particular strategy? Do they, given the same information, agree with one another? Are there systematic emphases in their judgments? Do they ever violate their own strategies?

Not only do these questions go unanswered, but, too often, they are unasked by researchers in writing who judge the writer's performance. Because a writing performance should reflect a writer's competence, anyone who attempts to elicit and judge that competence should heed Noam Chomsky's warning: the identifiable characteristics of a performance may not reveal an underlying competence, for performance is only what is observable, while competence is what is possible. Though language performance may only be a probable representation of one's competence, it is the only representation we have, and, for this reason, researchers have to be sure that the writing performance they elicit and judge represents the writing ability they hope to reveal.

Though most researchers recognize the complexity of the composing process for the writer, too many have ignored the process by which judges of writing reconstruct a piece of written prose. Too often grader training—epitomized by the "socializing of graders" procedure so popular with holistic judgments—has been concerned with making graders alike, or at least appearing alike, rather than with investigating their differences. When these differences are camouflaged or ignored, information that may lead to important findings goes undetected. It is these graders' differences, which I have observed and investigated as I have worked with graders, that cause me to make an important recommendation about the nature of the text given to writers.

At California State University I have been exploring compulsory essay exams designed to elicit personal experience responses. Such exams are enormously popular all over the country. However, the nature of an assessment based on personal experience can produce unintended results from readers. It is for this reason that topics and instructions for personal experience papers must elicit expository essays that *incorporate* narrative rather than essays that are pure narratives.

Although both narration and exposition could deal with personal experience, there is between them the distinct discourse difference that James Kinneavy has detailed. Pure narration is Kinneavy's expressive discourse, while exposition that incorporates narration is his persuasive discourse. It is, however, the essay's rhetorical features that clearly distinguish these differences. In exposition that incorporates narration, the writer makes an assertion early in the essay and then illustrates that assertion with personal experience. In pure narration, the writer does not state an assertion but rather may or may not imply it while describing a personal experience. (See the sample essays at the end of this chapter.)

The proposal—based on my findings that narrations are more likely to be misgraded than expositions that incorporate narrations—deserves serious consideration because so often topics on compulsory examinations require the test taker to draw on personal experience. There is a humane reason why this is so: the assumption that a writer needs to know the topic if he or she is to write about it. However, just as a writer needs to feel comfortable with a topic to perform competently, a reader also needs to feel comfortable with the topic to perform competently. Perhaps we might assume that just as the writer created the essay when writing it, the grader re-creates the essay when reading it. We might also assume, if we were to build on Walter Ong's proposition, that if the audience doesn't fit into the writer's fiction, that audience could easily misinterpret and misjudge the writer's presentation.

The assertion that an audience—a grader—could reasonably misjudge a writer's performance if unfamiliar or uncomfortable with the writer's presentation is reinforced by the "schema" assumptions underlying current research in reading. Lynne Reder suggests that a reader reconstructs meaning from a written passage only to the extent that "prior knowledge" gives the reader a "framework" for understanding whatever is being described or argued. The reading researchers are attempting to investigate reader comprehension and its causes, while I am interested in investigating reader (in my case, grader) miscomprehension and its causes. However, the assumption about the reader's "framework" underlies both their work and mine.

INITIAL OBSERVATIONS

My first hint that graders responded to pure narration differently from narration incorporated into expositions was prompted by data from the diagnostic and exit exams for first-term composition classes at Chicago State University and California State University at Los Angeles.[1] All the topics were personal experience topics, but some elicited pure narrations, while others elicited expositions that incorporated narrations. The narrations produced a greater grader variance than the expositions.[2]

Topics such as the following elicited pure narrations:

1. Tell us about an event that taught you something.
2. Things people do frequently tell about what the people are like. Write an essay in which you analyze one character trait of a person you know quite well.
3. How has a person changed your life?
4. How has someone involved with school (a classmate, teacher, or counselor) helped you?
5. Our closest friends and relatives sometimes display habits or attitudes that embarrass us or make us uncomfortable. Describe such a habit or attitude in a person you know.

Students did not respond to the topic with a stated assertion early in the essay. They merely described a single personal experience. On the other hand, topics such as the following elicited expositions that incorporated narration:

6. What is something that is work for you but play for another?
7. What are two or three things that you do better or worse than your boss?
8. How are family pressures on oldest and youngest children different?
9. Did you, as a high school student, find it necessary, comforting, dangerous, or dumb (choose one) to become part of a group?
10. How can your neighborhood serve as a model in the best or worst neighborhood contest?[3]

Students responded with an assertion stated early in the essay and then illustrated that assertion with personal experience.

On topics 1 through 5, students responded by simply telling a story. On topics 6 through 10, students responded by using a story or stories to support an assertion. This assertive focus forced the writers to develop their essays in the expository thesis and support format, even though they could and did expand the exposition with narrative examples. On exposition topics, writers created a thesis to provide a framework into which the reader could fit the example narrations. But the pure narrations had either no thesis or only an implied thesis. Therefore, in order to react to the written performance, the reader had to construct a framework; the grader had to create the thesis—from the topic or from a personal response to the topic.[4]

We might expect that graders will, in general, find fewer or tolerate more flaws in discourses they like and find more or tolerate fewer flaws in discourses they dislike. But the Chicago State and Cal State data encourage the speculation that varied responses are more probable in essays that are purely narrative and less probable in essays that incorporate narrations into expositions.

THEORY AND PRACTICE

Both theoretically and practically, it is important to account for how the units in the writing are perceived, measured, and evaluated. These tasks demand a useful measurement model and a reasonable discourse model. The measurement model I propose assumes what Georg Rasch asserts in *The Poisson Process as a Model for a Diversity of Behavioral Phenomena*. It is possible, by comparing an individual with other individuals in a similar situation, to identify a system in an individual's behavior. With the Rasch model, it is also possible to identify when an individual—in this case a grader—is not behaving systematically. The discourse model I propose is Jean Piaget's: a whole (which generates its parts) has external relationships that influence the internal parts. With Piaget's model, it is possible to explain why a judge who brings an external relationship to an essay may create a whole different from the writer's whole and, as a result, may misjudge the essay's internal parts.

The Rasch model is based on the assumption that people may not be consistent among themselves but that they are usually consistent within themselves and that consistency is observable when one compares individuals' performances in identical situations. Simply, the model identifies a grader's behavior by comparing the grader with other graders. Graders are asked to observe the same performances—in our case, essays—and classify what they have observed—in our case, flaws in the essays. What we find as different graders classify the flaws they observe in the same essays is hardly surprising: some see more flaws than others, some see the same flaws as others but identify them differently, and some have different thresholds of tolerance from others, but all seem to have pretty good reasons for what they observe and judge.

The observation framework designed to help graders categorize or classify what they observe is based on Piaget's assertion that a whole generates its parts. (The framework used in this study appears at the end of this chapter, following the sample essays.) The framework moves the grader from dimension 1, the flaws in the whole essay, through dimensions 2, 3, and 4, the flaws in the parts of the essay. Some may consider the observation framework flawed in that it seeks the vices in writing, not its possible virtues. There is, however, a theoretical reason for constructing the framework in this way.

The outstanding flaw theory concerns the relation of wholes and parts. Just as I assume that there must be a conception of the whole before a writer can generate functioning parts, I also assume that graders have a conceptualization of the essay as a whole; and because they have some idea of what they think a whole essay should contain, they can identify what it doesn't contain, that is, what necessary parts are missing. If the grader expects the essay to have meaningful, logical, and correct connections in its paragraphs, sentences, and words, the essay, made up of integrated parts, should have harmony among those parts. Becuase breaks in harmony cause blocks in communication, a flaw is likely to be a conspicuous feature for the grader.

This assumption can be explained by Platonic philosophy as translated by medieval theologians: a wrong, or a flaw, is not an entity in and of itself but is the absence of a right. With this principle, the flaw can be identified either through exclusion—the absence of what should be present—or inclusion—not only the absence of what should be present but the presence of an inappropriate alternative. In other words, the essay doesn't have something it should have, it has something it shouldn't, or both.

Drawing on the outstanding flaw theory, we ask graders in our program to read each essay twice, the first time to judge the whole essay in terms of whether it has a clear central idea that is reasonable and sufficiently developed and the second time to circle flaws and categorize them with marks in the columns at the right. After reading the paper a second time and recording each observed flaw, the grader makes an overall holistic judgment of good, competent, or incompetent.[5]

No a priori judgment is made on the performance the graders observe. Instead, the specifics they observe and how those specifics compare with the holistic judgments they make are compared.

As we compare the specifics that the graders observe, we find that these graders lie along a spectrum from harsh (the grader who observes the most flaws in the sample group) to lenient (the grader who observes the fewest flaws in the samples). Other graders fall between these points, and we can calculate a mean or an average on that spectrum:

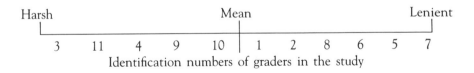

Harsh					Mean						Lenient
3	11	4	9	10		1	2	8	6	5	7

Identification numbers of graders in the study

Quite simply, we calibrate a grader's observations in much the way one calibrates the difficulty of a test item by observing the test takers' responses to that item: the easier the item, the more correct responses to it; the more difficult the item, the fewer correct responses to it. In our case, the harsher the graders, the greater their responses to the essay; the more lenient the graders, the fewer their responses to the essay. (Actually, we calibrate the graders' responses in each dimension of the essay.)

In the hustle and bustle of practical application at Cal State–LA, where we have a pool of 78 graders and give 2500 to 3000 exams each quarter, the system is quite efficient. We merely subtract a proportionate number of flaws from the graders above the mean and add a proportionate number of flaws to those below it. In other words, as in golf and bowling, we handicap the graders. As a result, we judge the essay irrespective of the person who graded it. Because we can compare one grader's numerical and holistic judgment with the consensus judgment of all graders, it is easy to spot an essay judged differently from what the group would have judged. In this sense, the essay does not fit the model and has to be regraded.[6] Fortunately, as we regrade we can see precisely what the previous grader had observed and how that grader classified the observations. Also, we can compare the grader with himself or herself by comparing each essay he or she has graded. If in one or two instances the grader's judgments are significantly above or below that grader's position on the spectrum, we say the grader does not fit the model; the grader does not come within the number of flaws that the statistical model predicts that grader would find. When there is a change in a grader's behavior with respect to a particular essay—when the grader violates his usual strategies for judgment—we consider the essay misgraded. And again, we can see precisely what the grader observed and how those observations were classified.

THE STUDY

I used 10 randomly chosen personal experience essays, all responses to the 10 example topics. Five were pure narrations of a single personal experience, and five were expositions that incorporated narrations, writers developing an assertion by means of personal experience (see sample essays). The essays were part of two grading sessions, one in Chicago and one in Los Angeles. There were 11 graders: 5 from Chicago and 6 from Los Angeles; 4 were high school teachers and 7 college teachers. The graders were informed of the topics and the test instructions and were also told that the writers had completed one course in college composition.

The results of the study were revealing. They are summarized in Table 1. Only 2 of the 11 graders, graders 4 and 6, did not misgrade. None of the personal experience expositions was misgraded. But it is more than significant—in fact, it is astounding—that, in 12 instances, 4 out of the 5 pure narrations were misgraded.[7] The details are shown in Table 2.

Essay 10 (topic: "How has someone involved with school helped you?") had the largest portion of misgradings: 5. These were graders 1, 2, 5, 7, and 11. Though the graders were more lenient than we would anticipate, none was particularly lenient on one dimension but generally lenient on all three

Table 1 Essays Misgraded

Grader	Essay

Grader	1N	2E	3N	4E	5N	6N	7E	8E	9E	10N
1										x
2										x
3			x		x					
4										
5					x					x
6										
7										x
8						x				
9					x					
10						x				
11					x					x

N = Narrative essay; E = Expository essay.

Table 2 Misgradings

Essay	Graders	Flaws expected	Flaws observed
10	1	13	6
	2	11	5
	5	8	3
	7	7	3
	11	14	6
5	3	17	32
	5	11	4
	9	12	6
	11	16	8
6	8	9	20
	10	13	4
3	3	10	19

functioning dimensions. For grader 1, we anticipated 13 flaws but received 6; for grader 2, we expected 11 but received 5; and for grader 5, we expected 8 but received 4. For grader 7, the most lenient grader, we predicted 7 flaws but received only 3; and for grader 11, we predicted 14 flaws but received 6. The graders seemed particularly sympathetic to the narration about a young Vietnamese being helped by a counselor's aide through a very trying personal experience (see the sample essay on page 163.).

Essay 5 (topic: "How has a person changed your life?"), which fit the statistical model least, is a narration in which a young girl tells of becoming pregnant, having the baby, and then being deserted by the baby's father. She now feels both responsible to and frustrated by the child. This essay received a mixed reaction; it was graded more harshly than predicted by one grader and more leniently by three others. We expected grader 3, a young woman who is divorced and supports herself and her young son, to find 17 flaws, but she found 32. Of these she found not the predicted 10 in dimension 4, mechanics, but 24—all commas, some in places where commas couldn't possibly exist. This grader was our harshest, but she was harsher even than we could predict. Grader 5, a young man from whom we expected 11 flaws, found 4 flaws, only 1 in dimension 4, mechanics. He ignored dialect differences, which he did count as flaws on other essays, and found no punctuation flaws at all. Two other graders, 9 and 11, both men, were more lenient than we predicted. For grader 9 we predicted 12 flaws but received 6; for grader 11, we predicted 16 flaws but received 8.

Essay 6 (topic: "Our closest friends and relatives sometimes display habits or attitudes that embarrass us or make us uncomfortable. Describe such a habit or attitude in a person you know.") also received mixed reactions. Grader 8 was harsher than predicted, grader 10 more lenient. This narration, which describes the writer's husband's "sloppy smoking," depicts the "ugly habit" as both "unhealthful and embarrassing." From grader 8, whom I later found out was a smoker, we expected 9 flaws; he observed 20. From grader 10, a nonsmoker, we expected 13 flaws; she found 4.

Essay 3 (topic: "Tell us about an event that taught you something.") was graded more harshly than we expected by grader 3. In this narration, the writer, a young woman, is just starting out on her own and depicts some harsh realities. Grader 3, much used to functioning on her own, appears to have had little sympathy for the situation and found 19 flaws; we expected her to identify 10.

CONCLUSIONS

On the basis of these findings, we may more than tentatively conclude that personal experience expositions that incorporate narrations will be more objectively graded than pure narrations that describe personal experience. When we consider current compulsory exams, we must decide if we want evidence of the writer's skill or if we want evidence that the writer's essay fits the grader's framework. If we do want to measure a writer's skill and we continue to encourage writers to use personal experience when they write, we should certainly create topics and test directions that elicit expository narrations rather than pure narrations.

Another viable conclusion in this study, though, is the usefulness of the Rasch model in identifying and accounting for graders' differences and the reasonableness of Piaget's model in explaining them. Moreover, the data of the study suggest an important reason why the holistic rating system for grading essays can be inadequate; namely, even similarly trained graders see different elements in the same essays, particularly in pure narratives. When graders convert their observations into judgments, their ratings can show intolerably large discrepancies.

Because we can see in holistic ratings only final judgments and not the specifics in those judgments, we have no way to answer important questions vexing researchers who want to trace ability changes in writers. Both Carol Sweedler Brown of San Diego State University and Frank Sullivan of Temple University have observed a change in graders' rating thresholds when raters considered essays as placement exams or as exit exams.[8] Brown found that students exiting a course received ratings lower than their entering ratings but were, in all graders' opinions, writing better essays. Sullivan observed that graders observed the same specifics but gave lower ratings when the essay was labeled "exit" and higher ratings when the essay was labeled "entrance." In other words, the graders observed the same flaws but judged flaws in terms of outside circumstances. In both cases, it would be difficult to trace improvement when better essays are rated lower because of the circumstances of the judgment and not the intrinsic qualities of the essay. It is much easier to trace improvement when flaws—reported irrespective of the observer—in an essay decrease.

Other questions plague researchers trying to identify and account for variances in the judgments of people in different disciplines. Take, for example, the interesting observations of Muffy Seigel of Temple University and Barbara Weaver of Anderson College as they have researched the responses of graders in different disciplines.[9] In Seigel's data, there was a similarity in the graders' holistic ratings, but graders from disciplines other than English indicated specifics very different from those noted by English teachers. In Weaver's data there is not only a difference between the specifics both groups noted but a wide difference in their holistic ratings. In my current research I have observed divergent responses to the same pieces from lawyers representing different areas of specialization in the law. Lawyers specializing in constitutional law, who observe the same five briefs, give not only identical ratings but also observe almost identical specifics in the briefs. Lawyers specializing in personal injury law observe, in the same five briefs, widely different specifics and give widely varying holistic ratings.

All of the intersting and important research questions these tentative findings raise go unanswered if we concentrate on trying to make graders alike rather than attempting to identify and account for their differences.

SAMPLE ESSAYS

Both of these essays are taken from the exit exams of first-term composition classes at California State University at Los Angeles. The first sample is essay 4 in the study. Like all exposition papers reported on here, this one was not misgraded. The second sample is essay 10 in the study, the essay with the largest portion of misgradings.

Exposition Incorporating Narration

Many neighborhoods throughout the city of LA are beautiful, well organized and respectable places. On the other hand there are some neighborhoods which can use a tremendous amount of cleaning up and construction. I happen to live in East LA and my neighborhood is one of the unfortunate ones, it can serve as the model for one of the worst neighborhoods in the city.

When I first moved to East LA in 1977 the neighborhood wasn't as filthy as today. The streets and houses were very clean and there wouldn't be many youngsters creatin problems. The neighborhood was filled with vegitation, from flowers of all textures and colors to many species of trees. The parks were always visited by people young and old.

In the 1980's many changes have taken place in our neighborhood, mainly toward the bad side. Many gangs have formed in our neighborhood which only leed to trouble and destruction. For example there was a situation were one of my friends wanted to get out of a gang. He didn't want to be like them, dope attics and trouble makers. The gang members came after him with clubs and nives; he had to be hospitalized in critical condition. Furthermore, they burned his house and beat up his brother. The police have no evidence for convicting them. They are still running around in the streets.

My neighborhood doesn't look livable anymore. The walls and some of the houses have been ruined by means of graffitti. Everywhere I go in East LA I will find buildings which have been scribbled on and destroyed. Furthermore, the parks are scary and filthy. The flowers are gone. The buildings smell bad. All of the equipments in the playground are broken. All of the grounds are littered.

I'm not saying that my neighborhood is in the worst but it sure comes very close. Even though my neighborhood is improving by means of construction and painting, it might not win the worst neighborhood contest but it sure can serve as a model for contest enterers.

Pure Narration

When I first came to the United States it was September 1979. The schools began to open everywhere. I was a junior in the high school even though I did not know English at all. I was very bashful and afraid about my new environment.

The first day in the school, I just stood in one place. I dared not move around I watched the other students talking, laughing and playing to each other. I felt very lonely. I thought that I was ignored and no body wanted to make friend with me. I missed my old friend and old teacher very much in that time. I wanted to go back my country immediately.

The bell rang. Everybody had to go to his classroom. My hand kept my schedule but I did not know where to go. It was a big high school which compared to mine. Therefore, I went back to counseling office and asked for help.

After fifteen minutes, there was a girl who went with my counsellor. They were taling and walking toward me. Then the girl spoke to me by Vietnamese. She said she would help me with the English. She would translate everything which the teachers said in the classes and help me how to do the homework. I was very glad to have her as my first friend.

Her name was Van Le Thanh. She was a really good student. She finished almost the advanced classes in the school. She had only three classes. The remainder of the time, she was a teacher's assistance.

She was with me in English and history classes. She sat beside me. When the teachers explained something, she took notes for me. Also I needed to take notes. If I missed some parts, she would give and explain her notes to me. She had not to be with me in math, chemistry and typing classes, because those classes did not need much English.

Besides the English and history classes, sometimes I needed her help in other classes. She was happy to do that.

She usually smiled when she explained something to me. If I did not understand, she would be happy to explain it again. She tried to help me as much as she could.

I really impoved when she was with me. After one semester, my counsllor thought that I could stand by myself and did not need any more help. Therefore she went backto the counseling office to help the other students. Although she did not help me any more, we still talked, played and shopped together. If I had some problems, I still could ask her. She was very glad to do that.

She was the best friend I ever had. I really learned very much from her. She was always nice to me and every body. I was lucky to have her as my first friend in the United States.

Note the distinct differences:

1. Essay length—narration, 460 words; exposition, 368 words
2. Sentence length—narration, 12.3 words per *t* unit; exposition, 10.2 words per *t* unit (mean counts)
3. Clause inclusion—narration, 17 dependent clauses; exposition, 7 dependent clauses

This fascinating lengthening and shortening, as the writers moved through different levels of discourse, has not escaped notice.[10]

OBSERVATION FRAMEWORK USED IN THE REPORTED STUDY

Dimension 1: Essay Development. The essay is flawed because
A. It does not focus on a central idea
B. It does not develop its central idea with sufficient detail
C. It is not well organized

Dimension 2: Paragraph Development. The paragraph is flawed because
A. A new paragraph should or should not begin
B. It needs a topic sentence
C. It does not develop its topic
D. It develops more than one topic
E. It is poorly organized
F. It needs transition from the preceding paragraph or to the following paragraph

Dimension 3: Sentence Development. The sentence is flawed because
A. Its content is faulty—illogical, contradictory, irrelevant, vague
B. Its style is faulty—repetitious, unclear, awkward, clichéd, trite
C. It needs transition from the preceding sentence or to the following sentence

Dimension 4: Mechanics
A. The usage is faulty
   1. Sentence mechanics: run-on or fragment
   2. Verb mechanics
      a. Verb-subject agreement
      b. Incorrect verb form
      c. Improper tense, mood, or voice
   3. Pronoun mechanics
      a. No or unclear antecedent
      b. Faulty agreement with antecedent
      c. Improper case
      d. Improper shift in person
   4. Noun mechanics

      a. No or incorrect plural form

      b. No or incorrect possessive form

    5. Modifier mechanics

      a. Incorrect comparative or superlative

      b. Adjective used as adverb

      c. Dangling participle

      d. Misplaced modifier

    6. Misspelled words

    7. Misused or missing word(s)

B. The punctuation is faulty

    1. Capital letter (unless addressed in sentence mechanics)

    2. Period (unless addressed in sentence mechanics)

    3. Comma (unless addressed in sentence mechanics)

    4. Question mark

    5. Semicolon

    6. Colon

    7. Quotation mark

    8. Apostrophe

    9. Underlining

   10. Parentheses

   11. Dash

   12. Hyphen

The testing instrument described can incorporate components different from the observation framework reported in this study. However, the dimensions in the framework do follow the discourse model and use the statistical model. The instrument is currently being employed for diagnostic and exit testing in a number of high schools, community colleges, and university writing programs, including these:

Anderson College, Anderson, Ind.; Barbara Weaver, Director

Bloom High School, Chicago Heights, Ill.; Leitha Paulson, Director

California State University, Los Angeles, Calif.; Rosemary Hake, Director

Chicago Board of Education, Time to Write Program, Chicago, Ill.; Pamela Pankey, Director

Oakton Community College, Morton Grove, Ill.; Karl Bentley, Director

Old Dominion University, Norfolk, Va.; Clare Silva, Director

Tinley Park High Schools, Tinley Park, Ill.; Marian Johnson, Director

Triton Community College, River Grove, Ill.; Lallie Coy, Director

The instrument is being initiated on an experimental level at the following schools:

Los Angeles Community College, Los Angeles, Calif.; Virginia Fick, Director

San Diego State University, San Diego, Calif.; Don Basile and Carol Sweedler, Co-directors

Temple University, Philadelphia, Pa.; Frank Sullivan, Director

These institutions have developed observation frameworks with different components in each of the dimensions used in essay grading. We, too, at CSU-LA have different components in the different writing courses.

NOTES

1. These classes rely a great deal on personal experience writing because they, like so many first-term compulsory composition courses, deal primarily with illustrative discourse rather than argumentative discourse.

2. The grader variances are identified by the computer, which acts, in a sense, as a second grader. The computer first calibrates each grader, than compares the grader's decision to a consensus decision. The variances are (a) an *anomaly* (the essay would have received credit in dimension 1, the structural parts of the essay, but would have no credit in dimensions 2, 3, and 4, the functional parts of the essay; or the essay would have received no credit in dimension 1 but credit in dimensions 2, 3, and 4) and (b) a *disagreement* (the essay received a credit from the grader, but the consensus judgment would have given it no credit; or the essay received no credit from the grader but would have received a credit from the consensus judgment).

3. Topics 1, 3, 7, and 9 were gleaned from Chicago State University's exams; topics 4, 6, 8, and 10 from California State University at Los Angeles's exams; topics 2 and 5 from the statewide English Placement Test, which is required of all applicants to the California State University system.

4. This speculation may hardly be news to those of us who have done any analytical work in literature. One need only contrast the number of seminars and conference meetings that investigate what short story writers mean with the number of seminars and conference meetings investigating what essay writers mean.

5. For information on calculating numerical cutoffs for good, competent, and incompetent test performance, see Hake; Wright and Masters; and Wright and Stone.

6. For a more complete explanation of statistical misfit, see Andrich and Hake.

7. The chi-square test is significant at the 2 percent level.

8. Both of these observations are unpublished; however, Sullivan's findings will be reported soon in Temple University's *Working Papers in Composition.*

9. At this writing, Weaver's impressive data (from Anderson College, Anderson, Ind.) are still being collected and analyzed.

10. Joseph Williams and I report on this phenomenon in "Syntactic Maturity, Discourse Difficulty, and Cognitive Ability," *Sentence Combining: A Rhetorical Perspective*, ed. Donald Daiker, Andrew Kerek, and Max Morenberg (Carbondale, Ill.: Southern Illinois UP, 1985).

REFERENCES

Andrich, David, and Rosemary Hake. "The Application of a Discourse Theory and a Rasch Model for Measuring in the Evaluation of Written Expression." *Education Research and Perspectives* 2 (1974): 51–61.

Chomsky, Noam. *Language and Mind.* Orlando, Fla.: Harcourt Brace Jovanovich, 1968.

Einhorn, Hillel. "Expert Measurement and Mechanical Combinations." *Organizational Behavior and Human Performance* 7 (1972): 86–106.

Hake, Rosemary. "With No Apology, Teaching to the Test." *Basic Writing* 1 (1978): 39–62.

Kinneavy, James L. *A Theory of Discourse: The Aims of Discourse.* New York: Norton, 1980.

Ong, Walter J. "The Writer's Audience Is Always a Fiction." *Publication of the Modern Language Association* 89 (1974): 9–15.

Piaget, Jean. *Structuralism.* New York: Basic Books, 1970.

Rasch, Georg. *The Poisson Process as a Model for a Diversity of Behavioral Phenomena.* Washington, D.C.: Institutional Congress of Psychology, 1968.

Reder, Lynne M. "The Role of Elaboration in the Comprehension and Retention of Prose: A Critical Review." *Review of Educational Research* 50 (1982): 5–33.

Siegel, Muffy. "Response to Student Writing from New Composition Faculty." *College Composition and Communication* 33 (1982): 302–09.

Wright, Benjamin, and Geofferey Masters. *Rating Scales Analysis: Rasch Measurement.* Chicago: Mesa, 1982.

———, and Mark Stone. *Best Test Design: Rasch Measurement.* Chicago: Mesa, 1979.

12

Current Research and Unanswered Questions in Writing Assessment

GORDON BROSSELL

What does research tell us about the construction and operation of writing assessment? What issues in writing assessment has research yet to address? These are fundamental questions for both theorists and practitioners—those attempting to extend the boundaries of knowledge about the measurement of writing ability and those whose task it is to design and implement assessment instruments and programs or to evaluate the progress and performance of student writers.

The growing insistence on large-scale writing assessment—indeed on academic testing—on the part of state legislatures and school systems has created a great need for reliable data on a host of factors affecting the measurement of writing skills. Bereft of the guidance of experimental research findings, testmakers are left to personal experience, hearsay, common sense, and professional wisdom. While such factors have traditionally had no mean influence on the making of writing tests, they cannot substitute for knowledge based on rigorous investigation of the specific variables inherent in assessment situations. That kind of knowledge, as well as the attempt to discover it, is the subject of this chapter.

The most extensive summary of research on writing assessment to date is that provided by Leo Ruth (*Properties of Writing Tasks*). This summary is concerned chiefly with topics and prompts (writing assignments and instructions to the writer) for writing performance tests, though it ranges necessarily into the broader field of composing behavior. Ruth reviews the sources of knowledge for designing writing prompts—psychometrics, professional wisdom, discourse theory, and research. His conclusion about research on writing prompts accurately describes the state of research of the whole of writing assessment:

A recent search of the literature conducted at the beginning of this study in the fall of 1981 confirms that there are few answers to the kinds of questions that researchers are asking about the nature of the effects of writing prompts upon performance. (Properties 63)

More recently, James Hoetker reached a similar conclusion in his review of the literature on essay examination topics. Both Hoetker and Ruth cite a number of questions that various researchers have posed as important for validating many assumptions made in theory and practice—questions about the rhetorical context of a writing prompt, the writing task presented by a prompt, the word choices elicited by certain kinds of prompts, and how writers read and interpret different prompts, among others. All these questions—and a multitude of others—are important ones demanding systematic investigation in assessment contexts. So far, however, researchers have produced only scanty data on writing task variables, often failing even to describe them in their reports, an omission Ruth decries:

The importance of including full information about the writing task variable cannot be overstated. There is a twofold loss when insufficient information is provided: It becomes impossible to make an independent judgment about the claims the researcher makes about the writing task characteristics, and it also becomes difficult to build a cumulative knowledge base about writing task properties and related effects. (Properties 65)

The cumulative knowledge base Ruth alludes to does not currently exist, though the beginnings of one are present in the widely scattered, disparate, and unsystematic research that has been done to date. What follows here is an attempt to provide a working summary of current research knowledge about writing assessment according to its major situational variables: topic variables, writer variables, and procedural variables.

TOPIC VARIABLES

Wording

Common sense alone would appear to be the only criterion necessary for determining that changes in the wording of a writing prompt make a difference in how writers read and respond to it. Certainly few composition teachers would disagree with William Harpin, a researcher who has studied writing assignments in elementary schools in Great Britain:

Substituting one word for another, though apparently a trivial change, may profoundly affect the way a child interprets the task—"Describe what you saw as you walked through the fog" gave very different results from "Describe what you felt as you walked through the fog." A similar effect is caused by the change from "What does this music make you think of?" to "What does this make you feel?" (109)

The formal assessment context is quite different from the classroom, however (though this point still eludes some people), and recent research calls into question any approach to lexical variations in writing prompts that is based solely on common sense.

Karen Greenberg studied the effects of different wording of essay examination topics on the writing of freshmen at the City University of New York. She designed four kinds of questions that varied according to the cognitive and experimental demands they placed on writers, hypothesizing that the effects of different levels of cognitive demands (demands for interpretation at the low end to evaluation at the high end) and experiential demands (demands for impersonal responses at the low end to highly personal responses at the high end) would be significant as measured by holistic scores of the essays. Specifically, Greenberg expected that low cognitive–high experiential questions would elicit essays that received significantly higher scores. None of these hypotheses was confirmed. She found no statistically significant effects for any of the variables (which included content and structural changes as well as lexical variations) on the qualitative ratings of essays or on scores for features such as syntactic complexity, errors in sentence control and word form, and essay length. Greenberg mentions four factors that may have prevented the writers in her sample from being influenced by her manipulated variables: previous training, test anxiety, the setting of the test, and lack of attention to the test instructions. Such speculations aside, the nonsignificant results of Greenberg's experiment—the first of its kind—stand in glaring contrast to the assumptions that underlie the professional wisdom attaching to composition topics.

In a study resembling Greenberg's that I conducted with Barbara Hoetker Ash, we sought to answer two specific questions about the wording of essay examination topics: Does it matter whether a topic is addressed to a writer ("you") or is couched in impersonal or neutral terms? And does it make any difference whether a topic's "charge" is cast as a question or an imperative? We combined personal and neutral manners of address with question and imperative charges to obtain different versions of topics, which we administered to freshman and sophomore students at four universities and community colleges in Florida. All statistical tests—conducted to determine whether differences in the holistic scores of the resulting student essays were attributable to any of the variables or to combinations of them—were nonsignificant. A critical reading of the essays likewise revealed little to suggest that writers had been helped or hindered by particular versions of topics. We also found that the subject matter of the topics (there were 21 different subjects) seemed of slight consequence in the judgment of the quality of the essays; we "came away feeling that as long as topics do not require special knowledge and are suited to the characteristics of the test takers, neither small syntactical variations nor subject matter has much of an effect on essay exam scores" (425). Our conclusion, like Greenberg's, contrasts sharply with conventional assumptions about the effects of lexical changes in writing prompts: "In sum, then, our study produced no evidence to support the contention that small changes in the wording of essay examination topics of otherwise similar construction affect writers or the holistic ratings given their essays" (425). What precise effects the wording of topics is likely to have on writers' understanding of topics and on their writing performance in particular assessments are not known.

Subject Matter

Clearly, what they are asked to write about makes a difference to writers, whether the context is the classroom or a writing performance test. But how much and what kind of difference are not at all certain. Ruth's NIE study includes a "philosophy of the assignment for writing assessment," which includes in its "synthesis of professional wisdom" these two injunctions for choosing subject matter:

1. The subject chosen must be potentially interesting to the teacher-reader or evaluator of the essays written.
2. The subject chosen must be potentially interesting to the student writers.

Precepts of this sort are not unhelpful, but they belie the complexity and unpredictability of the interaction of topic, writer, and context, a complexity that recent research has begun to investigate.

In developing essay examination topics for use on the Florida Teacher Certification Examination, another study in which I participated (Hoetker, Brossell, and Ash) experimented with student perceptions of writing prompts and the holistic scores given to student essays written on the same topics. We found that the popularity of the 33 individual topics field-tested, as judged by student responses to a questionnaire appended to each of the test packets, was unrelated to the scores on the essays. More to the point of the appropriateness of topics, we found that one topic that had worked successfully to elicit good writing in a college writing course was the cause of uniformly poor essays on the assessment. The apparent reason was that the topic—a "dream home"—was not at all conducive to the orderly, purposeful writing that must occur if one is to complete a timed essay test successfully. We also found that there was no difference in the mean scores of essays written on topics cast in "public" or "private" versions—topics asking for opinions on a public issue or demanding introspective reports on writers' inner lives.

Thomas Hilgers discusses the problem of unequal familiarity with content in the writing prompts used in recent composition research. Suggesting that writers' backgrounds and levels of intelligence interfere with a common understanding of writing topics, Hilgers recommends a set of procedures whereby all writers would receive enough information about a topic in order to overcome the problem of unequal familiarity. Aside from the practical difficulties of carrying out such routines in practical assessment contexts (something he notes in his report), Hilgers does not heed the fact that standard procedures for prompt development—screening and field testing—work to solve the sort of problem that concerns him. For example, we (Hoetker, Brossell, and Ash) eliminated the "dream house" topic (as well as two other topics) from our recommended test topic battery because it did not work well for writers in our sample. Good topics must match the characteristics of the writers who use them, and testmakers should identify and investigate writers' characteristics, such as previous training, education, cultural distinctions, and gender. Research knowledge of this kind can help testmakers to produce topics that are as uniform as those containing the additional information Hilgers would provide.

Mode of Discourse

Most research on modes of discourse supports both the belief that differences in syntactic complexity reflect differences in mode of discourse and the belief that narrative is apt to be less syntactically complex than argument. Studies by Perron, Rosen, San Jose, Crowhurst, and Quellmalz, Capell, and Chou are among those whose findings support this view. Although it is generally accepted that writing argument is more difficult than writing narrative, no experimental research evidence for such a difference was produced until 1981, when Freedman and Pringle found that 12- and 13-year-old students were able to realize the conventional schema for the structure of a story more successfully than the schema for the structure of an argument. Nearly all the students in their study embodied narrative structure in stories they wrote, but only 12.5 percent of them were able to embody classical argument patterns. Freedman and Pringle attributed the difference to the many opportunities students have to internalize the structure of narrative as opposed to the relatively few chances they have of doing so for the structure of argument, rather than to some inherent deficiency in understanding organization and form.

Some research on transformational sentence combining has prompted the notion that writing is generally better if it is syntactically more complex. This position has been attacked theoretically by Moffett, Holzman, and others, and recent experimental research also has discovered evidence to challenge it. Neilsen and Piche found that passages containing "mature" vocabulary were rated higher than passages containing "simple" vocabulary regardless of the level of syntactic complexity in the passages. Their data, they say, "do not confirm previous research findings which assert a relationship between syntactic complexity and quality of writing, but rather confirm other research which asserts no necessary relationship" (71). Thomas and Donlan, in a study of holistic and quantitative methods of evaluating student writing, found that the number of words in a written product was the variable most highly correlated with quality, despite the grade level of the writers. Other variables in their study included number of *t* units and words per *t* unit.

Length, then, is an important variable in writing on performance assessments. Nold and Freedman found in a study of reader response that the kind of essay affected the amount of writing produced: personal opinion topics elicited more writing and greater variation in response than did topics based on a comparison of quotations. Since all the topics in their study required writing in only one mode of discourse—argument—their results are less clouded by considerations of the differences that writing in another mode would have introduced. And those results showed that essay length was significantly correlated with essay quality. In my study of rhetorical specification in essay examination topics, I found that the effect of length on the holistic scores of essays was significant at the .001 level and that the longer an essay was in a 200- to 400-word range, the likelier it was to get a higher score. As reasons for the high correlation between length and score, I cited intrinsic motivation, previous training, willingness to use the full time limit in the assessment, and rater bias as possible contributing factors but concluded that a better explanation lies in the amount of information presented in the topics. Why some people and not others write longer and often better essays on writing assessments when topics supply (or omit) certain information is a matter for speculation and for further research.

Rhetorical Specification

Common professional wisdom suggests that people will write better if they know something about four elements of a writing task: purpose, audience, speaker, and subject—what is commonly called full rhetorical specification. Although this assumption has held for large-scale writing assessments, it has gone untested, at least until recently. I tested the hypothesis that essay examination topics providing information about all four elements—that is, having full rhetorical specification—would elicit essays judged of higher quality than those prompted by the same topics in less information-laden versions. I used three versions of six topics written at low, moderate, and high levels of "information load." The high-level versions, couched in scenario form, provided full rhetorical specification; the moderate-level versions contained a short introductory statement followed by a charge to the writer; the low-level versions were brief phrases only and left all rhetorical choices up to the writer. Moderate-level topics elicited the highest mean score. In addition, one topic ("violence in the schools") in its moderate-level version produced the highest mean score of any in the breakdown. I reported that the essays in this group were notably better than all others and speculated that the moderate-level version worked to help writers focus on the topic and to organize their essays more effectively than did the other versions. I suggested that essay examination topics providing full rhetorical specification may prevent writers from doing their best writing by inducing them to repeat given information needlessly and thus to waste time.

The question of the effect of audience on writing and on writers' perceptions has for some time been debated in the literature on composition and its teaching. Recently, Russell Long and Douglas Park have each analyzed the complexities of audience specification on writing assignments. Long calls for redefining audience as a created fiction instead of as a set of characteristics of some imaginary or real group of readers, a strategy that would force writers to pose and answer questions about what they want their audience to be. Park, too, argues that writers must create a context that readers may enter, maintaining that most of the time it is not possible for writers to separate a sense of audience from a sense of genre and convention. In Park's view, both experience as part of an audience—that is, as a reader—and an understanding of the various kinds of discourse and their purposes are necessary for developing a clear understanding of audience.

The role of audience in writing assessments is no less complex than it is in an instructional context, but it is grounded in the indisputable fact that writing on assessments will always be read by raters. Some writers may disregard a specified audience and write solely for raters; others may try to address both audiences simultaneously, whether or not they are compatible. Unfortunately, testmakers who wish to solve the dilemma of audience have little in the way of experimental research data to guide them. L. A. Plasse tested the influence of audience perspective on the assessment of twelfth-grade students' letters to four audiences: teachers, parents, students, and business people. The letters were scored holistically by raters representing the four audience types. Audience type was, in fact, found to be the significant factor in the assessment of the letters, and significant differences were found both among the means of the ratings of the letters according to audience and among the means of comment categories according to audience. The chief conclusion of the study—that audience and rater type affect the evaluation of writing—is hardly shocking, but it points directly to the importance of rater selection and training in writing assessments.

The interaction of the elements of rhetorical specification in writing assessments is just beginning to attract research attention. A study by Witte, Meyer, Cherry, and Trachsel sought to identify the influence of certain topic variables on writing quality. The researchers created a series of 12 variant assignments from an original single topic in order to represent three levels of audience specification, two levels of purpose, and two levels of content. Essays written on these topics by college freshmen were read and scored by raters representative of three training conditions—formal training, self-training, and no training. Statistical analysis of the resulting scores showed significant main effects for audience and purpose. As audience specification increased, the quality of writing increased as well. When purpose was more clearly specified, the quality of writing decreased. When the researchers tested for two-way interactions in the variables, they found that writing quality was highest when audience specification was highest and purpose specification was lowest and when purpose specification was lowest and content specification was highest. Tests of three-way interaction showed that the highest-rated essays were written on the topic in which audience specification was highest, content was specified, and purpose was left unspecified. The study provides evidence for the importance of specifying audience and content in writing assessment topics if not for specifying purposes, but, as the researchers maintain, it shows too the importance of obtaining experimental research data on the effects of topic variables before making pronouncements about topics.

HUMAN AND CONTEXTUAL VARIABLES

All writers are influenced in writing assessments by innumerable factors related to background and personality. Elements of culture, gender, ethnicity, language, psychology, and experience all bear upon the way different people respond to a writing task. The work of anthropologists, sociologists, linguists, and psychologists has shown that such influences are inevitable. Unfortunately, the current level of knowledge about such influences does not allow us to understand the precise ways in which human factors affect writers and their performance on writing assessments. A detailed look at even the rudiments of such influence is outside the scope of this chapter. We can, however, consider briefly two variables researchers in writing assessment have begun to address.

Topic Interpretation

The sociolinguist William Labov has called attention to the various ways in which an interviewee may interpret a simple question from an interviewer: as a request for information, a command for action, a threat of punishment, a meaningless utterance, or a request for display, among others. The possibilities for such interpretations are as likely to occur in a writing assessment as in an interview; in the latter situation, the respondent has at least the recourse of asking for clarification, something he or she would be prevented from doing in most writing assessments. Although the writing stimulus may be the same for every examinee in an assessment, each writer's understanding of it may be different. The idea that such an assessment is a fair measure of each respondent's performance is thus open to challenge. Labov himself has said:

> With human subjects it is absurd to believe that an identical "stimulus" is obtained by asking everyone the "same question." Since the crucial intervening variables of interpretation and motivation are uncontrolled, [such attempts to control the situation] are only the trappings of science: an approach which substitutes the formal procedures of the scientific method for the activity itself. (108)

One may argue that the same variables left uncontrolled—interpretation and motivation, among others—are in fact themselves subjects of assessment. That is, a test of writing performance, or a test of knowledge about using language, is, at least potentially, an implicit test of interpretive skill and motivation—though these are not in themselves sufficient causes of good performance. Given a writing task requiring no interpretation and given the highest level of motivation, a person who has not yet learned to write or has little knowledge of language use would still do poorly.

Such problems involving human and contextual variations in writing assessments have not prevented the testing enterprise from operating and, indeed, flourishing. But they point up the dangers of putting too much faith in assessment results apart from other evaluative data. The following currently accepted truths about writers and writing tests should now guide testmakers:

1. Different writers interpret features of writing prompts differently.
2. Testmakers and test readers agree on the interpretation of writing prompt features much more often than writers do.
3. Given the same prompts, writers will create different instructions for themselves at different points in the writers' development, differences that are not accounted for by test scores. (Ruth, "Current Research")

Research knowledge on how people read and interpret writing prompts is crucial to the sound development of writing assessment.

Writer Apprehension

Test apprehension is an important factor in writing assessments. But though the literature on the nature and treatment of test anxiety is interesting, it is not directly relevant here because researchers have not to date investigated the role of apprehension across a variety of writing types and situations. One recent study is a good example of the approach researchers should take to increase our understanding of test apprehension on writing.

Faigley, Daly, and Witte, in a study of college writers, tested the hypothesis that highly apprehensive writers would perform differently from writers with low levels of apprehension on standardized tests of writing-related skills and on two essay examinations. Their findings confirmed part of the hypothesis: high apprehensives scored lower on most measures of writing-related skills, but the quality of their writing was lower on only one of the two essay tests. The researchers report significant effects for apprehension with personal narrative essays but no effects with argumentative essays. The authors speculate that apprehensive writers may show more anxiety about expressing personal feelings and experiences than about arguing objectively for a particular point of view. Since previous research on apprehension has drawn measures of writing performance solely from narrative and descriptive essays, these findings argue strongly for future research on different essay types (and indeed across a variety of writing types and situations). Although writing apprehension and poorer writing should not be seen as mutually causative, they may reinforce each other in ways not yet disclosed by research.

PROCEDURAL VARIABLES

Although local testing conditions are apt to be unique, writing assessments often share certain similarities of scope, design, and instrumentation. Writing performance examinations, for example, typically include a writing stimulus, some instructions, a common environment such as a classroom or meeting hall, a time limit, and subsequently, a scoring system in which groups of raters evaluate the compositions according to established criteria and procedures. All of these factors can affect the outcomes of writing assessments, and some recent research indicates which procedural variables are likeliest to have certain effects.

Sarah Freedman explored the relative effects of three sources of variables on essay scores—essay, reader, and environment—and found that the essay itself contributed most significantly to the variance in scores. Of greater interest here, however, is her finding that the training of essay raters had the next largest effect on the essay scores. Reviewing tapes of her training sessions, Freedman discovered that different trainers influenced how raters scored papers. Raters trained by trainers who discussed the topics in some detail generally gave higher scores than those whose trainers simply discussed the meaning of a topic. Freedman concluded that training does in fact change rater behavior and pointed out that since raters can be trained to agree, they can also—intentionally or inadvertently—be trained to render higher or lower scores.

Raters themselves are subject to numerous forms of bias that can be reflected in the scores they give to writing samples. A study by Daly and Dickson-Markman, for example, found that essay raters may be influenced positively (but not negatively) by the quality of the essays they read prior to the essays used for rating. Although training can be designed to anticipate rater bias, some forms of bias are part of the very fabric of the reading task itself. Hake and Williams studied the effects of prose style on experienced high school, junior college, and university teachers of written composition. They assigned two versions of essays to be read and evaluated. Both versions were structurally similar, containing identical numbers of paragraphs and sentences and having the same organization, logic, and content. Stylistically, however, each version was different. One version was written in a simple, direct, concise fashion and stressed the verbal expression of a proposition. The other version was written in a more indirect, verbose, and complex style in which stress was placed on nominal expression—a style, Hake and Williams maintain, that characterizes the "inflated, prolix, indirect prose that all English teachers claim to condemn" (436). The researchers found that the nominalized versions of the essays elicited higher scores and more favorable comments than the verbal versions, though such differences stopped short of being statistically significant. What is striking about these findings is that they reveal an unexpected tendency of English teachers, who are presumed to know and agree on the basic elements of good style, if not on various styles themselves. These findings also demonstrate how the results of writing performance tests are to some degree subject to factors outside the control of a test.

Although the various scoring systems and rating procedures used in large-scale writing assessment aim to address the problem of standards, attention given to that problem is usually of an ad hoc nature and is often based on whatever wisdom seems most propitious at the moment. Research has produced a bare smattering of data on the question of standards. Ernest Spencer tested the hypothesis that inconsistency caused the bulk of intermarker unreliability and concluded that a shift to standards of consensus will realize greater overall improvement in the scoring reliability of assessment results than statistical standardizing alone will accomplish. Other research has sought to address other variables in the scoring of writing samples. Alan Branthwaite and his colleagues, in a "naturalistic" study of essay marking, found a significant positive correlation between the marks given out by university graders and their scores on a personality questionnaire. M. C. Mitchelmore presented a scientific formula for deciding the number of points to use on a rating scale in any given assessment situation. Lynn Winters investigated the relative validities of four essay scoring systems reflecting alternative conceptualizations of the writing process—general impression scoring, the Diederich expository scale, an analytic scale developed and used at the Center for the Study of Evaluation at UCLA, and *t*-unit analysis. Though all four systems produced highly reliable results, different systems produced different patterns of results, which, Winters suggests, may mean that the same scoring system cannot adequately describe the writing performance of each of the four groups in the study (high school writers and college writers of low ability and high ability). Three of the systems were associated with some differences in group performance, while a fourth, *t*-unit analysis, was not. Studies of this sort point out the difficulties in selecting a scoring system in large-scale assessments. Given particular goals—placement, prediction, evaluation of progress, diagnosis, achievement, measure of competence, experimental research, and so on—one scoring system may be more desirable than another, though there are as yet only limited research data to guide those who must make such determinations.

THE IEA STUDY[1]

A comprehensive and ambitious investigation of writing assessment in school has recently been undertaken by the International Association for the Evaluation of Educational Assessment (IEA), under the direction of Alan Purves and Sauli Takala at the Curriculum Laboratory of the University of Illinois. Initiated in 1980, the IEA study is intended to produce analyses of "the state of literacy" in the 16 participating countries as well as descriptions of the composition curricula in their schools. Preliminary results of the study indicate that the IEA model for classifying composition assignments has proved useful for several purposes at a fairly high level of generality (Purves, Söter, Takala, and Vähäpassi 396). For most American test administrators and researchers, the IEA models developed to guide data collection and the evaluation of student compositions will probably have greater value than the eventual cross-national comparisons.

Planning for the study has proceeded carefully. The articles and working documents from the project bombard readers with flowcharts, taxonomies, schematic models, and multidimensional matrices.[2] The IEA's approach has been both theoretical and practical. On the one hand, the staff has reviewed the literature on writing, learning to write, and evaluating writing and has settled on a model of the domain of school writing based on the work of Roman Jakobsson and other cognitive psychologists and speech-act theorists. On the other hand, it has gathered data on curricula and teaching practices, student writing habits, and national examinations in writing.

The IEA's rigorous categorization of topic characteristics makes much previous research on topics seem impressionistic. Fifteen factors involved in topic generation are identified—factors that may serve equally well for classifying topics already written—and in each factor are specified several "levels" into which have been incorporated the results of the preceding research into discourse theory and the nature of school writing.

The IEA's method of scoring composition assignments has yet to be decided, but it is clear that the system that is eventually approved will use multiple samples of student writing and will combine holistic judgments of quality, analytical ratings of various features of writing, and a good deal of purely descriptive data.

FINAL COMMENTS

Research in writing assessment is still at an inchoate stage of development and has yet to address in any systematic and careful way the numerous questions about and problems in large-scale testing and its implications. For example, we know that for a valid test of writing performance, multiple writing samples written on different occasions and in various rhetorical modes are preferable to single samples drawn from an isolated writing instance. But given the sizable and growing populations of test takers and the increasing costs associated with administering tests to them, the problems of collecting and scoring multiple writing samples are formidable. Until we find ways to reduce testing costs and to improve the validity of assessments, the whole enterprise is not likely to serve any purposes higher than routine sorting and certifying.

Good research in writing assessment is both rigorous and inventive. Careless, casually conceived studies or ones in which variables are not precisely identified and managed waste time and money. Studies that assume that research can follow a single, dominant mode of operation or design are apt to contribute little to our knowledge of the situational differences inherent in writing assessment. Writing assessment research is also situation-specific; that is, we cannot generalize its results until we understand how to regulate the major variables from testing site to testing site. And we will never be able to control these variables if our sources of information are compromised by faulty design and unclear reporting of results—problems that plague too many research studies now.

We must also remember that general-impression scoring, though a staple of holistic writing assessment, has limited value for research, allowing only for coarse discriminations of writing quality. Other more finely honed measures of writing performance are available, however. Analytic scoring of prominent features of writing in various modes is one such measure. Primary trait scoring, in which readers judge written text in terms of characteristics necessary to accomplish a specific rhetorical task, is another, capable of serving both diagnostic and evaluative purposes. And methodologies exist for measuring a number of rhetorical properties of written discourse, including syntactic fluency, cohesion and coherence, and elements of usage and mechanics. Assessment programs will obtain comprehensive, detailed information about writers' abilities only if they use appropriate assessment techniques and spend the time, effort, and money to use them well.

Writing assessment ought to reflect our best knowledge of how writing occurs and how it is best taught. That is, it ought to proceed from an understanding of writing as a complex process of discovering and conveying meaning, a process that involves rhetorical, structural, and mechanical choices governed by purpose and audience rather than by compositional rules. It ought to reinforce and even extend our instructional programs, not limit them to reductive skill-brokering, as is the unfortunate case in many institutions at present.

At the heart of the relationship between the assessment of writing and its teaching is the question of how to create the conditions of assessment that approximate the conditions under which good writing is known or is apt to occur. Some theorists suggest that an identifiable set of conditions is optimal for producing good writing: interesting topics, appropriate rhetorical specification, enough time to write, the opportunity to obtain responses to one's writing, a chance to revise a paper, and so on. Theory often fails to account for variations, aberrations, and idiosyncracies in learning styles, however, all of which confound the best efforts of teachers and assessors to instruct groups of writers and to measure their performance.

Research now demonstrates that logical and persuasive ideas about writing assessment are not always empirically verifiable. Research also proposes that writing for school, writing for assessments, and writing for all other circumstances are related, yet they are also compellingly distinct activities. Future research must address the question of how to understand the nature of this complex but enticing proposition.

NOTES

1. I am indebted to James Hoetker for an initial draft of this section.
2. For a full account of the IEA's preliminary work, see the 1982 special issue of the British journal *Evaluation in Education*, which is the chief source for this summary.

REFERENCES

Branthwaite, Alan, Mark Trueman, and Terry Berrisford. "Unreliability of Marking: Further Evidence and a Possible Explanation." *Educational Review* 33 (Feb. 1981): 41–46.

Brossell, Gordon. "Rhetorical Specification in Essay Examination Topics." *College English* 45 (1983): 165–74.

———, and Barbara Hoetker Ash. "An Experiment with the Wording of Essay Topics." *College Composition and Communication* 35 (1984): 423–25.

Crowhurst, M. C. *Syntactic Complexity in Two Modes of Discourse at Grades 6, 10, and 12.* ERIC Doc. ED 168 037. Washington, D.C.: U.S. Department of Health, Education, and Welfare, 1978.

Daly, John, and Fran Dickson-Markman. "Contrast Effects in Evaluating Essays." *Journal of Educational Measurement* 19 (1982): 309–16.

Faigley, Lester, John Daly, and Stephen Witte. "The Role of Writing Apprehension in Writing Performance and Competence." *Journal of Educational Research* 75 (Sept.–Oct. 1981): 16–21.

Freedman, Aviva, and Ian Pringle. "Why Students Can't Write Arguments." Ottawa: Carleton U Linguistics Dept., 1981.

Freedman, Sarah W. "Influences on Evaluators of Expository Essays: Beyond the Text." *Research in the Teaching of English* 15 (1981): 245–55.

Greenberg, Karen. *The Effects of Variations in Essay Questions on the Writing of CUNY Freshmen.* New York: City U of New York Instructional Resource Center, 1981.

Hake, Rosemary, and Joseph Williams. "Style and Its Consequences: Do as I Do, Not as I Say." *College English* 43 (1981): 443–50.

Harpin, William. *The Second "R": Writing Development in the Junior School.* London: George Allen & Unwin, 1976.

Hilgers, Thomas. "Experimental Control and the Writing Stimulus: The Problem of Unequal Familiarity with Content." *Research in the Teaching of English* 16 (1982): 381–90.

Hoetker, James. "Essay Examination Topics and Students' Writing." *College Composition and Communication* 33 (1982): 377–92.

———, Gordon Brossell, and Barbara Hoetker Ash. *Creating Essay Examination Topics.* Tallahassee: Florida State Department of Education, 1981.

Holzman, Michael. "Scientism and Sentence-Combining." *College Composition and Communication* 34 (1983): 73–79.

Labov, William. "The Logic of Nonstandard English." *Linguistics and the Teaching of Standard English to Speakers of Other Languages or Dialects.* Ed. James E. Alatis. Monograph Series on Language and Linguistics No. 22. Washington, D.C.: Georgetown UP, 1969.

Long, Russell. "Writer-Audience Relationships: Analysis or Invention?" *College Composition and Communication* 31 (1980): 221–26.

Mitchelmore, M. C. "Reporting Student Achievement: How Many Grades?" *British Journal of Educational Psychology* 51 (1981): 218–27.

Moffett, James. *Teaching the Universe of Discourse.* Boston: Houghton Mifflin, 1968.

Neilsen, Lorraine, and Gene Piche. "The Influence of Headed Nominal Complexity and

Lexical Choice on Teachers' Evaluation of Writing." *Research in the Teaching of English* 15 (1981): 65–73.

Nold, Ellen, and Sarah Freedman. "An Analysis of Readers' Responses to Essays." *Research in the Teaching of English* 11 (1977): 165–74.

Park, Douglas. "The Meanings of 'Audience.'" *College English* 44 (1982): 247–57.

Perron, J. D. *The Impact of Mode on Written Syntactic Complexity.* Athens, Ga.: U of Georgia Studies in Language Education, 1977. Part 3: Fifth Grade.

Plasse, L. A. "The Influence of Audience on the Assessment of Student Writing." Diss. Storrs, Conn.: U of Connecticut, 1981.

Purves, A. C., A. Söter, S. Takala, and A. Vähäpassi. "Towards a Domain-Referenced System for Classifying Composition Assignments." *Research in the Teaching of English* 18 (1984): 385–416.

Quellmalz, Edys S., Frank J. Capell, and Chih-ping Chou. "Effects of Discourse and Response Mode on the Measurement of Writing Competence." *Journal of Educational Measurement* 19 (1982): 241–58.

Rosen, H. "An Investigation of the Effects of Differential Writing Assignments on the Performance in English Composition of a Selected Group of 15- to 16-Year-Old Pupils." Diss. London: U of London, 1969.

Ruth, Leo. "Current Research in Writing Assessment." 2nd Annual Conference on Writing Assessment, National Testing Network in Writing. Tallahassee, Fla., Mar. 1984.

———. *Properties of Writing Tasks: A Study of Alternative Procedures for Holistic Writing Assessment.* NIE Final Report G-80-0034. Berkeley, Calif.: Bay Area Writing Project, 1982.

San Jose, C. P. M. "Grammatical Structures in Four Modes of Writing at the Fourth-Grade Level." Diss. Syracuse, N.Y.: Syracuse U, 1972.

Spencer, Ernest. "Inter-marker Unreliability in SCE 'O' Grade English Composition: Is Improvement Possible?" *Scottish Educational Review* 13 (May 1981): 44–45.

Thomas, David, and Dan Donlan. "Correlations between Holistic and Quantitative Methods of Evaluating Student Writing, Grades 4–12." ERIC Doc. ED 211 976. Washington, D.C.: GPO, 1982.

Winters, Lynn. "The Effects of Differing Response Criteria on the Assessment of Writing Competence." ERIC Doc. ED 212 659. Washington, D.C.: GPO, 1982.

Witte, Stephen, Paul Meyer, Roger Cherry, and Mary Trachsel. *Holistic Evaluation: Issues, Theory, and Practice.* New York: Guilford Press, in press.

Bibliography

WILLIAM LUTZ

The works listed here are selected from a large and rapidly growing body of research literature on the evaluation of writing. I have chosen here what I judge to be the basic works with which everyone engaged in writing assessment should be familiar.

The works cover both theoretical and practical aspects and problems of large-scale writing assessment, but this list provides only a starting point. You are encouraged to go beyond it. After these works have been studied, use the bibliographies in many of them to direct you to further documentation.

This bibliography should prove useful both to people who are just becoming involved in writing assessment and to those who have had some experience in the field. It should also prove useful for anyone designing a writing assessment program and anyone who might want to refine and improve a present assessment program.

Anderson, Beverly. *Writing Assessment for the '80's*. Portland, Ore.: Northwest Regional Educational Laboratory, 1980.
This book presents the proceedings of a seminar on the assessment of writing proficiency attended by more than 90 measurement specialists. It includes essays on alternative methods of writing assessment, holistic evaluation, and primary trait scoring.

Breland, Hunter, and Judith L. Gaynor. "A Comparison of Direct and Indirect Assessment of Writing Skill." *Journal of Educational Measurement* 16 (1979): 119–28.
This article reports the results of a study conducted at a university by researchers of the Educational Testing Service. After comparing student scores on the Test of Standard Written English with scores on essays written by the students, the researchers conclude that the multiple-choice test is as useful as the essay in placing students in writing courses.

Brossell, Gordon. "Rhetorical Specification in Essay Examination Topics." *College English* 45 (1983): 165–73.
Brossell reports the results of a study designed to determine whether essay topics specifying full rhetorical contexts help students write better essays than less specific versions of the same topics. He found, among other things, that essay topcis did not themselves affect the quality of student writing on a timed examination and that the length of the essay significantly correlated with the score on the essay.

Brown, Rexford. "Choosing or Creating an Appropriate Writing Test." *Basic Writing: Essays for Teachers, Researchers, and Administrators.* Ed. Lawrence Kasden and Daniel Hober. Urbana, Ill.: National Council of Teachers of English, 1980. 105–16.
Brown lists and answers 10 questions that should be answered before designing or purchasing a writing test. He then discusses the strengths and weaknesses of various kinds of essay and multiple-choice tests.

————. "National Assessments of Writing Ability." *Writing: The Nature, Development, and Teaching of Written Communication.* Ed. Carl H. Fredericksen and Joseph F. Dominic. Hillsdale, N.J.: Erlbaum, 1981. Vol. 2, 31–38.
After reviewing the results of the findings of the National Assessment of Educational Progress for 1969–70 and 1973–74, Brown concludes that there is very little accurate, unbiased, concrete information about writing achievement in America. He suggests that there is a need for more and better information about students' writing ability and offers 10 suggestions for improving tests of writing.

Charney, Davida. "The Validity of Using Holistic Scoring to Evaluate Writing: A Critical Overview." *Research in the Teaching of English* 18 (1984): 65–81.
The author argues that the validity of scores derived from holistic ratings has not been adequately demonstrated. Even in carefully supervised reading sessions, the holistic rating given by any reader may be unduly influenced by superficial features of the writing samples. According to Charney, the validity of holistic ratings has never been convincingly demonstrated.

Chase, Clinton I. "Essay Test Scores and Reading Difficulty." *Journal of Educational Measurement* 20 (1983): 293–97.
This article reports the results of a study that compared the scores on two essays—each correct in spelling and grammar but one constructed to be at a difficult reading level and the other at a less difficult level—to see if different levels of conventional readability influence essay test scores. The study concludes that essays that were more difficult to read produced lower scores than the less difficult essays.

Cooper, Charles R., and Lee Odell. *Evaluating Writing: Describing, Measuring, Judging.* Urbana, Ill.: National Council of Teachers of English, 1977.
This is a collection of six monographs, each of which deals with a different approach to writing assessment. Of special interest is the essay on holistic evaluation by Charles Cooper and the essay on primary trait scoring by Richard Lloyd-Jones. Although the essays deal more with the theory of evaluation than the practical problems, it is an indispensable work for anyone involved in writing assessment.

Culpepper, Marilyn M., and Rae Ramsdell. "A Comparison of a Multiple-Choice and an Essay Test of Writing Skills." *Research in the Teaching of English* 16 (1982): 295–97.
This article reports the results of a study designed to assess the validity of a multiple-choice writing test as compared with an essay test and concludes that a combination of both types of scores might be the most effective means of determining students' placement in writing courses.

Davis, Barbara Gross, Michael Scriven, and Susan Thomas. "Student Writing Performance." *The Evaluation of Composition Instruction.* Inverness, Calif.: Edgepress, 1981. 67–98.
This is an essay in an important book on the evaluation of writing instruction that

provides an excellent brief introduction to the major issues involved in the theory and practice of writing assessment, especially when such assessment is to be used to evaluate composition instruction or a composition program.

Diederich, Paul B. *Measuring Growth in English*. Urbana, Ill.: National Council of Teachers of English, 1974.
Diederich discusses the procedures for the reliable assessment of writing using writing samples, stresses the use of appropriate statistical procedures, and provides a sequence of steps to be followed in designing, administering, and scoring a writing test, as well as the statistical analysis to follow in reporting the scores. The book includes sample student papers and a scoring guide for evaluating student essays. This book remains the classic introduction to writing assessment.

Dixon, John, and Leslie Stratta. "Changing the Model for 'Examining' Achievements in Writing." *English in the Eighties*. Ed. Robert Eagleson. Adelaide, Australia: Australian Association for the Teaching of English, 1982. 61–68.
The authors reject the traditional approach to assessing writing proficiency by having students write an essay on a topic revealed at the time of testing and propose instead gathering "exemplar" folders of students' writing. They discuss using two kinds of writing, narratives based on personal experience and arguments about moral or social issues, and suggest criteria for assessing such writing.

Fagan, William T., Charles Cooper, and Julie Jensen. "Measures: Writing." *Measures for Research and Evaluation in the English Language Arts*. Urbana, Ill.: National Council of Teachers of English, 1975. 185–206.
This essay lists 13 measures of writing useful for research in writing, giving the validity, reliability, and normative data on each as well as the age range of students for whom each measure is appropriate. It includes a standard corpus of contemporary American expository essays, evaluation scales, tests, indices of syntactic maturity, and analytical tools.

Freedman, Sarah W. "Influences on Evaluators of Expository Essays: Beyond the Text." *Research in the Teaching of English* 15 (1981): 245–55.
In a study of the effects of three variables on holistic scores given to expository essays, Freedman found that the essay topic and the training of readers can affect scores assigned by readers. She also found that analytic scores add little information over the holistic scores.

———. "Student Characteristics and Essay Test Writing Performance." *Research in the Teaching of English* 17 (1983): 313–25.
Freedman reports the results of a study of the effects of students' attitudes toward essay topics on their performance on essay tests. She found that college freshmen at more selective schools perform best on holistically scored writing tasks and that regardless of school, those who claim to write better or worse than their peers do so.

———, and Robert C. Calfee. "Holistic Assessment of Writing: Experimental Design and Cognitive Theory." *Research on Writing: Principles and Methods*. Ed. Peter Mosenthal, Lynne Tamor, and Sean A. Walmsley. White Plains, N.Y.: Longman, 1983. 75–98.
This study examines how a reader in a holistic reading reaches a judgment about a writing sample. In examining this issue, the authors also show how a combination of cognitive

theory and experimental design procedures can provide a framework for constructing an efficient and informative research design.

Godshalk, Fred I., Frances Swinefold, and William E. Coffman. *The Measurement of Writing Ability*. Princeton, N.J.: College Entrance Examination Board, 1966.
This is the classic study that developed the scoring procedure called holistic assessment. The study concludes that the reliability achieved by having five different readers score five essays on five different topics written by one student can be matched by the reliability achieved on a 20-minute essay scored by two readers and the scores combined with a well-designed multiple-choice test. The researchers also found that multiple-choice tests are valid predictors of writing ability if the tests are well-designed but that the addition to prediction from the essay is real but small. This is an important but complex study, essential to the field of writing assessment.

Gorrell, Donna. "Toward Determining a Minimal Competency Entrance Examination for Freshman Composition." *Research in the Teaching of English* 17 (1983): 263–74.
Gorrell reports the results of a study to determine the best measures for determining an acceptable level of writing proficiency for placement in the regular freshman composition course. After comparing student scores on a standardized reading test, ACT English and ACT Social Studies tests, a cloze test, a holistically scored essay, and an essay read for an error count, she concludes that the best results were achieved combining the score on the holistically read essay with the ACT English score.

Greenberg, Karen L. "Competency Testing: What Role Should Teachers of Composition Play?" *College Composition and Communication* 33 (1982): 366–76.
Greenberg examines the issues and models in testing minimum writing competency and discusses methods of assessing the validity and the reliability of various types of writing tests. She argues that composition teachers must have input into every phase of a competency testing program.

———. *The Effects of Variations in Essay Question Format on the Writing Performance of CUNY Freshman*. New York: City U of New York Instructional Resource Center, 1981.
Greenberg reports the results of a study to determine whether essay questions that offer students a variety of options for structuring their essays and ask students to discuss their personal experiences would improve the quality of their essays. Essays were examined for overall writing quality, syntactic complexity, frequency of sentence-control errors, and essay length. She found that overall writing quality was not significantly affected by the type of essay question to which students responded and concludes that more research on essay test topic development is necessary.

Harnett, Carolyn G. *Measuring Writing Skills*. ERIC Doc. ED 170 014. Washington, D.C.: GPO, 1978.
Harnett discusses the results of a pilot study at one college. Using seven measures such as the Test of Standard Written English, the Nelson-Denny reading test, holistically scored essays, primary trait scored essays, and peer evaluation of essays, Harnett concludes that further study is needed to determine which measure or combination of measures is best.

Hirsch, E. D., and David P. Harrington. "Measuring the Communicative Effectiveness of Prose." *Writing: The Nature, Development, and Teaching of Written Communication.*

Ed. Carl H. Frederiksen and Joseph F. Dominic. Hillsdale, N.J.: Erlbaum, 1981. 189–207.

This article describes the theoretical basis for a new method of measuring the quality of prose on a single appropriate scale called intrinsic communicative effectiveness, which is derived from the actual effects of a piece of prose as compared to its potential optimal effects on a competent audience. The results are preliminary, and it is not clear whether this approach to assessment will be appropriate or acceptable, but the results are promising.

Hoetker, James. "Essay Examination Topics and Students' Writing." *College Composition and Communication* 33 (1982): 377–92.

Hoetker reviews the available literature on essay examination topics and concludes that little is known and little research has been conducted on the issue of constructing topics for essay examinations. He urges that more research be conducted on this issue.

Hogan, Thomas P., and Carol Mishler. "Relationships between Essay Tests and Objective Tests of Language Skills for Elementary Students." *Journal of Educational Measurement* 17 (1980): 219–27.

This is a report of the results of a study to determine the relationship between objective and essay measures of writing skill at the elementary school and high school level. The authors found that student performance on a standardized multiple-choice test of writing and a free-writing sample correlated significantly.

Hoover, Mary Rhodes, and Robert L. Politzer. "Bias in Composition Tests with Suggestions for a Culturally Appropriate Assessment Technique." *Writing: The Nature, Development, and Testing of Written Communication.* Ed. Marcia Farr Whitman. Hillsdale, N.J.: Erlbaum, 1981. Vol. 1, 197–207.

The authors examine the problem of linguistic and cultural bias inherent in the assessment of writing skills and the consequences of this bias. Among their recommendations to solve the problem of bias in composition tests are the elimination of objective or normed tests of composition, greater emphasis on reading and writing instruction in elementary and secondary schools, and the elimination of composition tests at the college level.

Houston, Robert. "Standardized Tests of Writing Ability: A Primer." *Freshman English News* 10 (Fall 1981): 20–22.

An essential introduction to reading the test manual for the teacher and tester of writing, this article provides a clear introduction to the special vocabulary and technical concepts of testing as they apply to standardized multiple-choice tests of writing.

Howerton, Mary Lou, Milton Jacobson, and Rosemary Selden. *The Relationship between Quantitative and Qualitative Measures of Writing Skills.* ERIC Doc. ED 137 416. Washington, D.C.: GPO, 1977.

In this study, student writing samples were scored for such quantitative qualities as number of words, number of sentences, and mean number of words per sentence. Essays were each scored by two readers using the Diederich scale, and the results were correlated with the quantitative qualities. The results indicated that quantitative and qualitative measures of writing skills are significantly related.

Hughes, David C., Brian Keeling, and Bryan F. Tuck. "Effects of Achievement

Expectations and Handwriting Quality on Scoring Essays." *Journal of Educational Measurement* 20 (Spring 1983): 65–70.
This article presents the results of a study that found that handwriting quality and scorer expectations influence essay scores. However, unlike previous studies, this study found no support for the suggestion that untidy writers may have an advantage if the scorers had high expectations for them.

Huntley, R. M., Cynthia Schmeiser, and Richard Stiggins. *The Assessment of Rhetorical Proficiency: The Role of Objective Tests and Writing Samples.* ERIC Doc. Ed 173 419. Washington, D.C.: GPO, 1979.
This is a report on the results of a study using the ACT English Usage Test, an experimental objective test to assess rhetorical proficiency, the SAT Verbal Test, and the Test of Standard Written English, and three student writing samples, each scored by four readers. The results indicated a moderately high correlation between objective measures and writing samples but also showed that the skills measured by the two types of instruments were different.

Lederman, Marie Jean, Susan Remmer Ryzewic, and Michael Ribaudo. *Assessment and Improvement of the Academic Skills of Entering Freshmen: A National Survey.* New York: City U of New York Instructional Resource Center, 1983.
The authors report on the findings of a national survey of 1269 colleges and universities. Of the responding institutions, 85 percent perceive poor academic preparation of incoming freshmen to be a serious problem, and a substantial percentage of these freshmen are viewed as needing assistance in the basic skills areas. More than 9 out of 10 institutions offer basic writing courses, and the most common method of placing students in these courses is through locally developed tests.

Lyman, Howard B. *Test Scores and What They Mean.* Englewood Cliffs, N.J.: Prentice-Hall, 1979.
This is the best introduction to the theory and practice of testing available to the nonspecialist. In addition to explaining test and statistical theory in clear, simple terms, there is a chapter called "Testing and Social Responsibility" and a glossary that defines technical terms in simple language. This is an essential work for anyone involved in writing assessment.

McCready, M., and Virginia Melton. *Feasibility of Assessing Writing Using Multiple Assessment Techniques.* ERIC Doc. ED 220 871. Washington, D.C.: GPO, 1982.
The authors report the results of a survey of all 50 state education agencies and selected city agencies concerning their large-scale writing assessment practices.

Mullis, Ina. *The Primary Trait System for Scoring Writing Tasks.* ERIC Doc. ED 124 942. Washington, D.C.: GPO, 1976.
Mullis presents the rationale and procedures of primary trait scoring used by the National Assessment of Educational Progress in the national assessment of writing in 1974. She discusses identifying important writing skills, developing writing tasks, scoring guides, and scoring procedures. Sample exercises, scoring guide, and sample responses are provided.

Myers, Miles. *Procedures for Writing Assessment and Holistic Scoring.* Urbana, Ill. National Council of Teachers of English, 1980.

This book presents in great detail the procedures for conducting a holistic scoring of writing samples, from designing the essay topic to reporting the scores. It also includes actual student writing samples and analyses of their scores.

Nystrand, Martin. *Assessing Written Communicative Competence: A Textual Cognition Model.* ERIC Doc. ED 133 732. Washington, D.C.: GPO, 1977.
Nystrand proposes a textual cognition model of written communicative competence by extending the cloze procedure from reading to writing. The model proposed assumes that the cloze procedure provides a valid measure of the extent to which writing makes sense to an intended audience. The author recommends that the model be more fully developed with further research.

Odell, Lee. "Defining and Assessing Competence in Writing." *The Nature and Measurement of Competence in English.* Ed. Charles Cooper. Urbana, Ill.: National Council of Teachers of English, 1981. 95–138.
Odell discusses possible definitions of competence in writing, warning that achieving such a definition is not easy. He stresses that competence in writing must involve discovering what to say and then conveying the message through language that is appropriate to one's purpose and audience. He argues against multiple-choice tests of writing and urges instead using writing samples that reflect the writing process and the best writing students can produce.

Polin, Linda G. *Effects of Time and Strategy Use on Writing Performance.* Los Angeles: UCLA Center for the Study of Evaluation, 1980.
Polin reports that a study found that time was not a significant factor in writing performance on an essay, whereas planning and revision could affect the quality of the essay. She suggests that the scoring procedure used would produce different results depending on the writing directions provided.

Popham, W. James. *Modern Educational Measurement.* Englewood Cliffs, N.J.: Prentice-Hall, 1981.
This basic textbook on test theory and statistical theory explains basic concepts in simple language. Popham uses many examples and sample problems to explain the more difficult concepts and procedures.

Purnell, Rosentene B. "A Survey of the Testing of Writing Proficiency in College: A Progress Report." *College Composition and Communication* 33 (1982): 407–10.
Purnell presents the results of a survey of 134 members of the Conference on College Composition and Communication concerning writing assessment at their colleges. Placement testing is widely accepted and appears to be on the rise, and the majority of the respondents (80 percent) indicated that they considered a writing sample to be an indispensable part of a test of writing ability.

Smith, Laura. *Measures of High School Students' Expository Writing: Direct and Indirect Strategies.* ERIC Doc. ED 171 796. Washington, D.C.: GPO, 1979.
Smith reports the results of a study in which students wrote two essays and completed a multiple-choice test on writing, with the essays scored holistically and analytically. Correlations between scores on the essays and the multiple-choice test were moderately positive, while high correlations were found between the analytic and holistic scores.

———, Lynn Winters, Edys Quellmalz, and Eva Baker. *Characteristics of Student Writing*

Competence: An Investigation of Alternative Scoring Systems. Los Angeles: UCLA Center for the Study of Evaluation, 1980.

This study contrasts three methods for placing students into freshman composition or remedial writing classes: a test combining multiple-choice and essay scores, an essay scored holistically, and an essay scored according to analytic scale. The researchers conclude that the three methods produce different placement decisions.

Spandel, Vicki. *Classroom Applications of Writing Assessment: A Teacher's Handbook.* Portland, Ore.: Northwest Regional Educational Laboratory, 1981.

Although designed for use by the classroom teacher in scoring student writing assignments, this book provides a good introduction to holistic, analytic, and primary trait scoring procedures. Detailed procedures, scoring guides, and actual student writing samples are provided, as is a discussion of the relative strengths and weaknesses of each scoring procedure.

————, and Richard J. Stiggins. *Direct Measure of Writing Skill: Issues and Applications.* Portland, Ore.: Northwest Regional Educational Laboratory, 1980.

This book provides basic information on designing and developing a writing assessment program using direct measures of writing. It compares holistic, analytic, primary trait, and *t*-unit analysis methods of writing assessment, and it also discusses how to choose a testing method appropriate to the purpose of testing.

State of New Jersey Basic Skills Council. *Scoring the Essays for the New Jersey College Basic Skills Placement Test.* Princeton, N.J.: Educational Testing Service, 1982.

This report describes the six-point scale used in the holistic scoring of essays written as part of a statewide testing of all college freshmen and gives examples of student essays in each score range.

Steele, J. M. *The Assessment of Writing Proficiency via Qualitative Ratings of the Writing Samples.* ERIC Doc. ED 175 944. Washington, D.C.: GPO, 1979.

This is a report of a series of studies on reliability and validity in the assessment of writing samples using qualitative rating scales. The author found that increasing the number of writing samples per student to three significantly increases reliability, but increasing the number of readers per sample beyond two does not greatly increase reliability. He also found that using improved training materials for readers improves the reliability of their scores.

Stiggins, Richard J. "A Comparison of Direct and Indirect Writing Assessment Methods." *Research in the Teaching of English* 16 (1982): 101–14.

Stiggins compares and contrasts the advantages and disadvantages of measuring writing proficiency directly through writing samples and indirectly through multiple-choice tests. He considers such factors as purpose of testing, components of writing to be assessed, and practical matters such as testing costs, scoring, and reporting procedures. Stiggins concludes that choosing a method for testing writing proficiency must take into account all the advantages and disadvantages of each method as well as the best way the results of the chosen method can be used.

————. *A Guide to Published Tests of Writing Proficiency.* Portland, Ore.: Northwest Regional Educational Laboratory, 1981.

Stiggins reviews 51 available standardized tests of writing, including both direct and indirect measures. He provides such information as reliability, traits measured, administration time, suggested uses of results, and evidence of validity. The tests reviewed range in level from grade school through college and adult education.

Troyka, Lynn Quitman. *An A Posteriori Examination of the Evaluation Scale of the Writing Assessment Test at the City University of New York.* New York: City U of New York Instructional Resource Center, 1982.
Troyka presents a research-based refinement of the criteria used in the CUNY scale and discusses the creation, evaluation, and refinement of a holistic scoring scale for large-scale writing assessments.

Tyler, Ralph W. "Testing Writing: Procedures Vary with Purposes." *Literacy for Life: The Demand for Reading and Writing.* Ed. Richard W. Bailey and Robin Melanie Fosheim. New York: Modern Language Association, 1983. 197–206.
After discussing the strengths of using a writing sample and the weaknesses of multiple-choice tests, Tyler outlines the seven steps to be followed when testing writing. He stresses that by following established procedures it is possible to construct writing tests using a writing sample and achieve the same degree of reliability and objectivity in the results as can be achieved using a multiple-choice test.

Veal, L. Ramon, and Sally Ann Hudson. "Direct and Indirect Measures for Large-Scale Evaluation of Writing." *Research in the Teaching of English* 17 (1983): 290–96.
The authors present the results of a comparison of the validity, reliability, and costs of several direct and indirect measures of writing. The direct measures examined include holistic, analytic, primary trait, and mechanical counts in the scoring of writing samples; the indirect measures examined include four currently available standardized multiple-choice tests. The authors conclude that the choice of an appropriate measure of writing proficiency depends on the scope and purpose of the writing assessment as well as the resources available.

White, Edward M. "Mass Testing of Individual Writing: The California Model." *Journal of Basic Writing* 1 (1978): 18–38.
White describes the California State University and Colleges English Equivalency Examination used to grant credit for freshman composition to students who have not taken the course. He presents actual essay questions used in past examinations, the scoring guides used when reading the essays, and sample essays illustrating the range of scores assigned by readers.

———. *Teaching and Assessing Writing.* San Francisco: Jossey-Bass, 1985.
This is an indispensable work for anyone involved in assessing writing. With great clarity, White covers in careful detail all aspects of designing a writing assessment program, from developing an essay topic, to how to conduct an essay reading, to how to do the statistical studies necessary to ensure a sound assessment program.

Wiener, Harvey S. "Sample Writing Tests." *The Writing Room.* Ed. Harvey S. Wiener. New York: Oxford UP, 1981.
Wiener describes the writing samples of various postsecondary writing tests.

Index